Narrating the Women, Peace and Security Agenda

CHRISTINE CHINKIN
AISLING SWAINE
MICHELLE BARNETT

Pg 149 for begues
→ how is this helpful?
Do this helpful

OXFORD STUDIES IN GENDER AND INTERNATIONAL RELATIONS

Series editors:
J. Ann Tickner, American University, and Laura Sjoberg, University of Florida and
Royal Holloway, University of London

Narrating the Women, Peace and Security Agenda

Logics of Global Governance

LAURA J. SHEPHERD

OXFORD

UNIVERSITY PRESS

OXFORD
UNIVERSITY PRESS

Oxford University Press is a department of the University of Oxford. It furthers the University's objective of excellence in research, scholarship, and education by publishing worldwide. Oxford is a registered trade mark of Oxford University Press in the UK and certain other countries.

Published in the United States of America by Oxford University Press 198 Madison Avenue, New York, NY 10016, United States of America.

© Oxford University Press 2021

Library of Congress Cataloging-in-Publication Data
Names: Shepherd, Laura J., author.
Title: Narrating the women, peace and security agenda :
logics of global governance / Laura J. Shepherd.
Description: New York, NY : Oxford University Press, [2021] |
Includes bibliographical references and index. | Contents: Stories of the women, peace, and security agenda—Tools to think with : narrative, discourse, logics—Ownership and origin stories—Narratives of success—Narratives of failure—Narratives of tensions and pressures— Silences, secrets, and sensibilities—Resisting narrative closure.
Identifiers: LCCN 2020044149 | ISBN 9780197557242 (hardback) |
ISBN 9780197557259 (paperback) | ISBN 9780197557266 updf |
ISBN 9780197557280 oso | ISBN 9780197557273 (epub)
Subjects: LCSH: United Nations. Security Council. Resolution 1325. |
Women and peace. | Women and human security. | Women—Violence against—Prevention—International cooperation.
Classification: LCC JZ5578 .S54 2021 | DDC 303.6/6082—dc23
LC record available at https://lccn.loc.gov/2020044149

DOI: 10.1093/oso/9780197557242.001.0001

1 3 5 7 9 8 6 4 2

Paperback printed by Marquis, Canada
Hardback printed by Bridgeport National Bindery, Inc., United States of America

For Brian and Joe. Then, now, always.

Contents

Acknowledgments

I never intended to spend my career writing about UNSCR 1325, and what has become known as the Women, Peace and Security agenda, yet here we are. I feel on some level that this book has been in development since the completion of my PhD research. When I began my doctoral research project, many years ago, I hadn't heard of United Nations Security Council resolution 1325, nor did I appreciate the significance of the adoption of a resolution by the Security Council under the title of "women and peace and security." I wanted to write a thesis on the articulation of gender violence as a matter of international security, elaborating parallels between the sovereignty and autonomy of (some) human subjects and the sovereignty and autonomy of (some) states, and the role of violence in maintaining a system that selectively and contingently affords the right of self-determination. I had planned to argue that gender violence could only be effectively articulated as a matter of international security if it were to be recognized as a violation of the right to security and bodily autonomy by the highest institutions of global governance. The discovery of resolution 1325 in the course of my research somewhat took the wind from my sails, I must confess. But I rallied and ended up writing a similar sort of thesis based on a critical reading of UNSCR 1325, at the conclusion of which I swore I never wanted to work on UNSCR 1325 again. Yet, as I said, here we are.

I cannot possibly thank all of the people who have guided, supported, and encouraged me and my research. Even just this book, five years in the making, has accumulated debts I cannot repay. But it is important to try. First, the formalities: the research presented in this book was made possible by a Discovery grant from the Australian Research Council (DP1606100212), for which I am extremely grateful. In the spirit of sharing failures as well as successes, I originally submitted this project to the Future Fellowship scheme, in which iteration it was roundly rejected. I dusted it off the following year and submitted it to the Discovery scheme, where it was successful. This project was an attempt from the beginning to "fail better," which, now I come to think of it, is not a bad analogy for its subject matter.

The research presented here was entirely contingent on the generous participation of all the people in New York who gave up their time to meet with me and talk about the WPS agenda in all its guises. Given that you all made involvement contingent on anonymity, I can't name names, but you know who you are. You have my deepest appreciation and admiration for your tireless and frequently thankless efforts.

This book, and its author, benefited enormously from the insight, care, and organizational skills of the extremely brilliant Caitlin Hamilton, who worked for many more years than we anticipated on this project, which we just couldn't seem to bring to a close. There's always more interesting stuff to say, I guess. Cait, I couldn't have done this without you; the project would have been so different, and much diminished, without your contribution. Thank you.

I have presented bits of this book all over the place, and each time I have received generous feedback and comments that have made me rethink my analysis, sharpened the arguments, and generally helped me see how the work might be improved. I am particularly grateful to colleagues in the Department of International Relations at the Australian National University, the Department of International Relations at the LSE, and the Department of Government and International Relations at the University of Sydney, for attending my presentations as the book itself began to take shape and engaging so constructively. Special thanks are due to Evelyn Goh, Megan MacKenzie, Nicole Wegner, and Roxani Krystalli, all of whom took the time to read and discuss aspects of this research with me and in doing so contributed immeasurably to the book. Mistakes and omissions, naturally, remain my own.

I write out these acknowledgments in extraordinary times. In our house, we have taken to referring to this period as "unprecedented-global-pandemic-times," in a gesture of unseriousness to counter what is always, these days, the seriousness of our deliberations on, and in, pandemic life. My plans to complete and deliver this book, perhaps even launch it in New York, were completely overshadowed by the global health crisis of Covid-19. None of us expected to be here, to be grappling with these issues, to experience being suspended in this strange and broken time. And yet, again, here we are.

I have spent the last six months holding my people a little closer, being a little more grateful for every privilege I enjoy, all the while acknowledging that I am a little more exhausted and depleted than I have ever been before and so I need my people a little more. I am so thankful to share my life with my husband and son, for all the ways in which they surprise, delight, and support me, and for all the times they reduce me to helpless laughter at the dinner table. I have boundless appreciation for my family of origin and my family of choice, for the feminist peace crew, and for the extended network of people who nourish me with love and generosity. It is in these relationships that I am constituted and held. It is in these relationships that I am. And I am so very grateful.

Laura J. Shepherd
Sydney, Australia
1 July 2020

1

Stories of the Women, Peace and Security Agenda

Representatives of women's civil society organizations convened in New York in 2000 to encourage the UN Security Council to examine the impact of armed conflict on women and girls and to recognize the importance of women's participation in peace and conflict prevention. The adoption of resolution 1325 was a huge achievement, and the agenda has been elaborated over the intervening twenty years in a series of related resolutions. Thanks to sustained advocacy from women's civil society organizations, it is now impossible to ignore the gendered dynamics of international peace and security. We have resolution 1325 and the other resolutions, and that's important in and of itself. It's not perfect, but we didn't have those resolutions, this agenda, twenty years ago. The WPS agenda has really changed how the UN thinks about peace and security, and women on the ground can use the resolutions to put pressure on their governments, to make them take the agenda seriously. We've got a long way to go, though, before we see full implementation of the agenda. The major problems we have are a lack of resources and political will. Some people still don't really understand what the agenda is all about, or they try to make it about everything, which makes it hard to focus. Also, we need to be careful about putting too much emphasis on one aspect of the agenda. It's all there in the resolutions; we just need to work on implementation. And of course, we're working within the limits of the UN system; the Council really only wants oversight of things related to peace and security. But we can influence the process sometimes. We all know each other, and we know who to call if we need to get that piece of paper on someone's desk before that meeting. Often, I've just been lucky, I've been in the right room at the right time. But you know, we can't talk about that.

Narrating the Women, Peace and Security Agenda. Laura J. Shepherd, Oxford University Press (2021). © Oxford University Press. DOI: 10.1093/oso/9780197557242.003.0001

I'm in a midlevel office around East 44th Street, ten minutes or so from the United Nations (UN) building. My eyes are gritty with jet lag. I tilt my head to one side, inquiring. I give an encouraging smile: *share your stories with me, please.* Every conversation I had, on this and other visits, was a version of this conversation. Every story I was told was a version of the story I've just outlined. In my efforts to understand the formation and diffusion of the Women, Peace and Security (WPS) agenda across UN Headquarters (HQ) in New York, I learned how narratives form and travel across institutions, how these narratives hold together sticky arrangements of discourse that produce particular political affordances and forms of (in)action. I learned how WPS emerges through narratives as a knowable policy agenda, and also what insights analyzing this agenda through narrative and discourse theory might yield for other, similarly complex, policy agendas in global politics. I learned the stories of the WPS agenda, as well as learning what possibilities, what *realities*, are produced in and through these stories. This is a book about those stories and the worlds they contain.

The WPS agenda is a policy agenda that is anchored in, though not encompassed by, the ten UN Security Council resolutions (UNSCRs) adopted under the title of "women and peace and security."[1] UNSCR 1325, the first WPS resolution, was adopted in October 2000; it represented the culmination of concerted feminist activism around women's rights and needs in conflict and conflict-affected settings. The resolution's principles were foreshadowed in a press release (SC/6816) issued on the occasion of International Women's Day, 8 March 2000, by the then president of the UN Security Council (UNSC), Ambassador Anwarul Karim Chowdhury from Bangladesh (Hudson 2010, 12). Ambassador Chowdhury's statement reminded the UN and its member states that "peace is inextricably linked with equality between women and men" (United Nations 2000). The particular impact of conflict on women was recognized by the Security Council a few days in later in a Presidential Statement outlining the humanitarian dimensions of the maintenance of international peace and security, which included a reaffirmation of the need to consider the protection of civilians, as well as introducing the idea that women and girls might have "special situations" in conflict and conflict-affected settings, necessitating specific attention and training (S/PRST/2000/7, p. 2). These March statements foreshadowed the content of the October resolution, which came to be recognized as the foundation of the WPS agenda at the Council.

UNSCR 1325 also builds on existing international agreements and declarations regarding gender equality and the status of women, including the Beijing Declaration and Platform for Action (A/CONF.177/20/Rev.1) and the Windhoek Declaration and the Namibia Plan of Action on Mainstreaming a Gender Perspective in Multidimensional Peace Support Operations (A/55/138-S/2000/693). The Beijing Platform for Action, in particular, is a significant document in the history of women's rights, including in the context of peace and security. The text covers twelve areas across which the status of women and the issue of gender equality require sustained attention, including armed conflict. The document was the outcome of the Fourth World Conference on Women, held in Beijing, China, in September 1995. The provisions in the Beijing Platform for Action section on armed conflict (Section E) include a number of strategic objectives that informed—and continue to inform—the development of the WPS agenda. For example, the need to "increase the participation of women in conflict resolution at decision-making levels and protect women living in situations of armed and other conflicts or under foreign occupation" (United Nations 1996, strategic objective E.1) and the need to "promote women's contribution to fostering a culture of peace" (United Nations 1996, strategic objective E.4) have been directly taken forward and integrated into the principles of the WPS agenda.

Resolution 1325 contains a number of provisions that are clearly related to the Beijing Platform for Action, notably its commitments to increasing women's participation in decision-making in peace and security governance; its calls for all parties to armed conflict to respect the relevant mandates of international human rights law and international humanitarian law (including in regard to protection afforded to individuals displaced to refugee camps and settlements); and its emphasis on "[m]easures that support local women's peace initiatives and indigenous processes for conflict resolution, and that involve women in all of the implementation mechanisms of the peace agreements" (S/RES/1325, para. 8b). Each of the ten resolutions adopted by the UN Security Council under the title "Women and Peace and Security" since the adoption of UNSCR 1325 has slightly different priorities and emphases (see Appendix 1 for a summary). Together, the resolutions comprise the policy architecture of the WPS agenda and develop the various provisions and principles of the agenda to which member states of the UN are bound to adhere by virtue of the authority of the UN Security Council.

The provisions of the ten resolutions tend to be grouped thematically into four "pillars": the participation of women in peace and security institutions and decision-making, the prevention of sexual violence in conflict and gender mainstreaming in conflict prevention, the protection of women's rights and well-being in conflict and conflict-affected settings, and gender-sensitive relief and recovery efforts (though the explanation of the pillars is not uncontested; there is a discussion to be had about the consolidation of the agenda around these pillars, and why the fourth pillar is so rarely included in debates about the WPS agenda, on which I elaborate in Chapter 6). These pillars were foreshadowed in the UN System-Wide Action Plan published as part of a report of the Secretary-General to the Security Council on the theme of WPS in 2007 (S/2007/567, para. 42) and then consolidated in the 2010 Secretary-General's report (S/2010/173).

Across the various pillars, the resolutions have mandated specific actions for member states and UN entities alike, which has affected the development of the WPS agenda over the past two decades. Resolution 1888 (2009), for example, contained provisions for the creation of the office of the Special Representative of the Secretary-General on Sexual Violence in Conflict and the associated UN network, UN Action on Sexual Violence in Conflict. In turn, resolution 2122 (2013) identified UN Women as the key UN entity providing information and advice on participation of women in peace and security governance; this resolution also included important provisions regarding the accountability of other UN entities in the implementation of the WPS agenda. Resolution 2242 (2015) connected several "new security challenges," including forced migration, climate change, and terrorism and violent extremism, to the WPS agenda, while also highlighting the relevance of the WPS agenda to all UNSC country-specific items of business and establishing the Informal Experts Group on WPS as a mechanism for providing advice on WPS-related matters to the Council. These two initiatives, in particular, stand to have a significant impact on how the Council integrates WPS work into other areas of practice.

Beyond the UN architecture, the policy agenda has proliferated enormously. UN member states have National Action Plans (NAPs) to guide the implementation of the WPS agenda at country level, there are Regional Action Plans (RAPs) governing WPS in regional organizations, and many guidelines and protocols have been developed by intergovernmental organizations such as the North Atlantic Treaty Organization (NATO) and the Organization for Security and Co-operation in Europe (OSCE). Little unifies these diverse policy artifacts beyond the invocation of the suite of WPS resolutions as a touchstone, as these different forms of institutionalization reflect the priorities and preexisting peace and security practices of the terrain in which they are conceived. NAPs, for example, tend to reflect national "interests" and concerns, including in their engagement with security matters that fall under the auspices of the WPS agenda. Beyond the immediate national context, Katrina Lee-Koo and Barbara Trojanowska (2017) have written on WPS in the Asia-Pacific, for example, adding to studies of WPS and Association of Southeast Asian Nations (ASEAN) (Davies, Nackers, and Teitt 2014), and there are some important studies on WPS in the African Union (Haastrup 2019) as well as WPS in the European Union (Guerrina and Wright 2016). These studies draw out regional practice and together generate insights about similarities and differences across the different contexts. Attending to the various articulations of the WPS agenda in national and regional settings functions as a useful reminder that ultimately it is an object of political contestation like any other policy framework or governance regime.

The WPS agenda has motivated and mobilized magnificent efforts in transnational, national, and local contexts. In many locations, women's organizations and peace organizations work on WPS-related and WPS-adjacent initiatives, often without reference to a NAP and frequently with very limited resources. In Afghanistan, for example, women's organizations "have played an instrumental role so far in outreach and awareness raising, training and capacity building, and facilitating engagement between women and other important actors at the community level" in efforts to counter violent extremism, without much in the way of support from the national government (Safi 2016, 126; for a related analysis of countering violent extremism initiatives in Nigeria, see Nwangwu and Ezeibe 2019). In Solomon Islands (George 2016; George and Soaki 2020) and Sri Lanka (Singh 2017); in Liberia (Martín De Almagro 2018a; Basini and Ryan 2016), Finland (Jauhola 2016), and Australia (Lee-Koo 2014, 2016); and across South Asia (Rajagopalan 2016; Manchanda 2017) and South America (Drumond and Rebelo 2020), the WPS agenda is being shaped and reshaped, told and retold. These activities bring the agenda to life and are an essential component of the ways in which the agenda can be apprehended and known. In and through these "local" contexts, various imaginings are visible; all kinds of different stories can be told, of what the agenda is, what it can be, and how its implementation can transform unequal societies and move communities from conflict to durable peace.

This research proceeds from the premise that the stories that are told about the WPS agenda constitute it as an object of knowledge. In this book, I encounter WPS as a policy agenda that emerges in and through the stories that are told about it, focusing solely on the world of WPS work at the UN HQ in New York (noting, of course, that many other equally rich and important stories could be told about the agenda in other contexts). Part of how the WPS agenda is "put into discourse" (Foucault [1976] 2000, 11), formed as (and simultaneously forming) a knowable reality, is through the narration of its beginnings, its ongoing unfolding, and its plural futures. These stories account for the inception of the agenda, outline its priorities, and delimit its possibilities, through the arrangement of discourse into narrative formations that communicate and constitute the agenda's triumphs and disasters. The story with which I opened this chapter is both the story of the WPS agenda and the story of this book; I break down this story over the chapters that follow to show how its constitution and its retelling over time organizes the agenda in particular ways and with specific political effects.

This history of UNSCR 1325, and its articulation of the WPS agenda that grew from its adoption, are as familiar to anyone long working on the agenda as the alphabet, the rules of grammar and syntax, or the spelling of their own names. I know the codes of the UN documents by heart, the years and numbers of the resolutions, and the way that I have learned to express my understanding of its "pillars"—of violence prevention, rights protection, political participation, and post-conflict reconstruction—is largely consistent over time. There are certain elements that must, in my telling at least, be present, and which signal a particular politics: I personally cannot tell this story without mention of feminist activism, women's organizations, or civil society, without an emphasis on women's agency and contribution to peace work. The more times I have written out this story, the more familiar its cadence and structure have become, and the more I have come to realize that *how* I narrate WPS is as politically significant as the claims I make about its possibilities and limitations.

Most of the literature on UNSCR 1325, particularly the early scholarship, recounts some version of the WPS "origin story," as I have come to think of it (see, for example, Hill, Aboitiz, and Pouhlman-Doumbouya 2003; Cohn, Kinsella, and Gibbings 2004; Shepherd 2008a; Tryggestad 2009; Hudson 2010). Attentive to the productive power of discourse as I am, the recitation of this story across multiple texts and multiple venues began to intrigue me; I became alert to the small differences in its narration and wondered how and in what ways the realization of the WPS agenda was affected by its telling.

I wondered whether, for example, it was commonly understood at the United Nations Security Council in New York—across the street and separated by a number of robust security barriers and checkpoints from the somewhat drafty and dingy room in which I sat to hear the account that opens this section—that UNIFEM's cleverness had been instrumental in getting the resolution "in blue" (as draft text for UN Security Council resolutions is marked). I wondered whether it made a difference to Council members when they were negotiating UNSCR 1325 that the Beijing Platform for Action and the Windhoek Declaration had already made much of the case for the resolution, or whether this claimed degree of institutional authority and legitimacy meant more to the civil society actors, who were (understandably) fearful of having their concerns and ideas dismissed, than it did to the members of the Council back in October 2000. I wondered how it was that this—or some version of this—coalesced into my own WPS story, to be told and retold across a career's research and writing, and how different my contribution might have been if I had learned by heart a different story.

These are some of the questions that prompted me to undertake the research presented here. I recognize that evaluating the effectiveness with which an agenda is implemented, across both national and international settings, is an important and worthwhile endeavor, but there is always a prior consideration for me. This consideration drives me to understand not only *why* the WPS agenda may succeed or fail, but *how it becomes possible* to know WPS (on the difference between "why" and "how-possible" questions, see Doty 1993, 298). The political affordances created through the discourses marshaled in service of the dominant or regularly repeated stories of the agenda are an integral part of the explanation of its formation. Essentially, I propose that to know the agenda, we must know its stories. Thus, the core questions driving the investigation presented here are: 'What are the narratives of the WPS agenda that are told at and around the UN HQ in New York, site of the UN Security Council and thus architectural "home" of the formal elaboration of the WPS agenda?' and 'How do these narratives shape and inform the ways that the agenda is encountered, acted upon, and imagined into the future?'

It is my hope that the methodology I develop here might have broader applicability. There is much disciplinary interest in governance and the kind of governance constellation—across national, regional, and transnational contexts—of which the WPS agenda is an example.[3] Considering the WPS agenda as an artifact or manifestation of global governance, a governance regime or system, connects the insights presented here to the study of global governance more broadly; the WPS agenda is proximate to, and even imbricates, various other formal and informal mechanisms that regulate human activity through institutions and less immediately obvious configurations of norms and expectations. There are regimes related to, and distant from, the WPS agenda that have similarly multilayered and decentralized governance arrangements: women's rights regimes, for example, and particularly the governance of violence against women (VAW), might yield useful insights if analyzed using a narrative approach. Environmental governance is another policy area that could be explored in terms of the logics of its constitution; so, too, is peace and security governance, engaging issues such as terrorism and violent extremism. Whether the logics are the same across different contexts is an empirical question, but the approach I deploy in this book could reveal the narratives, discourses, and logics of other regimes of global governance. Thus, I hope that this book might contribute to disciplinary ways of apprehending and comprehending complex governance systems.

In the remainder of this introductory chapter, I offer a brief explanation of how I understand the political significance of stories and storytelling, drawing on narrative theory. I follow this discussion with a brief elaboration of the ethics and politics of working with narrative. The inevitable partiality of narrative accounts and the decision to focus on the UN in New York are just two of the ethical tensions that run through the project presented here, and I explore these tensions not in an effort to resolve them but rather to acknowledge the work that they do in prompting my thinking around the issues that arise in the course of this analysis. In the final section, I explain the argument that I make in this book and outline the development of this argument over the course of the chapters that follow. Ultimately, I hope to show that the arguments I put forward make both a theoretical and an empirical contribution: in the former to the broader study of policy formation and implementation in the use of narrative and discourse theory, and in the latter to the study of the WPS agenda more specifically as I capture its stories and lay out in this work the potentialities these stories create.

The politics of storytelling

A significant body of work on narrative has developed a complex and nuanced understanding of the concept of narrative and of the political significance of storytelling.[4] I use the concept of narrative and the idea of storytelling here because of their resonance with practice. Narratives, and stories within them, are *told*: the practices of narration, or storytelling, represent a particular form of communication. Narratives represent events and experiences in a particular sequence or order, capturing within a narrative formation one or more recognizable stories (Abbott 2008, 13). The communicative act of narration composes stories into particular formations, such that sense or meaning can be communicated through the sharing of those formations and that sense or meaning potentially can be socialized. Intuitively, narrative and story are inflected with an interpersonal life, a social dimension: "storytelling" implies a storyteller and an audience to whom the story is told; similarly, narratives can have one or more narrators, but their articulation and reception are intrinsically social. In this way, the concepts of narrative and story perform a different function than the concept of discourse, which does not necessarily carry with it the sociality and relationality I wish to invoke.[5]

Although story and narrative are often used interchangeably in writing or conversation, it is conceptually useful to think of them as distinct and to posit a relationship between narrative and story that sees narrative as a particular configuration of a story (or multiple stories)—a sequenced representation of events or experiences (for others who follow this approach, see Culler 2002; Abbott 2007, 2008; Ryan 2007), which could be organized differently. Narrative thus exceeds story, while story, in this view, is the arrangement of discourse that is told within a narrative. The organization of discourse in service of narrative can therefore be thought of as a process of stabilization; discourses coalesce into the particular story formation of a recognizable and communicable narrative. Narratives can thus be apprehended and analyzed as sticky arrangements of discourse, as assemblages or partially and temporarily fixed configurations that cohere over time to present a story: "Most narratologists agree that narrative consists of material signs, the discourse, which conveys a certain meaning (or content), the story, and fulfils a certain social function" (Ryan 2007, 24). This idea—that narrative is "storified" discourse with a particular function (or multiple functions)—is a productive foundation for analytical engagement with narrative.

Narratives are central to meaning-making practices, though I do not presume either the universality of storytelling as a social practice or the existence of a universal story form (for a discussion of this claim to universality, see Abbott 2008, 1–3; Fernandes 2017a, 4–6). They have a privileged place in the communicative practices of Western Anglophone cultures; stories are a way of learning and of passing on learning.[6] As indicated previously, stories can be considered fundamental to the social self; "we are *homo fabulans* because we interpret and tell stories about who we are or want to be, and what we believe" (Wibben 2011, 43).[7] Perhaps most significantly, stories make ontopolitical claims: "[M]aking a statement about what *is* is always already to find oneself within an understanding of the *is*, as such" (Dillon 1998, 35; emphasis in original). Narratives can illuminate much about the assumed *is* of social research—in this case, the WPS agenda—and, through a process of careful analysis, a focus on narrative can show not only the shared understanding of "the *is*" but also the political implications of that understanding. In part, this is through showing the presences and absences in a given story: illuminating what is not told and therefore what is not part of "the *is*" of the object of study.

Narratives are always partial and necessarily exclude much in their telling; if there is a single unifying dimension of narrative as a form of communication, it might be that narratives cannot represent (or re-present) a story in its totality. The process of representation through narrative (or any other mode of communication) is always selective. The shape and form of narrative, and therefore the organization of event or experience into story, is always political, as narrative is composed of representational practice—of discourse. According to this view, power holds story and discourse, structuring each in relation to the other, and produces narrative (and simultaneously is itself reproduced in and through narrative); it is precisely the question of what can be known (or is knowable) that narrative analysis can encounter productively, as narratives that purport to offer explanations of a specific social or political event.

Storytelling may be conceived as a deliberate form of political intervention (for different expressions and interrogations of this, see Dauphinee 2013; Fernandes 2017a, 2017b; Lipton and Mackinlay 2016), but even without the structuring of a declared political project to mark the act of narration as a form of praxis, narrative is political. Narratives are produced by and productive of sticky arrangements of discourse into stories that perform ordering functions in, and of, our worlds. To know our worlds, then, "we need to know narrative, and to trace out limits and possibilities that attend the larger effort to understand why ours is an experience best captured somewhere between story and discourse" (Puckett 2016, 289). This research therefore takes as its object of study the multiple compositions of story-discourse that constitute the WPS agenda at the UN HQ in New York, and explores these narratives to trace out the "limits and possibilities" of the agenda as it is known, told, and made manifest in the narration of its events and experiences.

Whose stories count?

I have already outlined the concept of narrative that informs and animates the research presented here. I take as central to the concept of narrative its partiality. Narrative is not only partial because of its fabrication through representational practice, but also because of the context into which narratives are articulated. Power structures narratives within a given text, but narratives are also enacted into social, political, and institutional contexts that themselves are produced by and productive of particular configurations of power. These configurations of power function to legitimize, authorize, and value certain narratives over others. I want to address explicitly the fact that this book focuses on a specific, elite set of narratives—those produced by people working on WPS at and around the UN HQ in New York—and thus risks reproducing the authority of, and value afforded to, these narratives over others.

The idea that certain forms of knowledge are privileged over others is not new within the academy. Those working at the "margins" of international relations (IR) as a discipline (cf. Steans 2003) have offered consistent and insistent critiques of the kinds of disciplinary knowledges, and disciplining mechanisms, that have constituted the "mainstream." These efforts at critical engagement are manifest in a "volume and variety of work whose principal business is to interrogate limits, to explore how they are imposed, to demonstrate their arbitrariness, and to think *other*-wise, that is, in a way that makes possible the testing of limitations and the exploration of excluded possibilities" (Ashley and Walker 1990, 263; emphasis in original). The epistemic authority afforded to particular theoretical accounts of world politics reproduces a discipline that is structurally disinclined to attend to "margins, silences, and bottom rungs" (Enloe 1996), while the methodological fetishization of rationalism creates a disciplinary "toolbox" ill-suited to a focus on people and their stories.

International relations as a discipline privileges science (Smith 2000, 2004). As Patrick Jackson notes, science is "a notion to conjure with in the field of IR" (2010, 9). Scientism lauds such conjuring; ours is conventionally a discipline of abstraction, hypothesis testing, and quantification of the social world, in the name of "rigor" and "objectivity." Science is not seen as the same order of thing as storytelling. Adherence to a regulative ideal of science in IR research determines the parameters of the discipline and "assumes only that which is manifested in experience, that emerges from observing 'reality', deserves the name knowledge. All other utterances have no cognitive and empirical merit: they are mere value statements, normative claims, unprovable speculations" (Bleiker 1997, 64). The hierarchies of knowledge production thus created and perpetuated through disciplinary and disciplining techniques (peer review, publication, presentation of research) situate science "within the true" (George Canguilhem quoted in Bleiker 1997, 64), within the domain of what is thinkable and knowable, which is a precondition for evaluation of the actual claims presented (true/false, valid/invalid). Most narrative accounts of world politics, until relatively recently at least, were not included in this domain.

Thus, "fact narratives" of world politics are privileged over "fictive narratives," objective privileged over subjective. Such an arrangement demands that so-called personal narratives of events or experiences must be filtered, marshaled, and ordered into scientific form before they can be ascribed the status of Truth. An individual's stories may count as knowledge, but only once they have been apprehended by Science, rendered objective and docile in what Donna Haraway calls the "god trick of seeing everything from nowhere" (1988, 581). The value statements and beliefs that infuse research at every step (determining what literature is surveyed, what questions are deemed important, whose knowledge is apprehended, whose experiences are curated) are glossed over in the creation of scientific validity, in line with the "origins myth" of Science itself, which "recommends that we understand everything but science through causal analysis and critical scrutiny of inherited beliefs" (Harding 1986, 36).

One of the most violent ways in which events and experiences have been disciplined is through colonial practices of research. The subjugation of *kinds of knowing* in the academy cannot be separated from the use and application of *ways of knowing* to shore up systems of domination through time. "The ways in which scientific research is implicated in the worst excesses of colonialism remains a powerful remembered history for many of the world's colonized peoples" (Tuhiwai Smith 2012, 1). The reproduction of binary oppositions—researcher/researched, knower/known, subject/object—through the production of knowledge in service of "Western civilization" (Tuhawai Smith 2012, 62–67) creates subject positions into which colonizer and colonized are interpellated and from which it is, or is not, possible to speak with authority and have one's story heard. It is to this reproductive knowledge economy that Gayatri Chakravorty Spivak gestures when she proposes that "that the subtext of the palimpsestic narrative of imperialism be recognized as 'subjugated knowledge'" (1988, 25). The idea that this violent history can be undone simply by "giving voice" to colonized and subjugated peoples obscures the politics of narrative and the very endeavor of research itself. The use of storytelling as a political intervention can "become implicated in the formation of new kinds of subjectivity that accord with Western liberal modes of domination" (Fernandes 2017b, 645–646).   A DIFFERENT small

There is therefore, and necessarily, an ethics to working with narrative that demands careful negotiation. Anna Agathangelou and Lily Ling discuss the dangers of appropriating the narratives of others in their brilliant essay on the disciplinary politics of IR. They offer a critique of White Western feminist theorizing that presumes to speak for women of color even as such theorizing is presented as potentially progressive, even emancipatory:

> Such epistemic, political, and personal violence pervades the House of IR. The US academic self-righteously presents the woman of color as a victim of "Third-World" patriarchy in need of "First-World" feminist rescue without questioning either her right or place to do so. (Agathangelou and Ling 2004, 38)

The hierarchies and dynamics of exclusion and oppression that structure academic IR as a discipline are thus reinforced through the recognition of "'First-World' feminists" as legitimate and credible experts on relations international, speaking for, and speaking out about the need to "rescue," "Third-World" women. To "give voice" in this way is often to simultaneously deny agency, and in work on narrative this is a particularly pressing concern (see also Edkins 2013, 290).

In the narratives of the WPS agenda, there is frequently a clear articulation of the significance of mobilizing efforts undertaken by women's civil society organizations. These organizations, credited with driving the agenda forward in 1999 and 2000, are diverse and global. Most of the WPS work undertaken prior to the adoption of UNSCR 1325 and in the two decades since has not happened in, nor is it even mostly visible at, the UN HQ in

New York, as I have touched on already. The knowing and seeing of this work is also racialized, along the lines of the discipline of IR more broadly, where it is assumed that theory is developed in the Global North and tested in the Global South. "While individuals and organizations from the Global South are acknowledged and celebrated for their WPS work in local contexts, the authorship of the relevant reports and documents—at the global level—lies . . . with the relevant international body" (Basu 2016a, 366). The racial and spatial politics of the WPS agenda (see Pratt 2013; Martín de Almagro 2018a; Parashar 2019; Hagen and Haastrup 2020) are thus implicated in the production of knowledge about the agenda, and I am wary of this book perpetuating the exclusions and limitations of the WPS agenda that I seek to critique.

There are many sites at which the narrative constitution of the WPS agenda could be, or could have been, examined. I have chosen to focus on the narratives curated, collected, and co-produced at UN HQ. These are obviously just a small part of the WPS "whole," a story so complex and wide ranging that it would be impossible to attend to all its dynamics, actors, and tropes in a single book (or even across the span of a career). WPS stories exist in local, national, regional, and transnational spaces and places, at the so-called grassroots and in elite institutions of governments; these stories feature many different actors with varying levels of access to power and who enjoy different levels of privilege. These stories border, and sometimes intersect with or are even represented within, the WPS stories at UN HQ, but are not encompassed by them; WPS exceeds the narratives I examine and, conversely, the narratives I examine necessarily exclude many WPS stories.[8]

There is no satisfactory resolution to the problem of exclusions and limitations in the specific case of my research on narratives at once structured and riven by racial, gendered, and class power, nor to the ongoing issues of partiality and privilege that come with working on narrative in general. There is no easy answer to the question of whose stories count or the question of how to address the multiple relations of inequality and domination that validate me, a White Western feminist researcher, to write this book. Linda Tuhiwai Smith proposes that research should proceed according to the principle of "getting the story right" and "telling the story well" (2012, 226). There are so many stories to tell about the WPS agenda, and such profound political implications to draw out from those stories. I hope that in this book, I can at least tell this story well.

A narrative of Women, Peace and Security

The first time I went to New York, to talk to UN staff and civil society actors about the WPS agenda, it was July 2013. The contrast between the humid, crowded city streets and the quiet cool of overly air-conditioned offices was disconcerting. The entire experience was disconcerting, and so different to the bloodless and prim description of the research process that I had outlined in the grant application that funded my presence there. I remember being overwhelmed and overawed, and also mildly affronted by my own abiding sense that I didn't belong in those spaces. Visiting again in the years that have passed between then and now, visiting the same people and the same offices (though not necessarily in the same configurations, as people move around from post to post, from organization to organization, while remaining in the general orbit of WPS work), I feel the same but different: an insider/outsider.

I can claim some expertise in this area, some—occasional, partial, provisional—"insider" status after many years of research on WPS. I wrote my doctoral dissertation on UNSCR 1325, adopted in 2000 after a debate on a new thematic area for Council business: "women and peace and security." I have spent nearly fifteen years working on and with this resolution and those that came after. I have written many articles and a couple of books, and I have traveled back and forth from Sydney to New York, growing increasingly—though never completely—comfortable with navigating those bureaucratic and institutional spaces held and animated by the WPS agenda. And I have listened to hours and hours of WPS stories.

I have learned much from these stories. I have learned the language of "women, peace, and security," the significant dates, the acronyms, the alliances, and the antagonisms. I have learned how meaningful a pause can be, or a raised eyebrow, in the recounting of an event or experience. I have learned the power of the knowing nod, as a response to the phrase that begins, "Well, of course you know . . . ." *Of course <nod>*. This is a benefit of the time I have spent in these spaces, a privilege of the assumption of expertise that structures my own engagement. I have learned what is taken for granted in WPS circles in New York, what is and is not featured in a shared history, what counts as "common sense" among these clever, committed, and altogether *human* advocates for the agenda. Fundamentally, I have learned how central storytelling is to my own understanding and to the development of a shared understanding of what the agenda has been, is, and could be.

All of the research participants that I have worked with over the years have generously shared their time, and their tales of WPS activity, with me. I have read the science of WPS—its resolutions, reports, and research—and I have heard its stories.

> Science explains how in general water freezes when (all other things being equal) its temperature reaches zero degrees centigrade; but it takes a story to convey what it was like to lose one's footing on slippery ice on late afternoon in December 2004, under a steel-grey sky. (Herman 2007, 3)

The formal documentation and informal communications of WPS share, and thus socialize, not quite the sensation of losing one's footing on slippery ice, per David Herman's eloquent formulation, but certainly more than can be apprehended through simply listing provisions, mandates, and recommendations from research or policy. The narrative formation of the WPS agenda is the focus of this research because I believe that we stand to learn much from investigating how WPS emerges through storytelling practices as a knowable policy agenda, a "thing in the world" that we can apprehend and understand.

In this book, I analyze these data as stories of the WPS agenda, examining the arrangement of discourse in the formation of particular stories. I argue that the form of these stories is structured through four powerful sets of logics:[9] logics of (in)coherence, logics of (im)possibility, logics of (dis)location, and an ambivalent logic of practice. The parenthetical modifiers in these logics are not an affectation; these logics are intrinsically plural, resisting closure. The function of the parentheses is to emphasize plurality and undecidability, to hold in mind when reading that these logics cannot be reconciled. A singular logic of coherence would tend toward organizing discourses that in turn reproduce the agenda as whole and integrated, and—conversely—a logic of incoherence would tend toward organizing discourses that reproduce the agenda as multiple and dis-integrating. The argument I make here is that *both* of these logics structure the discourses that in turn comprise the narratives of the WPS agenda. They are not "either/or" but "both/and." Similarly, a logic of possibility would tend to structure the narrative of the agenda according to its representation as manageable and operationalizable; impossibility renders its opposites—and *both* are evident, both are "true" in the stories of WPS that I recount here. Logics of (dis)location produce the space/place of the agenda, situating or "homing" the agenda in New York and at the UN, on the one hand, and on the other hand, reproducing its projection elsewhere, to spaces/places beyond and outside of the elite institutions of global governance. This relates to, but is not exhausted by, what I identify as an ambivalent logic of practice. It is ambivalent because it structures the attachment of radically different values to the concept of practice; literally, its valence, or emotional register, is both "good" (representing authenticity, experience, and credibility) and "bad" (subordinate to formal knowledge, expertise, and authority). These four sets of logics are evident in, and resonate across, the diverse and disparate discourses that I identify within the ways in which the agenda is narrated. These logics have a plurality that cannot be reconciled, and together they produce and structure the (un)imaginable future(s) of the agenda.

This is not the argument that I thought I would make in this book. Until I was about halfway through writing the book, I thought I would produce a neat, and—yes—singular argument about what the WPS agenda *is*, how it emerges through its narration as a straightforward, knowable policy agenda in world politics with particular characteristics or qualities deriving from the logics that structure its fields of discursivity. My early work on UNSCR 1325 found the kind of certainty, the kind of singularity and consistency, that I presumed I would find here as well. It was disorienting to sift through layers and layers of discursive practices, pages and pages of texts and transcripts, only to find when I arrived at a conclusion that I had no satisfactory conclusion to offer. Writing toward this singularity was exhausting and dishonest, and it was only when I began to consider the possibility that I didn't need to reconcile the plurality I couldn't make sense of that this plurality began to make sense. The irreconcilability of these plural, or ambiguous, logics, precludes the realization of the agenda as a singular, essential "thing in the world." There is no "true" WPS agenda that practitioners, activists, and policy makers can apprehend and use as their guide; there is only a messy and contested space for political interventions of different kinds. As I show in the analysis that follows, much energy and resource is expended in efforts to reduce or resolve the agenda to a singular, essential "thing"—with singular, essential meaning. The argument I present here implies that those seeking to realize the WPS agenda might need instead to live with the irreconcilable, the irresolvable, and the ambiguous. I show how the narratives of the WPS agenda are organized according to these plural logics and argue that this plurality, the actually existing complexity, of the agenda cannot—should not—be used as an alibi for limited engagement or strategic inaction.

In Chapter 2, I outline a methodology for the investigation presented in the substantive analytical chapters (Chapters 3–7 inclusive). I begin Chapter 2 with a discussion of dimensions of narrative, distinguishing between working *on* narrative and working *with* narrative in the study of politics (broadly conceived). I situate the form of narrative analysis I use in this project in relation to different modes of narrative scholarship. Building on previous work on discourse analysis, I distinguish discourse from narrative and explain how I use both of these concepts in my analysis of WPS stories. I discuss the tools of narrative analysis and discourse analysis that I use to make sense of the data I have collected and introduce the concept of discursive logics. In the final section, I outline the design of the project presented in the book and explain the research process, providing an overview of the data that I analyze: twenty-four interviews conducted with people working on WPS in and around the UN; and more than ninety documents produced by the UN, including Secretary-General's reports on various dimensions of the WPS agenda and statements by UN Women and representatives of the NGO Working Group on Women, Peace and Security at the annual Open Debate on WPS (a full list of documents is included in Appendix 2).

Chapter 3, the first substantive analytical chapter, outlines the "origin stories" of the WPS agenda. One of the most prominent motifs in the data I have collected is a repeated, and repeatedly *coherent*, narrative of the history of the agenda, which tells of the advocacy surrounding the adoption of UNSCR 1325 in 2000 and anchors the agenda firmly in the passage of this resolution by the UN Security Council. The narration of this "origin story" is of critical importance in shaping what the agenda could and would become in the intervening twenty years. In particular, the "ownership" of the agenda by the women's civil society organizations that lobbied for the adoption of the foundational resolution is a touchstone of political activism around the agenda and has had a material impact on its implementation and related practices. I show how this narrative is comprised of discourses of significance, interconnectedness, and completeness, which manifest in turn each of the four sets of logics that I excavate throughout this analysis.

Chapter 4 examines the "success stories" of the WPS agenda, interrogating the ways in which the agenda emerges as a triumph of transnational advocacy, a step forward in the seemingly endless search for strategies to mitigate against gendered inequalities and discrimination, and the prompt for—or ally of—related policy initiatives such as the UK's Preventing Sexual Violence Initiative (PSVI) or the "feminist foreign policy" commitments of Sweden and Canada.

The discourses held in the stories of success include those about the anniversary of the adoption of UNSCR 1325, which I label the "anniversary effect," and discourse about success *in moderation*, which is about the "little wins" that the agenda can count. The third discourse relates the possibility of leveraging the agenda to achieve particular kinds of political change at the UN and beyond. Again, these discourses are structured by logics of (in)coherence, (im)possibility, (dis)location, and the ambivalent logic of practice I introduced previously.

In Chapter 5, I interrogate the challenges and obstacles that are a frequent theme in the WPS stories I have collected. Specifically, I examine the ways in which failure, limitations, and challenges are narrated in the WPS agenda, and juxtapose these "failure narratives" with the "success stories" presented in the previous chapter. I argue that the explanations of failure that are dominant in the narratives I examine frequently relate to material failures of implementation, which are in turn attributed to a lack of resources and/or a lack of political will by the actor(s) in question to take up the WPS agenda in earnest. I propose that these failure stories—or "failure rationales"—are problematic, as "political will" is so general an explanatory factor as to be impossible to counter (an argument in line with Jutta Weldes's treatment of "the national interest"; see Weldes 1996a, 1996b). Narrating the failures of the WPS agenda in this way therefore reproduces (and is itself reproduced by) logics of (im)possibility and (in)coherence. These logics are reinforced in and through discourses of (lacking) expertise and discourse about the scope of the agenda.

Chapter 6 investigates stories about tension in the WPS agenda, according to its narration across the data I have collected. These stories of tension are comprised of discourses about the way that the agenda has developed into a/an (un)settled set of principles and priorities; this discourse in particular is integral to the reproduction of the agenda's organization into "pillars" and the idea that there ought to be balance among them. This discourse is organized by logics of (in)coherence and (im)possibility. Further, there is a powerful discourse on (dis)connections within and between spaces and practices of the agenda and a discourse about the power of the Security Council that features prominently in the narration of tension, reproducing the logic of (dis)location. The final discourse I identify in this chapter is about "resolution fatigue," which posits that there is no appetite for further resolutions to be adopted under the title of "women and peace and security." This last discourse manifests the ambivalent logic of practice.

Chapter 7 explores the narration of silences, secrets, and sensibilities in the WPS agenda. This is an exploration of feelings, and perceptions, of absences or palimpsest: residual traces of different knowledge formations and the erasure or disciplining out of certain dispositions or modes of engagement. These stories are comprised of discourses about the limitations of data; about individual influences (and influencers); and about intuition, and ambition, both personal and on behalf of WPS as a knowable policy agenda. There are specific silences and absences that are alluded to in the data I have collected that have a formative effect on the political affordances generated by the WPS agenda; the "common sense" of WPS is that these dimensions should be left unspoken lest they provide cynics and skeptics with critical ammunition to undermine the agenda. I suggest that there may be positive political gains to be made from examining some of these silences and absences as constitutive of the WPS agenda and therefore as implicated in both its failures and its successes. This chapter weaves in a discussion of the politics of knowledge, scientism, and subjectivity and connects these with the four logics that run through each of the previous chapters.

In Chapter 8, I offer a brief conclusion. I revisit the elaboration of the logics I identify and reflect on the implications of these logics for the imaginable future(s) of the WPS agenda. I also revisit the contribution that the book hopes to make, both to research on global governance and to research on the WPS agenda. I situate the WPS agenda as a form of international policymaking and international policy practice constituted in and through the stories that are told about it, arguing that in order to apprehend WPS as a knowable policy agenda, due analytical attention should be paid to the ways in which it is narrated. Through analysis of narrative and discourse, it is possible to identify the logics that organize and (re)produce meaning in particular configurations and that therefore structure the horizons of possibility around WPS as a policy agenda. The plural logics I identify resist efforts to close down or narrow the meaning of WPS as a policy agenda in global politics, and so effective political engagement—the realization of the agenda—depends on sitting with, and finding productive potential in, multiplicity, polysemy, and ambivalence.

2

Tools to Think with

Narrative, Discourse, Logics

Narratives of the WPS agenda, through various discourses structured in accordance with specific logics, recount the formation of the agenda, the mobilization of support, and the varied implementation successes and shortcomings of the agenda, both at UN HQ and elsewhere. In this chapter, I outline a methodology for the investigation presented in the chapters that follow. I begin with a discussion of dimensions of narrative, distinguishing between working *on* narrative and working *with* narrative in the study of politics (broadly conceived). I situate the form of narrative analysis I use in this project in relation to different modes of narrative scholarship. Building on previous work on discourse analysis, I distinguish discourse from narrative and explain how I use each of these concepts in my analysis of WPS stories. I discuss the tools of narrative analysis and discourse analysis that I use to make sense of the data I have collected and introduce the concept of discursive logics. In the final section, I outline the design of the project presented in the book and explain the research process, providing an overview of the data that I analyze: twenty-four interviews conducted with people working on WPS in and around the UN, and more than ninety documents produced by the UN, including Secretary-General's reports on various dimensions of the WPS agenda and statements by UN Women and representatives of the NGO Working Group on Women, Peace and Security at the annual Open Debate on WPS.

The driving theoretical claim in this book is that the stories that are told about the WPS agenda—its narration within this particular institutional context—have profound and constitutive effects for how the agenda is encountered, known, and acted upon. In the previous chapter, I introduced the idea that storytelling is a political practice and a fundamentally human practice. We learn from stories, from the ways in which stories are told. In the context of this investigation, which explores the narration of the WPS agenda at the headquarters of the United Nations in New York, the stories

Narrating the Women, Peace and Security Agenda. Laura J. Shepherd, Oxford University Press (2021). © Oxford University Press. DOI: 10.1093/oso/9780197557242.003.0002

that are told about the agenda—the events that are made prominent, the actors, the timelines, and the points of contestation—are constitutive of WPS as a knowable policy agenda in world politics. Moreover, the specific ways in which the WPS agenda is narrated function to hold open the meaning of the agenda, to resist—in fact, to render impossible—the closure of the agenda around a single and stable meaning, thus shaping and informing the futures of the agenda. In this chapter, I develop the theoretical and conceptual framework that sustains such a claim.

Working on/with narrative: A theoretical framework

The narrative constitution of the object of study (in this case, the WPS agenda) proceeds according to the same dynamics, and with the same political significance, as the narrative constitution of the self as a political subject. Thus, in this section I show how working *with* narrative has afforded new insights in the study of world politics, to craft a theory of narrative that centers the concept of constitution. This approach allows me to link working *with* narrative to working *on* narrative, wherein the narratives of others are rendered visible as the analytical object, without giving up on the constitutive theoretical commitments I advance. I draw in examples of narrative analysis that forward similar theorizations of the world as narratively constituted and also highlight those that see, and treat, narrative differently.

International Relations (IR), the discipline in which I (somewhat uneasily) situate myself and my scholarship, is a particularly *disciplined* discipline. The idea of *a* discipline (noun), in the academic sense, clearly derives from the verb: both relate to establishing clear boundaries between what is right and good (behavior/research) and what is wrong and bad (behavior/research); both have ways to correct transgression when an uninitiated (or resistant) person strays. We are trained to recognize the boundaries of our discipline and to stay carefully within them, and the artifacts and agents of IR police those boundaries furiously, both explicitly and implicitly.[1] "Among other things, international relations students are quietly forbidden from looking for, let alone importing, valuable insights from art, fiction, and literary criticism" (Babík 2019, 4). Yet—and thankfully—an ill-disciplined, dissident series of scholars have refused to be bound by such strictures and have delighted in music, photographs, sculptures, murals, novels, and films as ways of encountering, and presenting encounters with, world politics (see, among many others, Bleiker 2009; Franklin, ed. 2005; Harman 2019; Shapiro 2009; Sylvester 2013, 2019; Weber 2011).

Though diverse, these studies proceed from a broadly similar set of theoretical assumptions about knowledge and its manifestations. Of relevance here is the assumption that, to varying degrees, the (so-called) fictive and the aesthetic are as rich a source of insight about world politics as other, more formally validated texts such as Presidential Statements and policy documents. Further, the fictive and the aesthetic are modes of expression that can allow access to knowledge about world politics that is otherwise closed off. Scholars have written novels (Dauphinee 2013; Jackson 2014), made films (Der Derian 2012; Harman and Welham 2017), and produced collage art (Särmä 2014) to explore the dynamics of power and authority that other research explores in more conventional ways. Of particular interest here, of course, is the work in narrative form. Such work disrupts the "secret assessment" that "[f]iction's insights are not . . . transferable to our actual world" (Inayatullah and Dauphinee 2016, 1; see also Inayatullah 2013).

Narrative accounts of world politics "facilitate an encounter between writing and reading that enhances de-reification by demonstrating the partiality of knowledge and the fractures that are inherent in our societies, in our subjectivities, and, by extension, in our scholarship" (Ravecca and Dauphinee 2018, 126). The worlds about which we write in narrative form are the same worlds about which we theorize in the scholarship that suppresses the "I," that makes a claim to objectivity and coheres in rationality, but they are invented differently, invested with different qualities and visible in different ways, such that they emerge as different, and differently imaginable, "things." Moreover, we ourselves are differently constituted in narrative. The "I" that engages in narrative writing from within a discipline such as IR is undone in, and by, the process of such writing in so much more visible a way than that which characterizes the "scientific" writing that is expected of disciplinary scholars (see Inayatullah 2011; Naumes 2015; Shepherd 2016a, 2018).

The "I"/researcher-self that authors these words is always already present in this text, whether acknowledged explicitly or not. As I have written elsewhere, the elements of this research "are inevitably shaped by my subjectivity and emerge in and through my research practice; they are informed by and inform my engagement with people, books, fields, offices, social mediascapes and seashores" (Shepherd 2016a, 10). The self/subject and the object of study are simultaneously constituted in and through the narrative account.

I recognize that I have made decisions and exclusions that influence this text, and thus I am visible here in conversation with the "object" of my study as a kind of palimpsest, both residue and structure. This theory of narrative collapses the distance between self and object, between experiential account and objective analysis. It is both/and; theoretically, *this* narrative, the one you hold in your hand or view on your screen, in keeping with other narrative forms, "challenge[s] both authenticity and authority through . . . complex negotiations of theory and experience" (Ravecca and Dauphinee 2018, 136).

I do not offer in this book a *personal narrative*, or autoethnographic, account of the diffusion and disturbances of the WPS agenda at the United Nations (though see Shepherd 2016a, 2018, for elements of the same). Instead, I engage with the narratives of the WPS agenda from this theoretical perspective: a theory of narrative that posits that "exposure and disclosure of the self/selves, rather than locating some idiosyncratic 'n of 1' or some *sui generis* entity, instead uncovers events, histories, cultures, and worlds" (Inayatullah 2011, 8). That is to say, accounts of the self, which are expounded through the narration of an "I-being," always implicate and are implicated in broader, and necessarily political, dynamics; "narratives . . . are accountable for the kind of work they do in unpacking or reproducing the official scripts attached to power structures" (Ravecca and Dauphinee 2018, 131). The subject realized through narratives of the WPS agenda is the agenda itself, and exploration of these stories too "uncovers events, histories, cultures, and worlds." Also, the stories that are told about the WPS agenda frequently feature an "I"-self, situate this self-as-subject in relation to multiple objects, and in so doing, produce and reproduce specific configurations of power: structures of authority, legitimacy, and credibility in relation to the telling. Narratives, in short, present and thus forge relationships between the self/subject and the context within which the self/subject is narrated; a political engagement with narrative draws out these relationships and complex connections between subjects and objects as they emerge as knowable (Ravecca 2019, 32).

The primary theoretical insight that I draw from this body of work on narrative, then, relates to the political function of narrative in, and as a form of, knowledge production. Narrative offers a particular construction of self/selves (subjects) and surrounding objects with which those subjects are held in relation: the "events, histories, cultures, and worlds" that Inayatullah sees revealed through narration (2011, 8). Embracing narrative form in one's own work opens up these relationships in generative and sometimes difficult ways.[2] Apprehending narrative in political analysis, therefore, encourages the researcher to investigate the dynamic interplay between (presented/narrated) self and situation such that both are constituted in the narration, evident in the formation of stories to tell. I carry this element—of narrative constitution—forward as a critical element of the theoretical framework currently under construction here.

In addition to those works that write in narrative form, working *with* narrative in provocative and productive ways, there are those studies that work *on* narrative, seeking to understand how the stories we apprehend about our worlds work to tell of our worlds and bring those worlds into being (Krystalli 2019). A foundational, and highly influential, contribution to this body of work is Annick Wibben's *Feminist Security Studies: A Narrative Approach* (2011). Extending the insights of poststructural work that acknowledge the ontological significance of language (which assumes that what we (think we) know about the world—including the world itself—is constituted through the ways in which we engage with the world; see Hansen 2006, 18–23), Wibben's book lays out both a methodological and a normative case for paying critical attention to how we make sense of experience through storytelling—and how we can interpret diverse knowledge claims as security stories. In order to understand security politics and practices, IR tends to focus its analytical gaze on policy documents, databases, and discussions of strategy, but Wibben argues that we can glean many fruitful insights from listening attentively to how people make sense of their security environments. For example, through her analysis of the narration of "9/11," Wibben concludes that

> [s]elected narratives, those that conform to and confirm the existing order because they can occupy a space within its confines, are re/circulated. It is a violent process of controlling and securitizing meaning because narratives arrest meaning. (2011, 64)

This is a political undertaking that unsettles the foundations of much conventional security studies scholarship, demanding that we pay analytical attention to the formation and re/production of knowledge about security rather than accepting our objects of study as extant a priori. The broader implications of this research are to encourage a focus on which narratives are "re/circulated" and how they function to invent orders.

Building on these insights, other scholars have used narrative analysis to good effect in understanding political institutions, including—and of particular interest to the present study—the United Nations and the WPS agenda.

Ingvild Bode (2019), for example, explores narrative accounts provided by senior women in the UN Secretariat and reflects "on how gendered power relations emerge and are sustained and resisted in practice. . . . The narrative form can explicate existing practices and the power relations they sustain, while also drawing attention to women's agency" (Bode 2019, 2). Bode's research sustains and furthers the theoretical claim regarding the utility of narrative in efforts to elicit the connections between self and situation, extending this insight to third-party narratives and also drawing attention to the ways in which narrators tell stories as part of their own interpretive engagement with the worlds they inhabit. How research participants situate themselves as characters in their own stories reveals much about how they make sense of their experiences and expertise (Bode 2019, 7) and also reveals much about how the operation of power is perpetuated and sustained.

A further theoretical claim relevant to narrative analysis is put forward by Maria Jansson and Maud Eduards (2016), whose work considers the disruptive power of narrative in the context of peace and security governance. Jansson and Eduards analyze the policy architecture of the WPS agenda—the collection of adopted UN Security Council resolutions, of which at the time of writing there were eight—through the lens of narrative, to examine the ways in which particular emergent or contingent narrative constructions force revision to, or reconfiguration of, dominant conventional narratives of peace and security. Specifically, the authors argue that the resolutions' representation of wartime sexual violence "undermines central security narratives that build on the idea or myth that war is undertaken to protect women and children" (Jansson and Eduards 2016, 599). More broadly, their analysis shows that bringing to the center those narratives that have been held at the margins historically, as is the case with feminist war stories in the wider context of warcraft and security strategies, offers a valuable opportunity for rupture and contestation of those structures that position certain knowledges as central (to theory and practice) and others as marginal (Jansson and Eduards 2016, 601).

Through engagement with existing scholarship that works with and on narrative, I have drawn out three claims that combine to constitute the theoretical framework of the investigation I present in this book. First, a narrative approach places the analytical focus on the co-constitution of the storytelling self and the situation or context. Narratives permit insight into how subjects render themselves knowable and how they conceive of, communicate, and therefore construct other subjects and the worlds they inhabit.

These insights are unique to narrative ensembles of knowledge in the social sciences because the "I"/researcher-self is so often written out of our knowledge products.[3] Further, these insights are transferable to the analysis of the other subjects that are constituted in and through narrative. As narratives of the WPS agenda present an account of, for example, the formation of a new UN entity or the experience of negotiating a new resolution, all subjects and objects and relational connections are produced in and through the discourses that comprise the story. Thus, storytelling is a process of narrative (co-)constitution.

Second, a narrative approach attends to *which* stories are told, and when, and which stories are (dis)counted, because exploring the political effects of organizing and communicating knowledge in narrative form reveals much about how power operates. As Wibben explains, narratives "are sites for the exercise of power; through narratives we not only investigate but also invent an order for the world" (2011, 2). Related to, but different from, discourse (as I elaborate further later), narrative has an iterative quality that affixes and affirms relationships between subjects and objects, and thus *every* narrative is on some level a story about power. "The framing of events in a particular narrative always has implications for action because it includes and excludes opinions and actors, while also limiting what can be thought or said, thus eventually imposing silences" (Wibben 2011, 3). Power flows through narrative, and produces worlds; by devoting a chapter to the stories of silences, secrets, and sensibilities of the WPS agenda, I examine what is included and what is left out of the agenda's narrative formation and thus can excavate the relations of power that dominate the agenda at this particular historical moment.

The third element of the theoretical framework I present here draws attention to the disruptive power of narrative. A narrative approach necessarily engages with the stories that have become accepted or dominant over time; when a researcher asks someone to recount an event or reflect on a phenomenon, those memories are usually told and retold in the same way. As Stuart Hall reminds us, "We mainly tell stories like we've told them before" (Hall 1984, 5). Telling, or bringing to light, new stories, or juxtaposing existing stories that conflict over or contest salient details, can be a way to deconstruct or challenge those power structures mentioned in the previous paragraph. Narratives are always partial and productive, and they thus always contain plural political possibilities. A narrative approach makes analytical use of this plurality, examining the different stories that are told about specific events or phenomena and exploring the different implications of each. This is not a reconstructive project per se, but in the juxtaposition of narratives, or the privileging of a previously subjugated narrative, it is possible to challenge existing structures of power and see different possibilities emerge. My reading of the WPS stories presented here reveals an intrinsic plurality in the logics that structure the discourses which are arranged into story formations, thus disrupting a desire for singularity and homogeneity that informs many knowledge claims about the agenda.

In this section, I have engaged with narrative analysis in order to assemble a theoretical framework that guides my research on narratives of the WPS agenda. The analysis presented in the remainder of this book elaborates these theoretical claims through the close examination of various narratives elicited both from relevant documents issued by the United Nations and in interviews with key actors working on and around the WPS agenda at UN HQ in New York. The theoretical framework outlined here brings together the social practice of storytelling within the analytical reach of the more familiar tools—within political science and international relations, at least—of discourse analysis. Thus, the next sections draws on narrative and discourse analysis to explain which concepts I bring to bear on the data with which I am working.

Concepts as tools to think with, part I: Narrative analysis

Starting with narrative analysis, I draw on Mieke Bal's distinction between "layers" of narrative that allow the analyst to interpret meaning in/from an assemblage of textual data. Bal proposes the analytical utility of three layers—text, story, and *fabula* (Bal 2017, 6)—but to avoid overburdening the conceptual framework under development here, I focus just on text and *fabula*.[4] Bal articulates a broad definition of "narrative text," proposing that we can identify a narrative text as one "in which an agent or subject conveys to an addressee . . . a story in a medium, such as language, imagery, sound, buildings, or a combination thereof" (2017, 5). The texts under consideration in the following chapters are primarily, though not exclusively, linguistic; nonlinguistic elements include, for example, images of the UN logo on the reports of the Secretary-General and the transcripts of the Open Debates, the physical architecture of the space at UN HQ, and the gestures and embodied expressions of the research participants during our conversations. Once the texts are determined, the *fabula* can be identified. The *fabula* is the "series of logically and chronologically related events that are caused or experienced by actors" (Bal 2017, 5), the conjuring of connections between objects and subjects to marshal meaning. While the discursive content of the texts might vary, the elements of the *fabula* remain the same; each text presents "a particular manifestation, inflection, and 'colouring' of a *fabula*" (Bal 2017, 5). In this analysis, I am trying to draw out and explicate the stories, and through those stories, the *fabula* of the WPS agenda at the United Nations. These *fabula* manifest in and through the stories that are told about WPS: the "tellings" of events and actors and relationships between them, the composition of stories in/through discourse. Centering events and actors in this theory of narrative draws attention to two further elements of the *fabula* that can assist in the construction of an analytical framework: temporal organization, relating to how the timeline is constructed; and characterization, in terms of how the actors within the *fabula* are constructed.[5]

First, temporal organization, as mentioned, concerns the ways in which time is represented *within* the narrative. "Time and space are . . . more than background elements in narrative; they are part of its fabric, affecting our basic understanding of a narrative text" (Bridgeman 2007, 52). In the narratives I examine here, motifs of temporality are of central significance, in at least two ways. First, the co-produced narratives elicited through interviews almost all present a telling back through time of the emergence of the WPS agenda at the United Nations, referring to the adoption of resolution 1325 and the subsequent development of the agenda. In part, this is a function of how the conversations unfolded with the research participants, but in academic work also the agenda's temporality is part of its narrative; scholars routinely invoke the adoption of resolution 1325 in October 2000 at the beginning of books and articles on the subject (see, among many others, McLeod 2013, 166; Otto and Heathcote 2014, 2; Basu 2016b, 255; Johnson-Freese 2019, 1). Thus, as part of the investigation presented here, the concept of temporality and temporal organization was used to understand how the narratives cohere and explored further to interpret the political significance and ramifications of this iterative return to the foundation of the agenda at the turn of the millennium. This concept is primarily used to inform analysis in Chapter 3, which examines narratives of genesis, but the pasts and possible futures of the agenda are also significant in organizing narratives of success and shortcomings. Temporal organization is therefore a useful tool to think with in understanding how the WPS agenda is narrated at UN HQ.

Characterization is the second concept that informs my analysis. This is of critical significance given the centrality in political analysis of the identification of relevant actors, all of which have varying capacities to directly or indirectly effect political change. The narrative universe of WPS at the UN HQ includes many characters, including member states (in general, and specifically), civil society organizations (again, in in general, and specifically), named individuals, the UN Secretary-General, and so on. These feature across the different texts at different times and are each understood to have different (more or less stable) attributes and to perform different roles in the diffusion or implementation of the agenda. The concept of characterization is useful because it reminds me that the emergence of these actors *as characters* is part of the narrative process and does not necessarily reflect an authentic or "real" self/subject. Such an approach "is concerned not so much with the validity and specific nature of any given mental representation but rather with its textual base" (Margolin 2007, 76). "Mental representation" is used to explain the process of forming an image of a character so that we—the reader of the narrative—can make claims or inferences about them. The texts I engage here present various characters and ascribe to those characters different characteristics and qualities: influence, authority, courage, and persistence, for example. These characters feature more or less prominently at different moments in the narratives and are constructed as responsible agents at key moments in certain stories that are told; this has an impact, in turn, on how change is perceived within the agenda and what are the conditions or horizons of possibility. These elements of characterization are drawn out in the context of the various narrative themes over the coming chapters.

In each of the analytical chapters that follows, I attend to one element or component of a broad and polyvalent set of WPS narratives. It is important to hold in mind both the plurality of the WPS stories that are told, even in and around a single site of practice such as the United Nations, and the simultaneous will to singularity that emerges in appeals to forms of "common knowledge" and common sense. Each of the chapters first (re)constructs and then analyzes an element of the WPS story, a process I call "identifying the *fabula*." I attempt to sum up, in two or three sentences, the essence of the story I present for analysis (the *fabula* is also presented in its entirety to introduce the book in the previous chapter). I then apply the techniques of narrative analysis outlined here, explicating the temporal ordering that structures the narrative, and the dynamics of characterization I identify, in order to map out the narrative formation. To analyze the content (the discourse and attendant logics), however, different conceptual tools are required. Thus, in the next section I develop a set of textual analytical strategies that I use to deconstruct and interpret the narratives with which I am working.

Concepts as tools to think with, part II: Discourse analysis

As I explained in the previous chapter, the conceptualization of narrative that I deploy in this research is inherently imbricated with discourse. Narratives can be apprehended and analyzed as sticky arrangements of discourse, as assemblages or partially and temporarily fixed configurations that cohere over time and have a broadly consistent, if contextually contingent, form, as outlined previously. If a narrative approach reveals the structure of the stories that are told—and informs the insights that can be gleaned from telling stories—then discourse theory offers the means to interpret the content and political affordances of those stories.

Discourses form the totality of that which can be apprehended about a knowable object; it is through discourses that objects (and subjects, and the relations between them) become meaningful. Different discourses configure those attachments of meaning quite differently, such that the narratives that can be woven around those subjects and objects are many and various. A simple example is that of the subject of women and the object of political leadership. In one discourse, the meanings attached to the subject of "woman" construct her as emotional, frail, weak, constrained by her femininity and her association with childbearing and domestic care, and thus less suited to political leadership than her male counterparts. A different set of attachments characterizes a counter-discourse that positions women as uniquely suited to leadership *because* of their femininity, emotionality, and association with care, pacifism, and nurture: a "women as peacemakers" discourse. There are myriad other discourses that configure the subject of woman in relation to leadership in different ways, and all can be narrated in stories about political events and phenomena that in turn help us make sense of the world. Discourse is, in a sense, the raw material of narrative.

Critical to my understanding of discourse is that its production does not presume the existence of a pre-discursive, agential subject. Assuming rationality and intentionality requires engaging with the possibility of an extra-discursive or pre-discursive reality, as it assumes that we can tell, as analysts, what policy makers and political elites are *really* thinking or doing outside of discourse. A poststructural discourse-theoretical approach does not speculate on motivations or intentions and thus moves further away from the presupposition of a rationally acting subject, rather than closer to it; scholars in this tradition study the conditions under which it becomes possible for actors to be seen to have "agency" and argue that identity is performatively constituted in/through discourse. There is nothing inherent in the concept of discourse that demands this kind of world view or research design; there are plenty of analysts of discourse who maintain a commitment to epistemic realism (the idea that there exists a reality independent of our encounters or imaginings). But as it is used by poststructural scholars of global politics, the concept of discourse does not rely on the existence of a pre- or extra-discursive realm, nor yet does it presume intentionality of actors even as it permits interrogation of the process of construction. Discourse describes "structures of meaning-in-use" (Milliken 1999, 231), but there is no presumption of an agent constituted outside of discourse that *uses* meaning. Rather, the subject-position of agent, and the condition of agency, are constructed in and through discourse. The agential subject is an effect of power as well as (rather than) its possessor or its dispossessed.

Deconstructive discourse analysis can show how subjects and objects emerge as known/knowable and how the discourse in question creates relational chains of meaning between these subjects and objects such that they are known/knowable in particular ways—according to particular logics. Logics organize a discourse and produce, through signification, the overarching semblance of fixity that allows for the expression of the known/knowable. These logics are never predetermined, and it is in fact part of the ethos of deconstructive discourse analysis that the taking apart of discourse is always a project of radical possibility. Because a deconstructive discourse analysis is motivated by a desire to show the processes through which meaning is constructed, it simultaneously shows how the construction of meaning is itself contingent and thus changeable. A deconstructive approach is a way of laying bare, or excavating, the logics of a text that create coherence and authority, and of surfacing the instability and tensions within the text (Derrida 1978, 278–282). The "center" or logics of the discourse that hold together certain possibilities, while precluding others, create instead of instability the appearance of totality (though of course such an appearance of totality is always precarious; see Laclau and Mouffe [1985] 2001, 96).

The idea that discourses are held together by logics is of central importance in this research. Logics are frequently assumed (or forced) to be singular, reducible to one side or another of a binary opposition; different logics of security, for example, take *either* the state *or* the human as the referent object, and different logics of gender construct masculine subjects as *either* aggressors *or* protectors (though these are of course intertextually articulated with other discourses and logics that constitute *some* masculine subjects as aggressors and *some* as protectors—"virtuous masculinity depends on its constitute relation to the presumption of evil others"; see Young 2003, 13). The way that I use logics here, however, takes inspiration from Cynthia Weber's work on "queer logics of statecraft" (2016, 38–46) and resists the closure or fixity of privileging one side of the dichotomy over the other. Thus, the logics I identify are plural, not singular.

Roland Barthes argues that the purpose of interpretation is to lay out the plurality of a text (1974, 5). In a particularly delightful turn of phrase, and drawing on his analysis of the representation of the subject of the *castrato*, Barthes argues that to force that closure or privileging, "to choose, to decide on a hierarchy of codes, on a predetermination of messages, as in secondary-school explications, is *impertinent*," as it denies the plurality and "non-decidability" of the workings of the text (Barthes 1974, 77; emphasis in original; see also the discussion in Weber 2016, 41–42). Weber interpolates Barthes's discussion of the "and/or" (as opposed to the "either/or" configurations discussed previously), as a way of holding open the plurality of the text, into her elaboration of "queer logics of statecraft," arguing that

> [i]n the (pluralized) *and/or*, meanings are no longer (exclusively) regulated by the slash that divides the *either/or*. Instead, meanings are also *irregulated* by this slash, and by additional slashes that connect terms in multiple ways that defy *either/or* interpretations. (Weber 2016, 41; emphasis in original)

Although Weber is theorizing the constitution of subjectivity specifically, and although I do not situate mine as a queer analysis per se, this articulation of the irreconcilability of plural logics is relevant to and inspires my excavation of the narratives of the WPS agenda.

The political affordances of the plural logics I identify, and the discourses they sustain, are similarly plural. As I discussed in the previous chapter, these logics produce and structure the imaginable futures of the agenda (and the unimaginable futures also); the logics "produce new institutions, new structures of understanding, and new practical orientations that are paradoxically founded upon a disorientating *and/or* reorientating plurality" (Weber 2016, 44). Critically, these logics and discourses can be mobilized in support of *both* the status quo configuration of power relations *and* their radical reconfiguration (Weber 2016, 44); through resisting reconciliation to a singular logic or series of singular logics, the logics I identify introduce "a kind of systematic, non-decidable plurality" into the discourses that I analyze (Weber 2016, 42), which are in turn held in sticky arrangements to form the narratives of the WPS agenda. The stories that are told (re)produce these undecidable logics, refusing attempts at reducing the agenda to a singular "thing." This plurality and multiplicity creates forms of political possibility and also demonstrates that to apprehend the emergence of WPS as a knowable policy agenda through its narratives is to situate oneself in relation to the intrinsic ambiguity of its constitution.

In order to excavate the logics of discourse, to apprehend the construction of meaning, a researcher can deploy textual analytical strategies in a deconstructive mode. For this investigation, I have selected Roxanne Lynn Doty's methods of analysis (1993, 1996; see also Åhäll and Borg 2013) involving the analysis of *predication* and *subject-positioning*. As Doty explains, "[T]ogether, these methodological concepts produce a 'world' by providing positions for various kinds of subjects and endowing them with particular attributes" (Doty 1993, 307). Crucially, this world then makes possible certain kinds of activities, outcomes, and sensibilities, while other possibilities are foreclosed.

Predication is the process through which characteristics or attributes are attached to subjects, the articulation—or linking—of "describing words" to "words described."[6] The predicate is the part of the sentence that bestows meaning on the subject. For example, consider this sentence: "Resolution 1325 is a groundbreaking document that draws attention to gender issues in situations of armed conflict and post-conflict settings." Here, resolution 1325 is the subject. Through the act of predication, the resolution is made knowable/known both as "groundbreaking" (a presumed positive quality or characteristic) and as a "document" (different from, for example, a "legal instrument," "treaty," or other kind of text). Further, the content of the resolution is made knowable/known through predication here; it "*draws attention* to gender issues in situations of armed conflict and post-conflict settings." The use of "draws attention" here is somewhat weak language; imagine how different the impact would be if the resolution were described as "mandating action on gender issues," for example, or even "*demands* attention." Different horizons of possibility are created even through these simple articulations. Finally, within the predicate, the juxtaposition of "armed conflict and post-conflict settings" implies both that there is a meaningful distinction between the two phases and that the resolution contains measures or advice applicable in both contexts. Predication thus goes hand in hand with subject-positioning.

In the process of subject-positioning, the subjects and objects of discourse are positioned in relation to each other. Subjects and objects emerge as knowable/known in part through their relationship with other subjects and objects: "What defines a particular kind of subject is, in large part, the relationships that subject is positioned in relative to other kinds of subjects.... Some of the important kinds of relationships that position subjects are those of *opposition, identity, similarity,* and *complementarity*" (Doty 1993, 306). Thus, subjects/objects become knowable, for example, through their textual articulation as like, or unlike, other subjects/objects within the text. Consider this sentence: "Issues related to gender and armed conflict had been raised by women's civil society organizations for decades, but took on a new and more authoritative form when enshrined in United Nations Security Council Resolution 1325." This sentence positions women's civil society organizations differently—and subordinately—to the UN Security Council, which in turn is constituted as "authoritative," thus implying that women's civil society organizations lack the necessary authority to drive debate around gender and armed conflict.

In the chapters that follow, I analyze the textual mechanisms of predication and subject-positioning in the discourse of the WPS narratives I identify. Through this kind of analysis, I can deconstruct the discourses captured in narratives, creating a layered methodology drawing in two kinds of textual engagement. The benefit of narrative analysis is that it draws attention to the ways in which individuals interpret, and communicate about, political events and phenomena in the form of storytelling, thus showing how these interpretive and communicate acts stabilize certain formations of knowledge into coherent and consistent structures—sticky arrangements, as I called them before—over time. Subjecting these formations to discourse analysis allows me to explore the constitutive effects of the component parts of WPS stories. This method of analysis is attentive to

> how a discourse *produces* this world . . . how it renders logical and proper certain policies by authorities and in the implementation of those policies shapes and changes people's modes and conditions of living, and how it comes to be dispersed beyond authorized subjects to make up common sense for many in everyday society. (David Campbell, cited in Milliken 1999, 236)

The "common sense" of WPS is thus what is at stake in this analysis, as I am exploring how the agenda is, and can be, known, in order to reveal the intrinsically plural possibilities that are generated through the narration of WPS as an object of knowledge.

Research design

This project unfolded over many years, and—as is so often the case—went through many variations before emerging as a project that applies narrative theory to independently and co-produced texts about the WPS agenda. I had initially intended to analyze the universe of WPS documents produced in and around UN HQ, capturing every WPS text produced by a UN entity over the last two decades. It became quickly apparent that this was a vast and unfeasible endeavor.[7] Beyond the technical obstacles to executing such a project, however, I also had a conceptual concern about treating all of those entities as equivalent and worried about flattening out important differences between, for example, how WPS was narrated by the Economic and Social Council versus the Counter-Terrorism Executive Directorate. This seemed to be a project of a different order, investigating how these different entities narrated their own WPS stories.

It would be impossible for any single project to map the totality of WPS stories told at and by the United Nations, and so I have had to limit the scope of the research presented here. This project focuses on the WPS stories narrated by the UN Security Council, in its resolutions and statements; by the Secretary-General, in the form of the regular reports on WPS; by UN Women, as the lead UN entity on the WPS agenda; and by individuals who work in and around the WPS agenda in New York, including both UN staff and civil society actors. "Narrative prototypically roots itself in the lived, felt experiences of human or human-like agents interacting in an ongoing way with their cohorts and surrounding environment" (Herman 2007, 11). This project treats the institution of the United Nations as a "human-like" agent because the various UN entities, including the Secretary-General, are proponents of narratives about WPS.

The data set of documents analyzed in this research includes: ten UN Security Council resolutions adopted under the title of "women and peace and security"; fifteen Presidential Statements issued by the UN Security Council between 2001 and 2016; twenty-eight reports by the Secretary-General on the topic of WPS, produced between 2002 and 2019; transcripts of forty-one Open Debates at the Security Council that incorporated statements or testimony from UN actors and various civil society representatives, from 2001 to 2019; and twenty-four largely unstructured interviews with UN staff and civil society actors working on and with the WPS agenda in New York.[8] A full list of the documents, and relevant URLs, is included in Appendix 2. The various chapters that follow all use the data differently, with certain categories of data being more prominent in some chapters than others.[9] The organization of the analysis into the thematic chapters presented here derived from preliminary engagement with the data, a form of open coding (Hutchison, Johnston and Breckon 2010, 289). The broad themes that emerged were origins of the agenda; successes; obstacles and limitations; tensions and points of contestation; and the barely articulated, hidden, or obscured (primarily applicable to the interview data rather than the documentary data, this theme manifests in research participants suggesting that there are elements or dimensions of WPS work and activity that are invisible, and also that there are WPS issues that they would rather not discuss). Each document or transcript was analyzed using the broad themes as a way of organizing the analysis and identifying within each theme key moments within the narratives and significant discourses, in a form of iterative interpretation. This stage helped construct the narrative presented in each chapter. I then subjected the discourses that emerged to the analytical techniques outlined previously, to examine the processes of predication and subject-positioning that produce meaning and lay bare the logics that hold the discourse together in a semblance of fixity.

The documents are referenced by code in the text that follows, as each UN document has a unique alphanumeric identifier. The full list of documents referenced in the book is provided in Appendix 2. Interview transcripts are identified by number only, with the first four digits of the number corresponding to the year in which the interview took place. I took the decision not to ask for permission to attribute information communicated in interviews from the research participants, partly because I wanted them to be able to speak freely and partly because one of the guiding commitments of this research is that the narratives are not attributable to any single individual. The form and content of WPS stories is part of how knowledge about the agenda is (re)produced and communicated, and thus how the agenda itself is (re)produced and communicated. While individuals share narratives and tell stories, the subject-positions that enable their narratives to be heard and interpreted as authoritative are also a function of the narratives themselves. Simply put, I am interested in the institutional stories about the WPS agenda, and these cannot be fixed to or contained within the account of a single individual.

A final word on foundations and futures

In research design, I have always been inspired by the words of Giovanni Sartori, who suggests that "there is no methodology without logos, without thinking about thinking" (quoted in Gerring 2012, xix). In this chapter, I have offered an account of my "thinking about thinking": what I think can be known, why and how we might study that which can be known, and what might be the effects of studying such stuff. I have long been of the view that it is through discourse that we can apprehend the world. Following Laclau and Mouffe, I argue that the question of whether an experience, event, or phenomenon *really* ("objectively") exists, independent of our will or understanding, is largely irrelevant in the context of political analysis, for what *can* be studied is the articulation of that experience, event, or phenomenon into discourse. This is essentially to remain agnostic on the question of foundations: "What is denied is not that such objects exist eternal to thought, but the rather different assertion that they could constitute themselves as objects outside of any discursive condition of emergence" (Laclau and Mouffe [1985] 2001, 108). Focusing on the process of constitution means focusing on discourse, which does not require taking a position on whether the discourse reflects or is founded on/in material foundations. It does, however, require careful consideration of how a researcher might apprehend and engage discourse and what the application of discourse theory and analytical strategies can reveal about the world.

In addition to elaborating the narratives of the WPS agenda, then, this book also shows how narrative, discourse, and logics as tools to think with can enable researchers to examine the political possibilities of plurality and multiplicity in complex policy agendas. This book is therefore both concerned with describing the narratives of the WPS agenda that emerge at and around the UN HQ and with exploring the political implications of the narrative constructs that I uncover. As this chapter has explained, the analytical framework guiding the research takes the form and content of stories about WPS as politically significant, enabling an examination of temporal organization and characterization within WPS stories as the first layer of analytical engagement. The second layer of analytical engagement draws on techniques from discourse analysis to excavate the architectures of meaning within the narratives I apprehend. Discourse analysis is well suited to the interrogation of meaning construction; paying close attention to the ways in which particular articulations are forged within components of narrative can illuminate how certain political possibilities are created through the stories that are told. This is leveraged using the concept of logics, specifically plural logics that resist reconciliation or reduction to a singular meaning or horizon of possibility.

The discursive formations that we identify as narratives are solidly coherent, through reiteration over time coalescing into "common knowledge" about the agenda and its promise and pitfalls. As Clare Hemmings explains in reference to her own narrative analysis of Western feminist theory, "[C]ommon sense glosses suggest views that are generally rather than only individually held, and an examination of these offers insights into the dominant narrative forms governing our perception" (2011, 16–17).[10] The theoretical claim advanced here rests on previous and well-developed claims about the ontological significance of discourse (Hansen 2006, 18 passim). Discourse is the concept that captures all that is, and can be, known, and in this chapter I have shown how discourses captured in particular formations—here identified as narratives—and organized in accordance with particular logics have particular kinds of political resonance and relevance. Narratives of the WPS agenda not only articulate common knowledge, and common sense, but also tell of the past and present of political action in the sphere of WPS, projecting its imaginable futures. In the remainder of this book, I sketch out these narratives and explore the political affordances of these telling stories.

3

Ownership and Origin Stories

One of the most prominent motifs in the narration of the WPS agenda is a repeated, and repeatedly coherent, story of the history of "the agenda," which tells of the advocacy surrounding the adoption of UNSCR 1325 in 2000 and anchors the agenda firmly in the passage of this resolution by the UN Security Council. The narration of this "origin story" is of critical importance in shaping what the agenda could and would become in the following twenty years. The "ownership" of the agenda by the women's civil society organizations that lobbied for the adoption of the foundational resolution is a touchstone of political activism around the agenda and has had an impact on its development over the past two decades. In particular, the reiterated attribution of authority over the agenda to women's civil society organizations has sustained the involvement of those organizations in both ritualized celebrations of that agenda (for example, in the annual Open Debates at the Security Council on the theme) and implementation efforts. In terms of the future of the agenda, the power of this narrative renders it almost unthinkable that women's civil society organizations would be excluded from WPS practices at the United Nations, and it is further unlikely that the ownership claims made by and on behalf of these organizations would be disputed. These ownership claims, deriving from the origin stories, thus have important constitutive effects on the future of the agenda and on the legitimacy and credibility of various WPS subjects.

In this chapter, I identify a story of the origins of the agenda and its ownership, articulated through the discussion of the *fabula* in the following section. This story is constructed through three particularly prominent discourses. The first concerns the agenda's significance, representing it as somewhat *sui generis* and drawing together dimensions of discourses of place and space to construct a situatedness for the agenda that is *both* at/in *and* beyond the UN Security Council. This discourse is structured by logics of (dis)location and an ambivalent logic of practice. The second is a discourse of interconnectedness, or its preclusion: on the one hand, there is an opening up of the agenda through the articulation of its connection to numerous other policy

Narrating the Women, Peace and Security Agenda. Laura J. Shepherd, Oxford University Press (2021). © Oxford University Press. DOI: 10.1093/oso/9780197557242.003.0003

platforms and conventions; on the other hand, there is a conservative impulse to constrain it to the text of the UN Security Council resolutions frequently enumerated as its foundation. Connecting to articulations of the history and heritage of the WPS agenda, and of resolution 1325 in particular, the invocation of other policy platforms and conventions in the context of WPS storytelling both creates links across diverse fields of practice and can act as a mechanism through which the WPS agenda is strengthened and legitimized. It also, however, functions to constrain the agenda within a narrow field of associated policy frameworks. I show how these discourses are underpinned by logics of (in)coherence and (im)possibility. Finally, and relatedly, there is a discourse of "completeness," which is about the comprehensive coverage of the agenda, and its full and complete codification in UN Security Council resolutions, versus the impetus to extend the agenda to include emerging and new issues relevant to WPS. I identify here again the ambivalent logic of practice in the disconnection between the agenda "on paper" and "in practice"; this logic is reinforced and interwoven with logics of (dis)location, (im)possibility, and (in)coherence.

Identifying the *fabula*

Representatives of women's civil society organizations convened in New York in 2000 to encourage the UN Security Council to examine the impact of armed conflict on women and girls and to recognize the importance of women's participation in peace and conflict prevention. The adoption of resolution 1325 was a huge achievement, and the agenda has been elaborated over the intervening twenty years in a series of related resolutions. Thanks to sustained advocacy from women's civil society organizations, it is now impossible to ignore the gendered dynamics of international peace and security.

This is something of a "David and Goliath" story, with women's civil society organizations depicted as the underdog, the subordinate, and the champions of women across the world, whose experiences during conflict had been hitherto ignored by the organization charged with maintaining peace and providing security. These women, tired of being silenced and marginalized and of having security defined for them, pushed not only for a seat at the peace table and a way to be heard, but also for a fundamental re-visioning of what security means and how it might be achieved. Through their collective action, they challenged the Security Council to acknowledge the rights of women in conflict-affected settings and sought recognition of the need to "mainstream" gender through the peace and security work of the Council and the United Nations more broadly.

The agency and drive of civil society organizations is credited with providing the impetus for the consolidation of the range of issues affecting women in conflict and the crystallization of these issues into a resolution (and, later, an agenda; see Porter 2003; El-Bushra 2007; Shepherd 2008a, 132–145; Cockburn 2013). As one research participant explained: "It's the only agenda on the security docket that is basically only there because of the activism of women and women's civil society" (Interview, 201905). The significance of women's civil society to the narrative of WPS cannot be overstated. Across resolutions, Presidential Statements, transcripts of Open Debates, Secretary-General's reports, and hundreds of pages of interview data, the reaffirmation of women's civil society as the primary architects of the WPS agenda is repeated over and over again. "Women, peace and security, the whole agenda comes from civil society" (Interview, 201907).

A near-perfect rendering of this account is captured in the 2015 Secretary-General's Report on Women, Peace and Security, delivered in October to celebrate the 15th anniversary of the adoption of resolution 1325:

> In 2000, when women peace activists took their call for a women and peace and security agenda to the Security Council, they were not only demanding the full and equal participation of half the world's population in addressing threats to global peace and security but also seeking a fundamental shift in how international peace and security is maintained and restored. (S/2015/716, para. 66)

Central to this narrative, as evident in the excerpt above, is the agency of women peace activists and the transformative nature of their interventions. This is another important part of the WPS story. It is not only that "[f]or the first time in its fifty-year history, the council recognised that women have a right to protection and a role to play in maintaining peace and security" (Naraghi Anderlini 2007, 7), but also that the resolution pressed for by these women—these "veterans of the struggle for peace" (S/PV.7533 2015, p. 11)— was nothing short of "visionary" (S/2014/693, para. 75).

The origin myth of the WPS agenda, then, tells of a group of extraordinary women taking canny advantage of political opportunities, convening in New York to make the institutions of power in the realm of peace and security listen to their demands and to change the way that peace and security were conceptualized and addressed within the international system. "We were offering an alternative, or a new opening as a pathway to adapt the institutions better to the changing nature of warfare: *Women in civil society build peace. They can make a difference. Work with them*" (Naraghi Anderlini 2019, 43; emphasis in original). The agency, and efficacy, of these women is central to the origin myth: "They wanted it. The reason they came 20 years ago, they came to the Security Council, because they want this guy to change that here. They were powerful. They made it" (Interview, 201901).

This story has clear consequences for the ideas about ownership that still hold the agenda in the space of civil society: "[T]his is an agenda that was born from the advocacy of women's civil society, and resolutions which are developed without any consultations with them or without reflecting the needs of civil society are seen as less than legitimate" (Interview, 201910). Similarly, the "contribution of civil society" is repeatedly invoked in UN documents about the agenda, including in WPS resolutions and Presidential Statements (for example, S/RES/2122, preamble; S/RES/2242, preamble; S/PRST/2007/5, p. 2). The ownership of the agenda by civil society is part of the ongoing story of WPS at the Security Council, reaffirmed in many tellings and thus sustained: "[T]he Security Council underlines the importance of a broad and inclusive political consultation with various components of civil society, in particular women's organizations and groups" (S/PRST/2005/52, p. 2).

The *fabula* accounting for the origins of the WPS agenda relies heavily on specific forms of characterization. The protagonists in this narrative are the UN Security Council and women's civil society organizations, also variously described as "women peace activists" (as above, and also, for example, in S/2014/693, para. 5) and "the women's movement" (for example, in S/2004/814, para. 27). There are supporting actors, notably the United Nations Development Fund for Women (UNIFEM), which was the primary UN entity working on women's empowerment and gender equality at the time of resolution 1325's adoption, and certain member states. The governments of Bangladesh and Namibia in particular are credited with important supporting roles; as mentioned in Chapter 1, under the leadership of Ambassador Anwarul Chowdhury, the Security Council issued a statement recognizing that "peace is inextricably linked with equality between women and men" (United Nations 2000) when Bangladesh held the presidency of the Council in March 2000. The Namibian government held the presidency in October and took forward the theme of women and peace and security, working closely with the women's civil society organizations and UNIFEM staff, who had been preparing all year—in fact, for many years—to push the issue onto the agenda of the UN Security Council.

Crafting the narrative in this way positions the WPS agenda as a site of contestation, of struggle over how peace and security governance mechanisms are formed and legitimized. The constant reiteration of the centrality and significance of civil society functions, maximally, to challenge the supreme authority of the UN Security Council in the realm of peace and security governance and, minimally, to articulate a narrative of production and ownership of the foundation resolution and subsequent agenda that competes with the narrative propounded by the Security Council itself (see Shepherd 2008, 133–159). As I discuss in Chapter 6, there are discourses that locate the agenda under the auspices of the Security Council, but these are always complicated by the counter-discourses outlined here. Thus, the logics of (dis)location, which deny any singularity to the space/place of WPS, are visible here.

Rendering the characters in this way has influenced both the way that the Security Council has engaged with the agenda since the adoption of resolution 1325 and the way that civil society has continued to engage with the agenda:

> Each October, since the passing of 1325, the NGO community has pressed for and succeeded in obtaining a review of progress on the implementation of the resolution's key provisions. Upon the first anniversary, in 2001, the council members expressed surprise. "Other resolutions don't have anniversaries," they said, to which the NGOs replied, "Other resolutions don't have a global constituency." (Naraghi Anderlini 2007, 7)

The above account perpetuates the characterization of civil society versus the Council, as well as the ownership claim articulated by civil society over the resolution: there is a sense in which the activism of civil society, in this telling, is what is keeping the agenda alive. "SCR 1325 is our tool, the tool of women's peace activists and human rights NGOs. It was our idea, not the Security Council's, and it is our efforts that have given it life since its adoption" (Ruby 2014, 181). It is not only ownership at stake, but also the responsibility for nurturing the agenda, sustaining its life; these are deliberately gendered terms I use to evoke maternality as a dimension of how these characters are constructed, for it is a gendered narrative. As Carol Cohn has eloquently argued, "the SC is at the center of UN power. Not coincidentally, it is also an overwhelmingly male and masculinist domain, devoted to the 'hardcore' issue of military threats to international peace and security" (Cohn 2008, 186). This is not, therefore, solely a story of plucky civil society organizations persistently speaking truth to institutional power; this is a gendered story of women pushing at the door of "the master's house" (Lorde 1984, 110).

The final element of characterization I wish to draw out is the way that this narrative renders the characters in somewhat monolithic terms: women's civil society organizations are frequently articulated as a homogenous group, eliding the many points of disagreement and contestation within that diverse group of actors (on this important point, see Naraghi Anderlini 2019, 46), while the UN Security Council is similarly indicted as an institution as a whole, ignoring the openness and support of the Namibian, Bangladeshi, and Jamaican governments. Opening up these characters and acknowledging the frequent tensions that emerge within as well as between these groups is important for the future of the agenda, a point to which I return in later chapters. Smoothing out the differences and glossing over the sharp edges of coalition politics is part of how the story is told, and each telling reinforces the need for consistent positioning and engagement. Critique is disciplined. One research participant recounted the frustration some felt—and continue to feel—with the manicured narrative of 1325's adoption that has emerged: "[She] said something along the lines of, 'Oh my God, would you just . . ., just stop with already with romanticizing 1325. There was so much we left out, so many things that we sacrificed'. It was so imperfect, but we've made it into this. . . . In the face of later things, it suddenly becomes this perfect object of civil society engagement" (Interview, 201911). The semblance of perfect solidarity told in the origin story of the agenda affects both the history of the resolution—as it is difficult to then correct for dissent and disagreement—and the future—as critical engagement can be read as challenging the very foundations of the agenda itself (see Otto 2014).

In addition to characterization, the linear temporality of this origin story is significant. There is a timeline, with significant moments, woven into the fabric of the narrative of resolution 1325's adoption in 2000. The beginnings of the timeline are less clear than its linearity. Some accounts trace the evolution of the agenda back to 1915: "In 1915 a bunch of women from around the world got together and came up with a vision that actually didn't translate until the Security Council resolutions in 2000 and beyond" (Interview, 201301). Others connect the momentum carried forward in 2000 to the UN World Conferences on Women, which were inaugurated in 1975 in Mexico City and then convened every five years until the conference in Beijing in 1995, which was of particular significance to the nascent WPS agenda (see Cohn 2008, 187; Shepherd 2008, 110). One research participant explained, "[W]e were really the voice of civil society at the UN, that was our voice, that was who we were, we're the voice of the women's movement at the UN, created in Mexico, reinforced in Nairobi, Beijing, whatever, that was very much who we were" (Interview, 201905).

The Beijing Conference, the fourth UN World Conference on Women, produced a Declaration and Platform for Action (A/CONF.177/20), which is referenced in all but two of the WPS resolutions (exceptions being UNSCR 1960 and UNSCR 2103), and which includes a chapter titled "Women and Armed Conflict," cited by many as the foundation of UNSCR 1325 (Naraghi Anderlini 2007, 5; Hudson 2010, 8; Barnes 2011, 16–17). Tracing time in neat five-year increments and connecting March to October in 2000 as a way of articulating ownership over the agenda, the story of consistent and coherent women's peace activism leading inexorably to the production of UNSCR 1325 is reaffirmed. There is a politics to this narration, however, a politics of both place and race. As "the women's movement" traversed space and time to convene in New York in 2000 (seemingly to take up residence between March and October, though this is in fact improbable—or at least only available to a privileged few), New York was thus reinforced as the epicenter of WPS endeavors. What is frequently missing from the citation and recitation of the Beijing Platform for Action as a linchpin of the WPS agenda, however, is any acknowledgment that "Africa was the source and venue for the establishment of the type of principles and policies articulated in UNSCR 1325 even before the emergence of this UN resolution on women" (Diop 2011, 173).

While mention is made in the origin story of the WPS agenda of the influence of the Windhoek Conference, held in Namibia in May 2000, the subsequent Declaration, and the Namibia Plan of Action on Mainstreaming a Gender Perspective in Multidimensional Peace Support Operations, it does not enjoy nearly as central a role in the narrative as the Beijing Platform for Action. Moreover, the Windhoek Declaration is articulated as part of the documentary heritage of resolution 1325 (S/RES/1325, Preamble) but, unlike the Beijing Platform for Action, is never mentioned again in the policy architecture of the agenda. Windhoek features in only one Presidential Statement (S/PRST/2007/5, p. 2) and one report of the Secretary-General (S/2018/900, para. 49), while Beijing is mentioned in six of each.[1] In combination with the elision of time between March and October in many narratives of resolution 1325, the writing-out of Windhoek and the failure to cite the African Platform for Action (adopted in 1994) as the primary inspiration for the Beijing Platform for Action represents place and race in the WPS story in not altogether unproblematic ways; although Beijing was a "world conference," it took place at a time when some feminist collectives and organizations in the Global South were expressing concern "about the imposition of what is perceived as an external agenda, and about whose interests are served by the [gender] mainstreaming project" (Baden and Goetz 1997, 10). Further, differences in political preparedness and positional authority meant that women of color in Beijing were not necessarily able to contribute to the deliberations and the outcome document as fully as other groups of women (Dutt 1996, 527). Thus, the incantation of Beijing invokes not only a particular policy platform—and it is important to remember that the Platform for Action was ultimately negotiated by government representatives—but a temporal linkage to the other UN conferences in the series, a spatial linkage through attachment to the UN, and a racialization of the agenda that positions African feminists as supplicants to the Security Council rather than drivers of this agenda.[2]

To conclude the narrative analysis of the WPS origin story in this section, I present just one further aspect of characterization: the powerful articulation of ownership communicated by those who tell these stories through the use of "we" and "our." Many of the people I interviewed for this research claimed ownership through the use of these pronouns:

> We were really building a field from scratch and a lot of the things that we did in those early years I think was obviously building on a huge amount of work that had already been done by feminists working in the UN system, after Beijing but also even before Beijing. (Interview, 201602)

Similar characterization is evident in the statements made by representatives of civil society at the Open Debates on WPS (see, for example, S/PV.5294 2005, p. 13; S/PV.6005 2008, p. 8; S/PV.7533 2015, p. 11). The overall effect is to unify everyone working toward the realization of the WPS agenda as a single—if diverse—entity. Among civil society actors, "we" statements help construct "NGOs . . . as a unit and as a force" (Interview, 201911), but among the WPS communities more broadly, this process of focalization infuses the narrative with a shared sense of both purpose and ownership, which is critical to the origin story.

In this section, I have outlined the *fabula* derived from the many WPS texts I collected and analyzed in pursuit of understanding the WPS origin story and narrative of ownership. In the section that follows, which applies discourse analytical techniques to the stories of origin and ownership, I examine the qualities of the WPS agenda as they are narrated through its origin story. I also explore the representation of the agenda as a governance framework, investigating how authority is constructed with the policy architectures through its positioning relative to other similar frameworks. The plural logics shaping the agenda through the dominant narratives I identify begin to emerge here: logics of (in)coherence, (im)possibility, and (dis)location, and an ambivalent logic of practice. ⟩ Debate @ authority

Discursive constructions of origin and ownership

The origin story of the WPS agenda constructs it not only as a known/knowable thing-in-the-world but as a particular *kind* of thing. This section first explores discourse about the significance of the WPS agenda. I go on to argue that the coalescing of the agenda into the often-cited four pillars is part of how it has taken form over the past two decades and that the implication of this distillation is to constrain specific understandings of what the agenda is and can be. Logics of (in)coherence and (im)possibility are particularly evident here, and also in the discourse of interconnectedness, the examination of which follows. Coherence in the agenda is complicated in part though attempts to link it to other governance mechanisms, which produces incoherence. This discourse functions to pre- and proscribe the broadening and deepening of the WPS agenda, inventing the agenda as fluid and encompassing, which has important implications for its possibility and potential. The final discourse relates the completeness of the agenda and brings into play an ambivalent logic of practice, which both attaches value to the resolutions "on paper" and devalues the resolutions themselves as political products of elite actors. Simultaneously, logics of (dis)location constitute the agenda as occupying particular spaces and places, both at/in and beyond the UN Security Council.

The significance of the WPS agenda

Resolution 1325 has been described in scholarly literature as "ground-breaking" (Tryggestad 2009, 539), "a landmark" (Cohn 2008, 185), "unprecedented" (Porter 2007, 17), "a watershed," and "a turning point" (Naraghi Anderlini 2007, 7). These modifiers elevate the resolution, and indeed the agenda more broadly, beyond "important," even beyond "significant." These descriptions communicate a sense of newness, a marker in an as-yet-uncharted territory. The break with convention, with the standard way of doing peace and security business, is further emphasized in the discourse of WPS origin stories. The resolution is described as a "tipping point" (S/PV.7533 2015, p. 11), an "extraordinary shift in the way conflict is addressed" (S/2011/598, para. 67). There is a definite sense of rupture or discontinuity in the way that the WPS agenda is constructed, a sense of the Council turning or inclining toward this new set of issues where previously there had been no such inclination.

The ability of the Security Council to chart a course in this new realm confers upon it clarity of purpose and intuition: "In its resolution 1325 (2000), the Security Council set out a *visionary* agenda for achieving gender equality as a prerequisite for peaceful, inclusive and just societies" (S/2014/693, para. 75; emphasis added). Notably, of course, it is not the issues that are new, but the placement of these issues on the agenda of the UN Security Council. It is this formalization of the process through which new issues are considered by the Council that gives rise to the moniker "the Women, Peace and Security agenda," which is not universally embraced:

> It's a thing, a big, solid thing now, this Women, Peace and Security agenda. For me, I was conflicted on the word 'agenda', and how I first thought about the idea of the Women, Peace and Security agenda, was not about our agenda, our side of the Council, pressuring the Council. But quite technically, Women, Peace and Security was an item on the Council's agenda. (Interview, 201911)

Another research participant similarly commented, "I feel really weird calling it an agenda. It's never been . . . everybody says that, but what is the agenda?" (Interview, 201906).

One of the ways in which the agenda is originated in discourse is as a collection of UN Security Council resolutions, in which "everything related to the Women, Peace and Security Agenda [is] . . . 1325 and all of the other Security Council resolutions" (Interview, 201301). In my own writing, I have referred frequently to the resolutions as the framework or architecture of the agenda, which affords the Council a degree of ownership and authority that others might contest: "[I]f I think of what matters in the world of issues related to Women, Peace and Security," said one participant, "I definitely think far beyond the Security Council" (Interview, 201911). There is no doubt, however, that the resolutions have a unique and particular significance in the origin story of the agenda; "1325," more so even than the other resolutions, is a nodal point within the discourse of the origins of the agenda, used as a shorthand, aide-mémoire, incantation. "1325 is just part of the conversation from day-to-day" (Interview, 201902). In many ways, across many conversations and documents, 1325 functions as a synecdoche; it *is* the WPS agenda, which ascribes power and authority to the Security Council as (technically and institutionally) author of the resolution. The logics of (dis)location begin to emerge here.

"I think there's something about Women, Peace and Security. As neat as those three letters [WPS] are, it is a very sprawling set of issues" (Interview, 201911). In my introduction to this book, I wrote about the seductive familiarity of the abbreviations, acronyms, and alphanumeric codes that comprise the vocabulary of the WPS agenda. As Carol Cohn comments in her influential analysis of nuclear weapons discourse, there is a thrill to "being able to manipulate an arcane language, the power of entering the secret kingdom, being someone in the know" (1987, 704). Repeatedly invoking "WPS" in my own work and conversations, I contribute to this exclusivity, this idea that there is an "expert community" of WPS people who can effectively decode those three letters. But part of what is revealed through analysis of WPS discourse is the extent of contestation over what WPS is.

A key dimension of the origin story relates to the originary or "real" meaning of the WPS agenda. There are evidently those who believe that there is a singular truth to the agenda, people who express concern about the "danger of taking the agenda off course if the political will, attention and desire to drive it is not informed by an understanding of where it comes from and what its *true origins* are" (Interview, 201909; emphasis added). It is hard, however, to find evidence for a singular, indisputable truth of WPS in the discourse. Some earlier, first-decade, accounts of the agenda in the Secretary-General's reports in particular produce the bifurcation that would later be identified as characteristic of the agenda. Consider, for example, the following:

> The significance of resolution 1325 (2000) lies in the way it links the impact of war and conflict on women on the one hand, and promotes their participation in various peace and security processes such as in peace negotiations, constitutional and electoral reforms and reconstruction and reintegration on the other. (S/2009/465, para. 77)

"On the one hand," here, women are visible as victims of violence, bearing the "impact of war and conflict," while "on the other," women are political actors, agents of change capable of meaningful participation in peace and security processes. The plurality of the construction of the subject of "woman" here defies singular explanations of the "real" meaning of WPS; this discourse is structured in part by logics of (in)coherence.

Similarly, there is contestation in the discourse over the constitution of WPS as a "rights" agenda as opposed to a "conflict prevention" agenda (for examples of academic research on this tension, see Hudson 2009, 2010; Harrington 2011; Heathcote 2011, 2012). Again, it is both. This is evident not only in the institutional discourse (see, for example, S/2015/716, para. 66; S/2017/861, para. 1, para. 69), but in the interview data co-produced for this project. Interestingly, several research participants articulated both understandings of the WPS equally emphatically within the same conversation: first "fundamentally the Women, Peace and Security agenda is a prevention agenda" (Interview, 201909), and then "[i]t's an equality agenda. It's a social justice agenda. And I think those are the origins that we need to take forward" (Interview, 201909); first "the WPS agenda has always been an agenda which promotes the rights of women affected by conflict and the organizations that promote their rights. So it is a rights-based agenda" (Interview, 201910), and then "we really had to go back to explain the narrative of 1325 being a conflict prevention agenda" (Interview, 201910). That the individuals I interviewed could not consistently articulate a singular truth about WPS lends credence to the conclusion that the agenda *has* no singular truth; in accordance with logics of (in)coherence and (im)possibility, it is rather a plural and yet somehow profoundly transformative agenda.

The transformative dimension of the agenda is widely agreed upon. Resolution 1325 is described as having "transformative potential" (S/2015/716, para. 22), while the agenda more broadly "contributes to transformative change" (S/2017/861, para. 1).[3] The transformative capacity of the agenda and its component resolutions is the nodal point around which the agenda coheres: "That is what the commitments of resolutions 1325 (2000) and 1820 (2008) are about: the transformation of society" (S/PV.6005 2008, p. 10). This has important implications for whether the "expectations and hopes" borne by the agenda can be realized (Interview, 201601). By shifting the discourse away from the concrete elaboration of potential foci for the agenda and those who work on it—human rights, security, conflict prevention, and so on—and articulating instead a commitment to (potentially limitless) "transformation," successful implementation of the agenda becomes exponentially more difficult, the agenda itself constituted as a utopian dream: "Not just fix the UN, fix the world, that's Women, Peace and Security" (Interview, 201403). The logics of (im)possibility organize this discourse.

Efforts are made to anchor transformation, however, in a substantive political commitment to demilitarization, to create a target for transformative efforts that is slightly more manageable, more feasible, than "the world." Linked explicitly to the ways in which the origins of WPS are narrated, transformation of the war system and the militarized societies that support it is embedded in the agenda. This happens in two ways. First, origin stories of the WPS agenda frequently cite Cora Weiss, director of the Hague Appeal for Peace, which was one of the founding members of the coalition that became the NGO Working Group on Women, Peace and Security, and her now-famous exhortation that "we are not just trying to make war safe for women" but to bring about an end to the war system itself (quoted in Cohn 2008, 199; see also Shepherd 2016b, 332; Hunt and Wairimu Nderitu 2019). Second, and more fleetingly, there are moments of possibility presented in the discourse of the organization. In 2015, for example, the Secretary-General's report on WPS recognized—in the context of articulating it as a prevention agenda—that the advocates for the foundational resolution were seeking nothing less than "a rollback of the escalating levels of militarization that was making homes, communities and nations less secure" (S/2015/716, para. 66).

Systemic transformation is thus articulated as the heart of the WPS agenda. But these discursive openings are rare. As one research participant commented:

We're not going to the core of the issue and saying, "Well, actually, WPS is really about opposing war." It's really . . . that's where feminists came from. . . . We oppose war. We oppose intervention in the name of women's rights. And what we really want to see is an end to patriarchy and capitalism. (Interview, 201912)

I return to this question of scope in Chapter 7, in which I explore the radical potentialities of the WPS agenda as they are articulated, or not, by those working in this space. In terms of how the agenda itself is constituted, however, there is one element I wish to explore here, as it has an impact on this question of what the agenda is and how, therefore, it might be encountered. This is the relational connection of the agenda with other policy platforms and conventions. The extent to which the agenda is articulated in relation to these other mechanisms and commitments depicts the agenda as a certain kind of thing; it is therefore important to examine the ways in which these relationships are constructed in the discourse as part of (or absent from) the origin stories of the agenda.

Connecting the WPS agenda to CEDAW and other frameworks

The WPS agenda is described as having not only an origin story but also a point of origin; as mentioned above, this coheres around the expression of a "truth" of the WPS agenda or a "core." For example, research participants talked of "core fundamentals" (Interview, 201403) and "core components of the agenda" (Interview, 20912), while the Secretary-General's reports articulate "core objectives of resolution 1325" (S/2009/465, para. 74) and "the core purpose of the women and peace and security agenda" (S/2018/900, para. 67). I elaborate in the following section on the discourses that support this process of constituting the agenda around a core purpose or set of issues and on the logics of (in)coherence that inform these discourses. In this section, I want to draw out the construction of the agenda as additive, explaining how the discourses of the agenda's development first posit the core and then expand the agenda through its connection to several other frameworks and areas of action, again organized in accordance with logics of (im)possibility and (in)coherence: "How do you get some kind of coherence with the post-2015 and all of these various agendas? All of these various other processes? Where does the agenda sit itself?" (Interview, 201403).

The connection of the WPS agenda to other areas of action at the UN should be read in the context of the recitation of the agenda's heritage in the foundational resolution and the policy relationships into which the agenda emerged; as mentioned earlier, these include the Beijing Platform for Action, the Windhoek Declaration, and the Namibia Plan of Action on Mainstreaming a Gender Perspective in Multidimensional Peace Support Operations, as well as the UN Charter. Paragraph 9 of resolution 1325, moreover, reminds "parties to armed conflict" of their obligations under numerous other conventions and treaties:

> the Geneva Conventions of 1949 and the Additional Protocols thereto of 1977, the Refugee Convention of 1951 and the Protocol thereto of 1967, the Convention on the Elimination of All Forms of Discrimination against Women of 1979 and the Optional Protocol thereto of 1999 and the United Nations Convention on the Rights of the Child of 1989 and the two Optional Protocols thereto of 25 May 2000, and . . . the relevant provisions of the Rome Statute of the International Criminal Court. (S/RES/1325, para. 9)

The inclusion of the Convention on the Elimination of All Forms of Discrimination against Women (CEDAW) and the Convention on the Rights of the Child in this paragraph reproduces the influence of the human rights architecture over the WPS agenda (see also Tripp 2006; Reilly 2009, 109–112; Arat 2015). As noted above, there is some contestation about the agenda as a rights agenda, but as is clear from the text of resolution 1325, the rights architecture is one of the constructs with which the agenda was interrelated from this first textual articulation.[4]

Connection to CEDAW has grown and strengthened over the past two decades. One research participant commented that it was "impossible" to think about the two frameworks existing in isolation: "I created a matrix to link it to CEDAW, because I go, I have it very difficult to think things are not really like that. For me, the CEDAW has to relate to this and execute. You don't have gender equality separate" (Interview, 201901). This is reaffirmed frequently in the Secretary-General's reports, all of which mention the Convention; further, all but two of the WPS resolutions reaffirm the obligations of state parties to the Convention (exceptions once again being UNSCR 1960 and UNSCR 2103), and three Presidential Statements similarly urge compliance (S/PRST/2007/40, p. 3; S/PRST/2011/20, p. 1; S/PRST/2012/23, p. 1). The function of this repeated invocation is to give "teeth" to the WPS agenda. Unlike the WPS resolutions themselves—which are binding but unenforceable under international law (see Chinkin 2019, 28)—CEDAW has a powerful accountability mechanism built in: "187 member states ratified it, it's probably the strongest accountability mechanism we have at this point" (Interview, 201402); "The Women, Peace and Security, it's not, how do you call it? CEDAW has the legal framework that governments have signed into. Women, Peace and Security, government haven't signed into. That's the biggest issue" (Interview, 201901).

Working consistently to form a discursive link between CEDAW and WPS has more than normative weight, then. The linkage perpetuates the agenda's possibility, through connecting it with this Convention on women's rights that has near-universal ratification; the connection also benefits the agenda through building in enforcement, most recently through General Recommendation 30 (GR 30). The text of CEDAW does not specify its applicability to situations of armed conflict; it focuses on economic, civil, and political rights such as employment, healthcare, inheritance, and political representation. In 2013, the Committee on the Elimination of All Forms of Discrimination Against Women, which has oversight of the Convention and which monitors the obligations of state parties, adopted a "general recommendation" on the applicability of CEDAW to women in conflict prevention, conflict, and post-conflict situations (see Patten 2018).[5] In the origin story of the WPS agenda, this is an important moment, as it also has a cohesive effect on the agenda, per the following:

> Implementation of commitments on women and peace and security at the national level should be grounded in human rights instruments, such as the Convention on the Elimination of All Forms of Discrimination against Women. The decision by the Committee on the Elimination of Discrimination against Women in 2010 to prepare a general recommendation on the protection of women's human rights in conflict and post-conflict contexts marks an important step in further *clarifying the obligations* of States parties to the Convention in those contexts and in providing *authoritative guidance* on the necessary legislative, policy and other measures to meet such obligations. (S/2011/598, para. 59; emphasis added)

GR 30, and association with CEDAW more broadly, rather than working *against* coherence by adding complexity to the agenda, function in quite the opposite way, to constitute the agenda as more coherent and therefore clearer and less complex.

The completeness of the WPS agenda

The WPS agenda is a promise: "a promise to women across the globe that their rights will be protected and that barriers to their equal participation and full involvement in the maintenance and promotion of sustainable peace will be removed" (S/2004/814, para. 121; see also S/2010/498, para. 3). The agenda is also "a framework for action" (S/2005/636, para. 5), a "mandate" (S/2006/770, para. 31), and "a critical, yet underutilized tool" (S/2016/822, para. 4). Along with the promise, therefore, comes a certain pragmatism, the idea that the agenda can be put to work like a tool, or that it manifests as a structure supporting women and the pursuit of peace and security in a straightforward and unproblematic way. Both discourses of promise and practical utility rely on the coherence of the agenda as a set of actions or principles; even where there is skepticism of discourses of transformation and promise, there is a logic of coherence in the discourses leveraged to express a more "realistic" orientation or mode of engagement (Interview, 201904).

Many of the people I spoke to in the course of this research were adamant that the agenda is settled, that "we" have agreed the principles and priorities of the agenda and that no "new language" is needed for the agenda to be successfully implemented or upheld (Interview, 201401): "[W]e've really mapped out conceptually what needs to happen for a gender-just peace, we just haven't implemented it" (Interview, 201401):

> I think it's important to not push for any more resolutions—I think we have everything that we need. Now we really need to focus on the implementation, and leave the policy side of things, you know, to itself. (Interview, 201606)

Consistently and over several years, the people I spoke with argued that the "policy level" or "policy side" of the agenda is complete. Their discourse, however, not only attributed to the WPS agenda policy architecture a coherence and comprehensive quality that is arguably open to contestation but also constituted the agenda as having a duality that is frequently reiterated in institutional discourse: through these articulations, the two dimensions of the agenda are constructed as policy and practice, hence the ambivalent logic of practice I identify within this discourse.

The tension between policy and practice is not unique to the WPS agenda, of course. But this seemingly ineluctable and persistent "gap" (see, among many other examples, S/2007/567, para. 34; S/PRST/2011/20, p. 1; S/2013/525, para. 76; S/PRST/2014/21, p. 3) reinforces a separation between the domains of the agenda such that other binaries are also strengthened, notably "rhetoric" versus "reality." For example, the 2015 Secretary-General's report comments on the "disconnect between the rhetoric and the degree of investment in relevant programming on the ground" (S/2015/716, para. 92; see also S/2016/822, para. 4). The concern here is that the reiteration of the "gap" affirms the plurality of the agenda such that it is not only constituted as Janus-faced—looking on the resolutions and Presidential Statements in one direction and in the other toward efforts to use the priorities and principles captured in those documents to inform activities and advocacy—but also as part of a system of oppositions that subtly undermines the significance of the written word of the agenda while valuing the practice (irrespective of the nature of the practice itself). This happens through the articulation of these binary oppositions: policy versus practice, rhetoric versus reality, words versus deeds.

I am not arguing here that the "gap" between the provisions captured in the resolutions and the ways in which those provisions are being interpreted and acted upon is unimportant. I am making the rather different argument that the articulation of a "gap" at all performs a number of political functions that are of equal significance and far less frequently interrogated. First, the "gap" implies a settled-ness or completeness within the agenda; if the agenda is dynamic, changeable, and fluid, then it lacks the necessary stability against which a gap can be measured. This forecloses development of the agenda in new and different directions. Second, the "gap" sustains and is sustained by the ambivalent logic of practice, in this instance valuing practice over policy, which takes attention away from policy-level negotiations and analysis, suggesting that effort is better expended in evaluation of implementation than in the possibilities that are afforded through the resolutions and statements that comprise the framework of the agenda. Together, these two effects constrain the imaginable futures of the WPS agenda, limiting the ways in which those working in this space encounter and use the agenda in their work: "[I]n the early days of 1325, . . . there was a lot of work about making . . . connections at all sorts of places. And I'm not sure now if, with a much more comprehensive policy framework, if that still feels as possible for people. I don't know. But when you got so much, when you arrive in a place with so much policy already in place, I mean, your imagination is maybe not as free to just find connections" (Interview, 201911).

Concluding thoughts on ownership and origin stories

In this chapter, I have explored the origin story of the WPS agenda and examined some of the claims to ownership that are narrated in the stories that are told in and around the United Nations Headquarters. There is similarity and resonance in the *fabula* I have brought to the surface across multiple texts. As shown, there are many variations of the origin story that feature similar characters and temporal ordering. Here is just one example:

> The adoption of the resolution was the culmination of years of concerted appeals and efforts, especially by civil society and women's organizations, to draw attention to and seek action to reverse the egregious and inhumane treatment of women and girls, the denial of their human rights and their exclusion from decision-making in situations of armed conflict. (S/2010/ 498, para. 1)

The elements of the *fabula* identified above are all present here: the ownership of civil society, the "years of concerted appeals and efforts," and the constitution of the agenda as concerning both rights and bodies of women and girls "in situations of armed conflict."

The constituent discourses of the origin stories and narratives of ownership are about the agenda's significance, its interconnectedness, and its completeness. Articulations of how important the agenda is, its landmark achievements in the field of women's rights (and peace and security), and its intersections with other related policy frameworks (or the lack thereof) represent the agenda in accordance with logics of (in)coherence and (im) possibility. Further, the discourse of completeness, in particular, creates an ambivalence or ambiguity about the spatiality and situatedness of the agenda: at the Council and in the resolutions, on the one hand, but also simultaneously "on the ground" and "in practice." Thus, an ambivalent logic of practice emerges, in conjunction with logics of (dis)location. These logics, all four, inform and shape the emergence of WPS as a knowable policy agenda and are of critical political significance, as without settling the question of what the agenda *is*—what it is about, what it seeks to achieve, and how—its effectiveness cannot be measured. It is this question to which I now turn, as the two chapters that follow deal directly with the question of measurement, focusing in turn on narratives of success and shortcomings.

4

Narratives of Success

This chapter examines the "success stories" of the WPS agenda, interrogating how the agenda emerges as a triumph of transnational advocacy, a step forward in the seemingly endless search for strategies to mitigate against gendered inequalities and discrimination, and the prompt for—or ally of—related policy initiatives such as the UK's Preventing Sexual Violence Initiative (PSVI) or the "feminist foreign policy" commitments of Sweden and Canada. Multiple articulations of success feature in the narrative of the agenda; for the purpose of identifying the *fabula*, I have organized these into two primary dimensions. First, the narration of the WPS agenda frequently cites the agenda itself as a success. This narrative element relates the emergence and consolidation of the agenda, and its rise to prominence as a governance framework, as a success, in line with the narration of the origin story of the agenda recounted in the previous chapter. The repeated narration of the agenda as evidence of its own success is not only tautological but also reinforces the idea that it can unproblematically be depicted as an ongoing struggle to provide structure to, and attain visibility of, gendered harms in conflict and conflict-affected settings. This creates discursive space for continued elaboration of an opposing position, enactors of which perform ongoing resistance to the agenda at the national or international level. The second dimension of the success story is the narration of moderate successes in implementation of the WPS agenda. These are the moments of change and, by implication, improvement to organizational structure or individual experience that the agenda has brought about. Over time, the ways in which these victories are presented, particularly in the Secretary-General's reports but also in the contributions and statements to Security Council Open Debates and even in interview data, rely more and more on quantitative data. Further—in terms of subject specificity—these successes are related increasingly to the prevention of sexual violence and women's participation in peace processes, while other dimensions of the agenda are less well attended.

This narrative, of the blossoming of the agenda and its moderate victories, manifested in the changes it has brought about, presents certain subjects

Narrating the Women, Peace and Security Agenda. Laura J. Shepherd, Oxford University Press (2021). © Oxford University Press. DOI: 10.1093/oso/9780197557242.003.0004

as the key characters in its narrative formation and also relates to discourse about institutional activity in the realm of the WPS agenda in particular ways. The stories identified here are comprised of three prominent discourses. First, there is a discourse about the "anniversary effect" of the institutional celebration of the adoption of UNSCR 1325 each year in October. The effect, and marking, of this anniversary reinforces the logics of (dis)location and the ambivalent logic of practice introduced previously. The second discourse I identify here relates to the idea of moderation evident in the *fabula*, and I characterize this as a discourse of "little wins." The diminution of success limits the possibilities afforded by the discourse making up the story of success, and this discourse is thus structured by logics of (im)possibility, in that each "win" is undermined by the elements left unrealized, the aspects of the agenda yet "un-won." The final discourse imbricated in the success story is one of leverage, both transnationally (across the institution of the UN) and nationally (as the agenda is used by women's organizations to pressure national governments to achieve particular advocacy and lobbying objectives). The logics of (dis)location are evident here, as the agenda is represented as belonging in and to both of these spaces simultaneously. Moreover, the articulation of the agenda in terms of its utility as a tool to effect change (the telling of which in turn constitutes and reinforces the subjects of the agenda and the relationships between them) operates in accordance with a logic of possibility, but the *need* to leverage the agenda to realize its own success constitutes it as impossible. Thus, logics of (im)possibility hold this discourse together.

The visibility of the agenda and its use in political mobilization are affirmed in recent research on the normative weight of WPS (see, for example, Hudson 2015; O'Rourke 2017; True and Wiener 2019); this can indeed be interpreted as a marker of success, as can the connection of the agenda to other, related, normative and policy frameworks. These discourses certainly reinforce the coherence and possibility of the agenda. They also, however, simultaneously operate according to logics of incoherence and impossibility, along with logics of (dis)location. While it is important to recognize and celebrate success, representing as it does a tremendous amount of hard work, advocacy, pressure, and the tireless commitment of many WPS actors, it is equally important to recognize that the things that are reported as success also shape the agenda, influencing how it is perceived, what is valued, and what is taken forward for future action. The success stories I recount here tend to reinforce state-led, Global North–dominated, articulations of WPS futures and to organize the resourcing of the agenda accordingly.

Identifying the *fabula*

We have resolution 1325 and the other resolutions, and that's impor-
tant in and of itself. It's not perfect, but we didn't have those resolutions,
this agenda, 20 years ago. The WPS agenda has really changed how the
UN thinks about peace and security, and women on the ground can
use the resolutions to put pressure on their governments, to make them
take the agenda seriously.

In the way that stories of success are told, there is a prior dimension to consider in accounting for the success of the various efforts and initiatives
within the agenda, and that is the existence of the agenda itself. Following
from the origin story elaborated in the previous chapter is the story of how
the adoption of UNSCR 1325 and each subsequent resolution is positioned
as a success in its own right; the achievement here is not the amelioration
of gendered inequalities and harms, nor the reconfiguration of gendered
power as it operates in peace and security settings, but rather the passage of
UNSCR 1325 and the rest of the resolutions that make up the architecture
of the WPS agenda. The WPS resolutions, and the weight afforded to them
as pronouncements of the UN Security Council, are positioned as successes
because their adoption was, in each case, by no means a foregone conclusion
(see Cook 2009; Jansson and Eduards 2016; Heathcote 2018).

This dimension of the *fabula* partly manifests in comparing the institutional culture of "peace-and-security-that-was" to where "we" are now. One
research participant, for example, commented:

When I think about the early days where we didn't even have any, not a
single gender advisor in [redacted] in New York, there was nobody.
[redacted] was just all people, men, and women, but all in dark suits with
no knowledge or understanding of gender at all. And you'd walk around the
halls and try to talk to them, and in those days it was like, "Well what are
you talking about, is it women or gender?," and they were kind of throwing
it back on us as like, "What is this thing called gender?," the level of ignorance, or agnosticism, I'm not sure what it is . . . was so high. (Interview,
201905)

Similarly, the early reports from the Secretary-General regarding the
successes of the agenda repeatedly recount the issues—the lack of gender
awareness, "ignorance, or agnosticism" that characterized UN work on

peace and security—that the agenda was adopted to counter. In 2004, the Secretary-General's report states bluntly that "[i]n no area of peace and security work are gender perspectives systematically incorporated in planning, implementation, monitoring and reporting" (S/2004/814, para. 118).

With the passage of time, the other WPS resolutions have also been held up as evidence of success. The adoption of UNSCR 1820, the second WPS resolution in the sequence, is celebrated in the Secretary-General's report the following year: "With the adoption of resolution 1820 (2008), the Security Council led the way in giving this issue the comprehensive and global attention it deserves" (S/2009/367, para. 56). The Security Council itself is of course produced through this narrative as an effective actor and champion of the WPS agenda. This is perhaps most clear in the (very lengthy) report of the Secretary-General to the Security Council in 2010, where it is suggested that "the adoption of resolutions 1820 (2008), 1888 (2009) and 1889 (2009) also illustrates the increased commitment of the Council to the issue of women and peace and security" (S/2010/498, para. 6). This sentiment is reinforced in a statement from the Open Debates, which "welcomes the advances heralded by those resolutions" (S/PV.6196 2009, p. 7). These constructions imply that the resolutions themselves are markers of success, suspending from consideration momentarily the fact that the resolutions require the mobilization of tremendous effort in order to themselves effect change in the world.

The emphasis in the WPS stories on normative change reinforces the significance of policy production:

> Remarkable achievements were made at the normative level in 2013: the Security Council adopted two new resolutions—2106 (2013) and 2122 (2013)—to make the women and peace and security agenda further operational; two high-level political commitments to combating sexual violence in conflict were made; a declaration on women's economic empowerment for peacebuilding was adopted by the Peacebuilding Commission (PBC/7/OC/3); and a criterion on gender-based violence was included in the Arms Trade Treaty. (S/2014/693, para. 2)

Many of the research participants that I spoke to in the course of this research held up the institutionalization of the agenda as a form, or marker, of success: "Five, six years [ago]," said one, "people would roll their eyes when you said what you were doing, like "Okay" (Interview, 201904). Broader contemporary institutional acceptance of the agenda is implied here, and the celebration of the adoption of resolutions and statements to buttress the foundational resolution. The political purchase of validating this kind of activity as success is explored further below, as "there's definitely the question of the institutionalization of these agendas and how once, once the UN and member states, et cetera, embraces them, embrace them, this is a victory. But in a way that's also the moment the agenda loses its political edge" (Interview, 201907).

Where observed change beyond the UN and beyond the policy framework is commented on, and is reported as success, the success is always qualified, undercut in every report of the Secretary-General by a reminder that there remains much to be done. Even the people I interviewed over the years sometimes followed the same structure in telling their stories of progress: "[I]f we could compare 15 years, [it's] much better, but the growth or the changes . . . [have] been very gradual[,] with lots of stagnation (Interview, 201604).[1] The successes are narrated as moderate in scope and are frequently reported as isolated achievements in the context of a broader evaluation of implementation. There are two elements of the success stories that I want to highlight here as being of critical political significance: first, (moderate, qualified) success in the domain of preventing sexual violence in conflict receives a lot of coverage, as does—more recently—the participation of women in peace processes (including mediation); and second, the monitoring and evaluation reported, particularly in the Secretary-General's reports, presents quantitative data as evidence of success, constructing the agenda, in accordance with a logic of coherence, as a manageable, measurable thing.

The "success" of the efforts under the auspices of the WPS agenda to prevent sexual violence take different narrative forms. On the one hand, in line with the story that the agenda itself is evidence of its own success, the adoption of resolutions focused on sexual violence in conflict is a claim to success. As mentioned previously, the adoption of UNSCR 1820 and subsequent resolutions is framed as evidence of progress and continued commitment: "The Security Council continued to remain seized of this issue, including by adopting a new resolution, 2016 (2013)" (S/2013/525, para. 3. Similarly, later reports comment, for example:

> Significant progress has been made in promoting efforts to address the conflict-related sexual violence agenda within the peace and security arena

through the consistent focus of the Security Council, strategic leadership in the United Nations system and more coordinated action of all relevant United Nations entities. (S/2015/716, para. 162)

On the other hand, the integration of the WPS agenda with the machinery of international law is articulated as part of this story, with the success of sexual violence prevention initiatives thus taking an alternative narrative form. In a statement to the 2016 Open Debate in June, for example, Human Rights Advocacy Director for MADRE and NGO Working Group member Lisa Davis linked the practices of the International Criminal Court (ICC) to the WPS agenda:

> The recent landmark conviction of former Chadian President Hissène Habré is a reminder that while the wheels of justice turn slowly, they do turn, and it is possible to achieve accountability for crimes that include rape and sexual slavery. The Security Council and other Member States should expand political and financial support to accountability efforts, including through referrals to the International Criminal Court and ensuring that those with arrest warrants against them face trial in The Hague. (S/PV.7704 2016, p. 9)

Similarly, the Secretary-General's reports make numerous references over time to the international legal frameworks addressing conflict-related sexual violence, even prior to the adoption of UNSCR 1820 and the subsequent bifurcation of reporting. (After the adoption of UNSCR 1820, the Secretary-General was required to report to the Council on sexual violence in conflict, according to the mandate of UNSCR 1820, separately from his report on the implementation of UNSCR 1325.)

The ICC is thus one of the characters identifiable in the *fabula* of WPS success, though playing a supporting rather than a central role. The characterization within these WPS narratives presents many of the same actors in much the same configuration as the origin stories outlined in the previous chapter, with a few notable cast changes. The UN Security Council is depicted in this narrative as sole arbiter of the agenda, adopter of resolutions—which, as shown, mark success—and thus as responsible for the agenda's success (or, one might suppose, the lack thereof, although this story is more complicated again, as I discuss in the following chapter). In addition to the representations included previously, the Council's dominance is reaffirmed through the claim that "[p]olitical will and consistent oversight by the Security Council are central to improving follow-up on the implementation of the women and peace and security agenda" (S/2015/716, para. 150). Interpreting the passage of a resolution as an unqualified success with greater significance than might normally be afforded a normative statement has doubtless affected the way that member states engage with Council business. For example, one research participant explained that "it's a badge of pride . . . for many of the non-permanent members to have got a resolution through the Council is something that they're very, very proud of" (Interview, 201911; on the engagement with WPS by member states at the Council see, in particular, Basu 2016b).

Member states actually feature more prominently in this narrative than in the origin story presented previously. From 2004 onward, the Secretary-General's reports feature multiple vignettes recounting the efforts by member states to implement the WPS agenda, as well as the various successes of the same. The 2004 report includes the first comments on successful implementation by member states (the Philippines, Australia, Canada, and Sri Lanka; see S/2004/814, para. 23) and goes on to praise other state-led initiatives, such as the creation of Friends of Women, Peace and Security—led by Canadian advocates for the agenda—and the installation of "working groups and task forces at the national level" in Canada, Colombia, the Netherlands, Norway, and Azerbaijan (S/2004/814, paras. 104–105). Even though member states are thus positioned as good workers toward the full implementation of the agenda, the overarching authority of the Council is still paramount, as the Council, and the UN system more broadly, is positioned as teacher/disseminator of WPS knowledge: "The United Nations system has paid particular attention to developing the capacity of Member States as well as its own to address the implementation of resolution 1325 (2000)" (S/2009/465, para. 25).

Another dimension of characterization relates to the construction of the civil society organizations and representatives that feature in this narrative. Per the discussion in the previous chapter, the representation of civil society in the origin stories of the agenda positions the plucky civil society actor in opposition to the conservative and close-minded Security Council. In this part of the WPS story, civil society actors are no less plucky but certainly a lot busier. Civil society actors feature in this story both as implementing agents— "in country"—and as experts on the issues captured by the WPS agenda. The NGO Working Group on Women, Peace and Security, a key actor in the WPS space in New York, is usually represented, or at least accompanied, by a member of a civil society organization at the Security Council Open Debates. These representatives claim a position of expertise from which to speak through the invocation of their personal histories, presenting their experiences as credentials to support their interventions (see, among many other examples: S.PV/5294 2005, p. 12; S.PV/6877 2012, p. 7; S.PV/8079 2017, p. 7). At the 2015 Open Debate, three women from various civil society organizations briefed the Council (testament to the "anniversary effect" I discuss later), and Alaa Murabit of the Voice of Libyan Women offered particularly personal, and personalizing, testimony:

> When I was growing up, my mother told me she always saw everything, courtesy of the two extra eyes she had in the back of her head. I made many attempts to disprove her, and needless to say, I was caught every time. What I did not know then was that my mother had just taught me a valuable lesson and that I would use it daily in my work as a peace and security advocate: that the very women who lead families and societies know first and best what is happening in them and how to address it. (S/PV.7533 2015, p. 9)

These women—and they are all women—thus ascribe a human face to the amorphous "women's civil society organizations" that feature in the origin stories.

The primary narrator of the success stories, however, is the Secretary-General, in part because of his structural positioning as rapporteur. He is required to account annually for the efforts made to implement the WPS agenda, mandated by the various WPS resolutions. Other relevant reports, such as the 2010 Report on women's participation in peacebuilding, were similarly mandated by WPS resolutions: "In its resolution 1889 (2009), the Security Council requested the Secretary-General to submit to it, within 12 months, a report on women's participation in peacebuilding" (A/65/354-S/2010/466, para. 1). The Secretary-General, through this process of characterization, is constituted as a vassal of the Council, which is an interesting reversal of organizational hierarchy. The continued presentation of the reports "pursuant to" various Security Council resolutions reinforces this relationship (see, for example, A/65/592–S/2010/604, para. 1; S/2012/732, para. 1; A/66/657*–S/2012/33*, para. 1). Although it is the Secretary-General who reports the small victories in the success stories and who affirms the position of the Council as the progenitor of success through the adoption of

WPS resolutions, it is the Council that is constructed as authoritative and credible, rather than the Secretary-General himself. Thus, logics of (dis)location inform this discourse. This is perhaps clearest in the Secretary-General's report of 2009, which suggests that the provisions of the WPS agenda related to reporting on sexual violence in conflict are applicable only to "situations of which the Security Council is seized" (S/2009/465, para. 1).[2]

The temporal organization of this *fabula* is both strong and significant. The stories of success frequently hinge on or otherwise make reference to temporal markers in the presentation of the narrative. In her work on the adoption of National Action Plans by member states, Jacqui True makes reference to a "period effect" (True 2016, 312), and in collaborative work with Michael Mintrom on transnational advocacy and policy diffusion, they coin the term "Beijing effect" in reference to the fourth UN World Conference on Women (True and Mintrom 2001, 43). Inspired by this formulation, I identify in the stories of WPS success a significant "anniversary effect." The temporal marker of the anniversary effect—initially rising to prominence before 2010 and then echoed in the buildup to 2015—does not function simply to produce more, or different, statements in the anniversary years. It is a powerful organizing force in the story of success, where the anniversary (any anniversary) is constituted as a moment of accountability and motivator/mobiliser of future action: "[I]t's a political opportunity for civil society to use what member states are particularly interested in to leveraging action' (Interview, 201401). Now, at the time of writing, "there is a working group on 2020, just focusing on 2020. Already, people are looking at plans and what to highlight, et cetera, and I think they're going to be meeting every month until next year" (Interview, 201902).[3] I examine in the next section the discourses that are drawn on to bring to the forefront the narrative about this anniversary effect. Its function in the story is to orient the agenda toward the future and to reinforce its linear temporality; this is a story of potentially endless celebrations of the WPS agenda, marked every five or ten years on the anniversary of the adoption of the foundational resolution.

This section has outlined the *fabula*, or presentation of events and characters in a particular configuration, of WPS success. The particular and individual narratives of successes in the WPS agenda over the past two decades vary, of course, but many of those individual narratives cohere around and into the story presented in this section: a story of the possibilities enabled by the very existence of the agenda, in which the adoption of the resolutions and the architecture of the agenda itself are counted a success.

It is also a story in which it is increasingly the case that what is counted as success—reported as such by the Secretary-General and even commented on by those working in this space—is that which can be counted: a reduction in instances of sexual violence in conflict, for example, or an increase in the number of female mediators trained and deployed. In the following section I delve into the discourses that are captured in the *fabula* to explore how meaning is constructed within these stories and value attached to certain forms of measurement and certain WPS subjects.

Discursive constructions of success

The stories of success have specific organizing logics and arrangements of discourse that are worth interrogating further. As noted previously, the articulation of the agenda as a success in itself is related to the origin story of WPS; this is reaffirmed through continued reference to what I have termed the "anniversary effect," which I discuss in the first subsection. I go on to present a more detailed investigation of how the "little wins" are constructed, and with what political effects. In the third subsection I examine the bolder but less frequent claims about structural reform at UN HQ as a result of WPS diffusion, paying particular attention to discourses about the increased visibility of WPS issues at UN HQ and the concomitant ability of WPS actors to leverage the agenda to effect change in various contexts.

The anniversary effect

The "anniversary effect" provides a clear and linear temporality to the agenda. As mentioned in the previous chapter, the celebration of the adoption of UNSCR 1325 each October is rendered discursively as part of the ownership claim over the agenda by civil society organizations. In the early 2000s, civil society actors worked hard to mark the anniversary of resolution 1325's adoption each year. It is highly unusual for Security Council resolutions to have anniversaries, and yet

> extensive celebrations and activities around the anniversary of 1325 occur every year at the UN. This Resolution has brought people together to discuss women and armed conflict and to lobby for increased inclusion of civil

society in conflict prevention, management, and post-conflict reconstruction to a degree that has never been prompted by any previous Security Council resolution. (Fuijo 2008, 220)

The anniversary effect could just as easily be dubbed the "October effect," as time in the WPS agenda is primarily measured in relation to October, the month in which UNSCR 1325 was adopted in 2000.[4] The Open Debate at the Security Council in October each year is a significant activity in each year's WPS activities; member states prepare statements to perform their WPS credentials, and those involved in WPS at UN HQ spend many months working with member states and civil society representatives to ensure that the debate is marked with the appropriate level of commitment and gravitas.

The discourse of the anniversary of the resolution reaffirms the significance of the anniversary as a temporal marker and contributes to the constitution of a temporality of WPS that begins in 2000. In the "notable" anniversary years—2010, 2015, 2020—huge effort is expended. "There was a lot of effort in the run-up to the 10th anniversary, in 2010, to make sure that they weren't just words on paper—that we actually in earnest started implementing it [UNSCR 1325]" (Interview, 201606). Then, "the 15 year anniversary was historic for the Security Council, the largest open debate in the history of the Security Council. Like literally diplomats were was sitting on the stairs. I've never seen anything like it. It filled over. . . . I mean, it was historic in so many respects" (Interview, 201909). This is reinforced by the Secretary-General's reports, which almost without exception reference to either an anniversary just passed or one in the future toward which the Council, the Secretary-General, and other UN actors need to be working (see, for example, S/2011/598, para. 3, which refers back to 2010, and para. 74f, which refers forward to 2015; S/2014/693, para. 4; and S/2018/900, para. 2, which looks forward to 2020). Two other notable "anniversary effects" are first, the length of the report presented in 2010 (an impressive forty-eight pages), and second, the fact that at the Open Debate in 2015 not only were there a record number of participants and speakers present, but it was also the first time that a head of state had chaired the Council's meeting on WPS. The president of Spain, holding the presidency of the Council in October 2015, presided over the debate, which ran over two consecutive days (see S.PV/7533 2015, p. 4).

The Open Debates cannot really be interpreted as "anniversary effects" in and of themselves, but the discourse around member state investment in the Open Debates is related to the success of the agenda *as* an agenda. Delivering a speech at the Open Debate, with or without firm commitments related to WPS, "tell[s] your domestic women's movement that, oh yeah, we're listening. So they're kind of like an easy win for member states. So, like a lot of areas of women's rights, you can get a lot of mileage with the rhetoric" (Interview, 201906). Member states perform their normative commitment to the agenda at the October Open Debates, and this investment is connected to the agenda's success in some of the discourse about the anniversaries:

> The 2015 open debate of the Council to review the implementation of the resolution had 113 participating speakers, the largest number in any debate in the Council's history. The outcome of the debate, resolution 2242 (2015), was adopted unanimously, and nearly 70 Member States made explicit commitments to implement the agenda. (S/2016/822, para. 4)

Notably, civil society representatives with whom I spoke in the course of this research were somewhat less persuaded by the presentation of the October performance as evidence of success, which I discuss further in the following chapter. There are logics of (dis)location evident in this discourse, as it represents a duality of space and place within the agenda: the Open Debates reinforce the association of the agenda with the Security Council and national government while simultaneously situating it within civil society, specifically the practices of "domestic women's movements."

The final dimension of anniversary discourse that I want to highlight is the artifacts of the Presidential Statements and the language that they use. The Presidential Statements are particularly interesting because they reflect awareness of the anniversary effect but also represent a lack of desire to adopt a resolution to further embed the agenda and its principles. Thus, this discourse also manifests logics of coherence and possibility, constructing the contents of the agenda and how its success can be measured. The first anniversary of the adoption of UNSCR 1325 is marked by the release of a Presidential Statement (S/PRST/2001/31), which essentially reaffirms the provisions of the resolution. The 2002 Presidential Statement "requests the Secretary-General to prepare a follow-up report on the full implementation of resolution 1325 to be presented to the Security Council in October 2004" (S/PRST/2002/32, p. 2), and the 2004 document is agenda setting in many ways. The statement is lengthy and detailed, encouraging activity across various domains, including production of National Actions Plans to guide implementation at the national level, and requesting the Secretary-General to submit to the Security Council in October 2005 an action plan, with time lines, for implementing resolution 1325 (2000) across the United Nations system, with a view to strengthening commitment and accountability at the highest levels, as well as to allow for improved accountability, monitoring and reporting on progress on implementation within the United Nations system. (S/PRST/2004/40, p. 3)

This was the genesis of the System-Wide Action Plan presented to the Council in 2005, which was then reported on in 2006, revised in 2007, reconfigured for 2008–2009, and eventually used to inform the set of indicators used to evaluate many of the "little wins" discussed in the next subsection. The Presidential Statements reinforce the anniversary effect and contribute to the representation of the agenda as a success in itself; though normative and not binding, the Statements show how change can be leveraged as a result of the agenda, as well as laying out the change necessary to improve its implementation.

Little wins

Many of the discourses that articulate success are almost tentative. The successes reported are always qualified and moderate; more always remains to be done (see, for example, S/2007/567, para. 1), and "[d]espite progress, obstacles . . . remain" (S/2009/465, para. 60).[5] It is as if the narrator is hesitant to claim significant success or lasting transformation, perhaps because the agenda is so wide ranging and also mandates deep structural transformation. The structure of the Secretary-General's reports over the two decades under consideration is remarkably consistent: the reports open with an acknowledgment of the mandate or scope, comment on the successes that the report presents, and invariably conclude that progress has been limited. The function of this discursive schema is to leave the reader with a sense of lack, of that which is left undone, rather than that which can be celebrated or conceived of as concluded. A strong logic of *im*possibility structures this discourse, along with a logic of incoherence.

A logic of coherence, however, underpins the tendency across the various sources of data to report progress in terms of easily grasped and quantitative measures; there is a certainty to numbers that strengthens the claim to *some* success, even where "gaps and challenges" remain (S/2013/525, para. 76). Reporting on progress (even slow progress) in the Secretary-General's reports becomes much more technical and indicator focused over time. The diffusion of the WPS agenda to other areas of Council business, which is relatively easily quantified by counting references to the agenda and its provisions, is articulated as a form of success, in both the Secretary-General's reports (for example, S/2004/814, para. 6; S/2015/716, para. 150) and the Open Debates (for example, S/PV.5766 2007, p. 9; S/PV.6642 2011, p. 7).

The ideational, or normative, dimension is captured in the idea of success as convergence around an idea or a set of ideas, reinforcing the logic of coherence: "[T]here is general agreement now, in a way that there wasn't, on women's place at the table, on the women's participation stuff" (Interview, 201403); "1325 is just part of the conversation from day-to-day" (Interview, 201902). The Secretary-General's reports also present diffusion across the organization as a form of success (S/2004/814, para. 116; S/2009/465, para. 26). As one research participant explained:

> [W]e've had staff say to us, in their evaluations of the trainings, "It was like a light that went on." Like, "Ding!" It was like, "My god, you know—I never looked at a conflict analysis the same way. I can see now when I read something, that if it doesn't talk about the impact on women and their role, and so forth, that I'm actually missing half the population, and the bigger picture." (Interview, 201606)

While there is an acknowledgment among those working directly in this space that others whose work intersects less frequently with the WPS agenda might not be "true believers," the idea that there is generalized "buy-in" to the agenda—that the agenda is "seen as adding value"—in a way that was not evident a decade ago came through strongly in the conversations that I had (Interview, 201904).

> The way that I have been trying to frame the issues is . . . there's a whole normative agenda, and we own it, because we work for the UN, but it's a given—it's not something you can question whether you have to do this—you have to do it, whether you think it's important or not—it's really irrelevant, because you're serving an organisation where this is the norm. (Interview, 201606)

When "it's not something you can question" (Interview, 201606), or when "it's just something that we have to do" (Interview, 201904), implementing the agenda is constituted as a series of unpleasant tasks, necessary but not necessarily supported or enjoyed: an "eat your greens" activity rather than the enactment of a shared commitment to a normative project of improving women's access to peace and security governance and investing in conflict prevention. "The analogy that I always make is that Women, Peace, and Security or gender to them is like going to the dentist, that they know it's good for them now, but it's still not necessarily how they want to spend their time, and they'd rather be doing something else" (Interview, 201905). This discourse thus represents and accounts for resistance in accordance to logics of (im)possibility: the successes of the agenda, as manifest in "little wins," are achieved at once because of and in spite of (a lack of) institutional commitment.

The construction of this discourse, which acknowledges on the one hand the diffusion of the agenda across UN HQ such that it is, increasingly, part of the "common sense" or "taken for granted" of the organization, and on the other hand the resistance that might still remain to the agenda and its provisions and principles, might contribute to the normalization of such resistance and the positioning of those dedicated to the agenda—the "true believers"—as forcing the institution to eat its greens or visit the dentist. Unsurprisingly, this is a highly gendered construct; most of the research participants—people in key policy or advocacy roles at or around the UN—were female, and this discourse constructs a maternal, caregiver role to these people. This discourse of success, then, at once acknowledges the "little wins" that have spread the ideas and ideals of WPS across the UN system and structurally positions those pushing for its further advancement as subordinate to the implied, and masculinized, father figure of the agenda, the UN Security Council. Of relevance here is the concept of "femocrats" advanced by feminist political science literature, coined to explain the challenges faced by women doing gender work in complex bureaucracies and governance institutions (see, for example, Sawer 1998, 2003; Subrahmanian 2007; True 2008); navigating stereotyped and gendered expectations about behavior thus informs and perpetuates logics of (im)possibility (for a detailed examination of these processes of navigation, see Eisenstein 1996).

As mentioned, much of the discussion of success recounts it as "prevention" (of sexual violence) success or "participation" (in peace processes) success. Part of this discourse involves a strong and repeated refrain about the importance of institutions, which is unexpected. The establishment of the ICC, for example, and the Rome Statute, which includes "[r]ape, sexual slavery, enforced prostitution, forced pregnancy, enforced sterilization, or any other form of sexual violence of comparable gravity" as crimes against humanity (Article 7g), provides a context within which sexual violence in conflict can be prosecuted. Moreover, while instances of sexual violence in conflict are not easy to count or track over time, the prosecution of such acts is much more amenable to reporting, both at the ICC and in conflict-affected countries (see, for example, S/2007/567, para. 31; S/PV.6984 2013, pp. 7–8; S/PV.7704 2016, p. 9). These prosecutions are reported as successes related to the WPS agenda (despite the fact that in the Bemba case, mentioned later, the verdict was eventually overturned. For a thorough discussion of the case, see Grey 2014, 2019; Koomen 2019):

> The trial in the International Criminal Court of Jean-Pierre Bemba, former Vice-President of the Democratic Republic of the Congo and leader of the Mouvement de Libération du Congo, in connection with events in the Central African Republic represents a critical test case for the principle of command responsibility for sexual violence as a war crime and a crime against humanity. (A/67/792–S/2013/149, para. 113)

This institutional articulation, which associates WPS with advances in jurisprudence and an implied commitment to the rule of law, strengthens the positioning of the agenda within the UN as an organization, a discursive move that is reproduced in the discourses of participation successes.

The 2015 *Global Study* was a significant stock-taking moment in the narration of the WPS agenda over time. One of the key elements of the study was the coverage given to women's participation in peace and security governance. The Secretary-General's report of the same year affirms this interpretation: "Perhaps the strongest message to emerge from the study is the remarkable impact of women's participation on all areas of peace and security. New evidence, added through research commissioned for the study, demonstrates clearly that the inclusion of women leads to more sustainable peace and enhanced prevention efforts" (S/2015/716, para. 8). When asked about the areas in which the WPS agenda has seen some success or gained traction, many of the research participants similarly commented on participation. "[O]n participation, we have seen that the UN, at least, has been able to make an impact over the last years," said one (Interview, 201904); another noted that "an area where there's been quite a lot of progress is in women's participation in peacebuilding" (Interview, 201908), while a third commented that "at the peace table for example, there have been significant gains. There are several processes, for example, where women's participation is much more significant and explicitly so as a goal of the peace negotiations" (Interview, 201604). The discursive construction of women's participation in peace processes as a marker of success of the agenda not only reproduces the association between women and peace but also focuses the discussion of success on that which is highly visible and easy to evaluate—if not easy, necessarily, to achieve. Thus, the agenda is represented as consolidating around these particular elements, constructing itself in accordance with logics of both coherence and possibility.

Visibility and leverage

I highlight three dimensions of visibility and leverage in this section. First, there is an institutional visibility, at UN HQ, that affords certain political opportunities. This is frequently described as a kind of "opening up" and "joining up" of the organization. Early reports of the Secretary-General make reference to, for example, the work of the General Assembly and the Economic and Social Council (ECOSOC) in their accounting of the agenda (S/2004/814, paras. 9–11; S/2005/636, para. 16); thirty UN entities reported back to the Secretary-General's office on the 2006–2007 System-Wide Action Plan (S/2007/567, para. 5). One comment provided in an interview in 2016 suggested that "the agenda has risen enormously in prominence and visibility in the last 10 years" (Interview, 201604; see, in addition to the madly proliferating literature on aspects of the WPS agenda, Rajagopalan 2016; Davies and True 2019; Basu, Kirby, and Shepherd 2020). As WPS intersects with other UN agendas, such as the Sustainable Development Goals and the Sustaining Peace agenda (see, for example, S/2017/861, para. 5), that prominence and visibility is growing, although—in part due to organizational restructuring and consolidation over the last five years—the number of entities reported on by the Secretary-General seems fewer. Across the organization, "communication has gotten better, for sure and that the content of the communication has gotten better" (Interview, 201403).

It is not just the UN in general that is more open and accessible, but the Security Council in particular. Pursuant to resolution 2242 (S/RES/2242, para. 5a), the convening of an informal group of experts to brief the Council in 2016, chaired by Spain and the UK together and with support provided by UN Women, is identified as a success, a way of ensuring that the Council is well informed about country-specific issues related to the agenda (S/2017/ 861, para. 87):

> The Informal Expert Group is an amazing idea. And it's really done well because it constantly reminds council members you got to ask, but it's only eight countries, it only covers eight countries. But they remind everybody ask about gender and they bring this data . . . all this information about what's going on on the ground and you get to ask the SRSG [Special Representative of the Secretary-General], did you talk to the woman opposition leader or the women minister of education there whatever? So they actually give them questions, it's made a big difference, and they draft material to go into resolutions and that's huge. That's made a big difference. (Interview, 201906)

The intention, reportedly, was "to facilitate a more systematic approach to its [the Council's] work in this area and enable greater oversight and coordination of implementation efforts" (S/2017/861, para. 88). The enthusiasm with which this initiative was met, and the repetition of its having "made a big difference," at least in the estimation of one research participant, suggests that the Council previously was closed and inaccessible. This aligns with a logic of possibility. Leveraging the agenda's origin stories and the ownership claims made by civil society to effect this kind of organizational change and increase the visibility of the agenda across the work of the Council is certainly part of this success discourse and is celebrated in documents and spoken discourse alike. It does, of course, reinforce the idea that civil society representatives and other "informal experts" are just that—informal—while the real, *formal*, expertise sits within the Council.

Second, there is visibility of the agenda beyond the UN, evident in the connection of the WPS agenda to other initiatives such as the PSVI and the "feminist foreign policy" platforms espoused by Sweden and Canada. Initially limited to enumerating the activities of states supportive of the agenda within the confines of the agenda itself—that is, related specifically to actions taken to implement the provision of UNSCR 1325 and subsequent resolutions—the Secretary-General's reports have, in recent years, connected WPS explicitly to these WPS-adjacent programs. Particularly of note given the strong emphasis on prevention (of sexual violence) successes, the UK's activities in this space, "inaugurated in May 2012 as the Preventing Sexual Violence Initiative" and with many manifestations (Kirby 2015, 457; see also Davies and True 2017), have had a significant impact on the ways that success is articulated. Former UK Foreign Secretary William Hague is described as "vigorously champion[ing] this cause" (S/2014/181, para. 10), and the UK's hosting of the Global Summit to End Sexual Violence in Conflict in June 2014 is lauded as further evidence of the commitment of the international community to addressing conflict-related sexual violence (S/2015/203, para. 9). Concerted effort and advocacy by the UK in the prevention (of sexual violence) domain is at least in part responsible for the focus on sexual violence within the agenda's accounting of success. Moreover, "the PSVI approach is best characterized as a relatively conservative rendition of WPS" (Kirby 2015, 461); the targeted focus on *specific forms of* violence—now emergent also in the association of WPS with countering terrorism and violent extremism (see S/RES/2242, preamble and paras. 11–13; S/2016/361, para. 90a; S/2017/249, p. 3; S/2018/250, para. 10)—reduces the visibility of conflict prevention more broadly, while producing a hyper-focus on sexual violence.

Relatedly, the visibility of UN member states in WPS activities is part of the discourse of WPS success:

Some Governments have appointed high-level champions for gender-responsive foreign policy and development cooperation. Australia established in 2011 the role of Ambassador for Women and Girls as an advocate for the promotion and protection of women's human rights around the globe and to ensure that gender equality is a central focus of Australia's diplomatic, peacebuilding and development efforts. In 2015, Sweden appointed an Ambassador-at-large for Global Women's Issues and Gender Equality to coordinate Sweden's feminist foreign policy, which aims at guaranteeing women's rights, including participation in peacebuilding and peacemaking and preventing violence. Such an explicit and strong political stand to promote gender equality and the human rights of women and girls marks a good practice that could be replicated by more governments. (S/2015/716, para. 100)

The language of "champions" and "leadership" (see also S/2017/861, para. 71) not only acknowledges the performance of commitment by these states—notably the UK, Sweden, Canada, and Spain (the last of which launched the Women, Peace and Security National Focal Points Network in 2017; see S/2017/861, para. 70)—but also elevates these states over others, which may be involved in equally important but less prominent initiatives (and in turn, these important but less prominent initiatives may be less prominent because they are less well funded). The overrepresentation of the Global North in this discourse about "WPS champions" and WPS-adjacent activity configures the global power structures of WPS—which organizes who/where "does" WPS to where/to whom WPS is "done"—in accordance with old, imperial logics of colonial domination, reinforcing the logics of (dis)location within the narration of the agenda.

Third, and related to (dis)location, the agenda's visibility enables WPS actors to leverage the agenda to effect change in various contexts at and beyond the UN in New York. This discourse represents civil society actors, rather than state actors, as the primary implementing agents of WPS provisions. Even the October statements at the Open Debates, in this account of WPS, are discursive materials for effecting change: "Taking the commitments that are made at the Council can be valuable to drive things in other forums, as you would normally use political statements" (Interview, 201911). What we see here is "civil society . . . trying to push an agenda, like, 'We want to develop a National Action Plan. We want to use these frameworks to be able to address protection issues, to be addressed for participation'" (Interview, 201902). The power of women and women's organizations to mobilize and use every tool at their disposal, including but not limited to the architecture of the WPS agenda, is affirmed repeatedly in the NGO Working Group statements to the Open Debates (see, for example, S.PV/5556 Resumption 1 2006, p. 2; S.PV/6877 2012, p. 7; S.PV/7428 2015, p. 6). Similarly, the Secretary-General's reports make frequent mention of women "making a critical difference" (S/2002/1154, para. 27) and using resolution 1325 to "demand a place in peace processes" (S/2010/498, para. 16).[6]

These organizations have galvanized awareness and commitment, developed important activities on the ground, helped to strengthen international standards, published important reports that have increased knowledge on this issue, shared essential information, formed effective coalitions on various initiatives and pressured parties in conflict to protect men, women and children from the scourge of sexual violence. (A/66/657*–S/2012/33*, para. 94)

Women, and women's civil society organizations, are doing a tremendous amount of on-the-ground work, both within and around the UN and in specific country settings (Björkdahl and Selimovic 2019; Jonjić-Beitter, Stadler and Tietgen 2020). They are leveraging the WPS agenda to achieve the kinds of change they want to see in the world; they are advising the Secretary-General and submitting to the Human Rights Council Universal Periodic Review (S/2015/716, para. 103) as well as briefing the Security Council (S/2014/181, para. 8; Interview, 201905), and frequently doing so with little to no stable or core funding (S/2013/525, para. 56).

This discourse (dis)locates the WPS agenda spatially and has implications for the credibility and authority of actor-subjects, interwoven as it is with an ambivalent logic of practice that constructs these efforts as the "real" WPS agenda even as the agenda's situation in the Council is reinforced. Civil society actors are extremely busy, expected to be "superheroines" (Maha Muna in Cohn, Kinsella and Gibbings 2004, 136), recounting their stories of courage in the face of adversity to affirm the legitimacy of the knowledge and expertise they bring (Cook 2016). The positioning of women, particularly the subject of "civil society woman," is not exactly in line with the vision of women's empowerment that the progenitors of the WPS agenda likely had in mind.

Concluding thoughts on success

This chapter has provided an analysis of the success stories of the WPS agenda. Normatively, it is vital to recognize and celebrate these successes, which are a result of hard work, relentless advocacy pressure, and tireless commitment. But analytically I recognize that these success stories are part of how the agenda is (re)produced. The agenda that emerges here is at once limited and limiting, reliant on the (unpaid, or at least undervalued) labor of civil society actors, while privileged state actors, all located in the Global North, are prominently and visibly associated with the agenda and its successes. Structured in accordance with logics of (dis)location and (im)possibility, these narratives of success reproduce tensions and plurality in the constitution of WPS subjects.

Further, the things that are reported as success also shape the agenda, how it is perceived in the moment, what is (has been, will be) valued, and what is taken forward for future action. As I have outlined, the bifurcation and consolidation of the agenda into prevention (of sexual violence) and participation (in peace processes) happens in significant part through the success stories I recount here. Recounted as areas in which "little wins" of the WPS agenda are evident, these two pillars come to dominate the stories that are told about the agenda at the UN and elsewhere, with the consequence of closing down discursive space both for the protection of women's rights (rather than their bodies) and for the articulation of broader dynamics of prevention: conflict prevention writ large. In a mutually reinforcing relationship, the quest for evidence of success drives the quantification of the agenda, which in turn leads to a disproportionate focus on that which can be quantified. And quantification is *seductive*:

> Under the evidence-based regime of governance, it is necessary to be counted to be recognised. Quantification makes issues visible and reveals the extent and scope of a problem. But things that are more easily counted and more often counted tend to be those counted in the future, while those that have not been counted or are hard to quantify tend to be neglected and thus disappear from view. (Merry 2016, 219)

It is not my concern only that other elements of the WPS "disappear from view" through the deployment of increasingly quantitative measures of success, but also that the very currency of knowledge about WPS is shaped and formed through these data-driven stories. These stories not only represent the terms of success as quantified data, they also represent WPS as a *quantifiable* knowledge object. Numbers are neat, and peace is not. Peace is messy, and complicated, and difficult to achieve.

Reinforcing the idea that the WPS agenda exists in two parallel tracks—one bloodlessly bureaucratic and simple, wherein the numbers of sexual violence prosecutions and women at peace tables are totted up as evidence of success, and the other human, complex, tangled, and frustrating, in which trial mostly results in error and is anyway under-resourced—are the two parallel locations of the agenda and its successes, per the logics of (dis)location identified here.[7] On the one hand, civil society actors labor for the success of the agenda and are commended (though not funded) for their efforts. On the other hand, the Security Council is reproduced as the patriarch of peace—or, more properly, security. Even in the accounts of success, the victories of this most bold and transformative agenda, the Council maintains the authority that is questioned through the civil society ownership claims and even through the member states' "leadership" and "championing." The Council directs the Secretary-General to tell his stories; it is the venue at which state representatives and civil society supplicants alike perform their commitment to the agenda each year in October. But—and this is a small hesitation, only because I am myself hesitant to leave this chapter on such a depressing and thoroughly *expected* conclusion—the Council is, as discussed, "opening up": "I do think that there has been a lot of push back on that but there has definitely been space pried open" (Interview, 201302). Logics of (im)possibility are evident here; the realization of the agenda's objectives, as they are narrated, is *both* possible *and* impossible, in accordance with the plural and polyvalent ways that these stories are told.

5

Narratives of Failure

In this chapter, I interrogate the challenges and obstacles that are a frequent theme in the WPS stories I have collected. Specifically, I examine the ways in which failure, limitations, and challenges are narrated in the WPS agenda and juxtapose these "failure narratives" with the "success stories" presented in the previous chapter. In the first section, in which I sketch out the *fabula* of these tales of failure, I show how the telling of these stories produces a collective subject jointly responsible for the limitations perceived in the agenda as it stands: "we" are all failing WPS at the UN. This construction reinforces the authority of the UN as well as its culpability as a WPS actor in the stories of these shortcomings, relevant to the logics of (dis)location that situate the agenda at/in the Security Council, and simultaneously disperses it spatially, locating it "in country" or "on the ground." The resolution to the acknowledged shortcomings is often presented as more frequent, more granular monitoring (in addition to further resources and stronger political will), which reinforces the construction of the agenda itself as a quantifiable knowledge object, as discussed in Chapter 4.

I go on to explore the arrangement of discourses that make up the stories I identify here. The primary discourse relates an explanation for the shortcomings of the agenda that focuses on a lack of funding or other kinds of resources and a lack of political will. The representations of failure that are dominant in the narratives I examine frequently relate to failures of implementation, which are in turn attributed to a lack of resources and/or a lack of political will by the actor(s) in question to take up the WPS agenda in earnest. I propose that these failure stories—or "failure rationales"—are problematic, as "political will" is too general an explanatory factor to be very useful in political analysis or intervention (an argument in line with Jutta Weldes's treatment of "the national interest"; see Weldes 1996a, 1996b). Narrating the failures of the WPS agenda in this way therefore constitutes the agenda as a knowable object, the success of which is contingent on the whims of implementing actors. I argue that this reinforces a realpolitik vision of the WPS sphere that strengthens a logic of impossibility regarding

Narrating the Women, Peace and Security Agenda. Laura J. Shepherd, Oxford University Press (2021). © Oxford University Press. DOI: 10.1093/oso/9780197557242.003.0005

the enactment of the transformative principles that the agenda purportedly captures (per the origin stories discussed in Chapter 3). Attributing those shortcomings to failures of resources and political will is somewhat reductive and reproduces the authority of the Security Council (and, to a lesser extent, UN member states) in the institutional architecture of the agenda.

There are other discourses at play, however, and I explore these here. Discourses about expertise, and discourses about the magnitude of the agenda, are of particular significance. Broadly speaking, the discourses about experts and expertise intersect with the discourses on resources and political will, as all construct the UN and its staff as an organization that *lacks*, in accordance again with a logic of impossibility. In an interesting parallel to the construction of the subject of "woman in need" in early WPS discourse (see Puechguirbal 2004; Shepherd 2008, 87–88), here it is the UN that lacks sufficient resources, agency, will, and expertise to deliver on the promise of the WPS commitments. The discourses marshaled in service of the stories of shortcomings construct the WPS efforts of UN entities and member states as limited at best, hampered by the inefficiencies of a complex and bureaucratic system, and tokenistic at worst, where WPS work is paraded before the Council one day each October and sidelined for the rest of the year. Unsurprisingly, the Council's authority is reinforced within these discourses, along with a subtle transfer of power to member states, whose passive or active resistance to aspects of WPS—or the agenda as a whole—shapes and influences the shortcomings that are identified (including indirectly through the withholding of resources and political will).

The magnitude of the agenda is articulated as a causal factor in the story of WPS failures (or, more generously, its shortcomings), in line with a logic of incoherence. Interrogating these discourses not only reveals that the size, or scope, of the agenda is widely held to be part of the story of shortcomings, but also that this story should account for failures of a different order: failures not of resources, will, or expertise, but *conceptual* failures. These are failures to properly *know* the agenda as a specified and settled set of principles and practices, to agree on these principles and practices, and to be certain about the parameters of the agenda and what is necessary for implementation. The conceptual failure, the failure of certainty—applied to the WPS agenda as a knowable object—thus reproduces the agenda in accordance with a logic of impossibility. These accounts of failure are often circular and recount the reoccurrence of shortcomings, the need to reiterate—or relitigate—that which was previously thought to be agreed upon. These discourses, in conjunction with the discourses discussed in the previous chapter, surface the plural logics of (in)coherence and (im)possibility I identify as particularly powerful in the narration of the WPS agenda.

Identifying the *fabula*

We've got a long way to go, though, before we see full implementation of the agenda. The major problems we have are a lack of resources and political will. Some people still don't really understand what the agenda is all about, or they try to make it about everything, which makes it hard to focus.

Locating the stories of shortcomings in the documentary history of the agenda reveals that most significant storytelling moments—the Secretary-General's reports and the annual Open Debates, as well as the less formal storytelling captured in co-produced interview data—are leveraged as opportunities to recount the limitations of the agenda's implementation. In part, this is a function of the structures developed around the agenda: the foundational resolution requested a report from the Secretary-General "on the impact of armed conflict on women and girls, the role of women in peace-building and the gender dimensions of peace processes and con-flict resolution" (S/RES/1325, para. 16), which was presented in 2002 and was met by a request to the Secretary-General in a Presidential Statement from the Council that the office "prepare a follow-up report on the full im-plementation of resolution 1325 to be presented to the Security Council in October 2004" (S/PRST/2002/32, p. 2). Thus, the Secretary-General's reports have been structured from the outset to provide an account of im-plementation, which necessarily requires reflecting on the areas where im-plementation has fallen short. The cadence of this story within the reports is quite consistent, with each of the reports concluding with some version of a statement that acknowledges shortcomings and notes: "Much remains to be done to ensure that the existing frameworks and the recommendations in Security Council resolution 1325 (2000) are fully implemented" (S/2002/1154, para. 67).

Similarly, the Open Debates tend to offer an account of both progress and unrealized potential, manifestations par excellence of the logics of (im)possi-bility that structure these narratives. Despite notable differences in *how* they tell their stories, the UN representatives (from the Office of the Secretary-General, or the Secretary-General himself; from UNIFEM/UN Women; from the Department of Peacekeeping Operations; and occasionally from elsewhere across the UN system) and the representatives from "civil society" (usually brought to the Council chambers by the NGO Working Group on Women, Peace and Security) tell the same stories during the Open Debates. Effort has been made, but "there is so much left to do" (S/PV.5766 2007, p. 3), "we have more distance to travel" (S/PV.7044 2013, p. 2), and "we still have far to go" (S/PV.8382 2018, p. 3). The metaphor of distance is frequently deployed in the discourse, a point to which I return below; in the *fabula*, what emerges is a story about an incomplete political project, a project that is effecting change but slowly, wherein the lassitude that characterizes progress is never fully explained but responsibility for the failures is assumed by an inclusive "we."

The characterization evident in the *fabula* speaks to a bureaucracy that encourages the formation of a strong and inclusive collective institutional subject. The Secretary-General in particular articulates the "we" subject as the entity of the UN system and interpellates civil society into this collective subject as well:

> *We* can no longer afford to minimize or ignore the contributions of women and girls to all stages of conflict resolution, peacemaking, peace-building, peacekeeping and the reconstruction processes. Sustainable peace will not be achieved without the full and equal participation of women and men. It is my hope that the Security Council, Member States, the United Nations system, NGOs, civil society and others will take further decisive action to ensure the participation of women and girls and fully incorporate their concerns into all our efforts to promote peace and security. (S/2002/1154, para. 68; emphasis added)

This paragraph links the Council, UN member states, the UN system, and civil society actors together and binds them in relation to the "we"-subject on whose behalf the Secretary-General speaks (see also S/2004/814, para. 121; S/2011/598, para. 32; S/2017/861, para. 111). In the telling of this story of shortcomings, therefore, "we"—WPS actors of all kinds—are implicated in failure and simultaneously subject to the evaluation of the Secretary-General, which reinforces the authority of that office while positioning all other actors as subordinate.

The responsibility for limited implementation, read as the primary short-coming of the agenda (which is significant in itself, and to which I return later), is a story of limited resources and a lack of political will. The explanatory potential of these factors is itself limited. Where, for example, the Secretary-General's report notes an urgent need for "strengthened political will" to enhance monitoring and evaluation of the implementation of UNSCR 1325 (S/2010/498, para. 8), underlying resistance to implementation is erased from the story. In the interviews I conducted, limited resources and a lack of political will were frequently and consistently cited as inhibitors of success: "[T]wo factors are the lack of political will of governments specifically, and second is the lack of dedicated funding for national level implementation" (Interview, 201402); "I mean it depends a little bit on the appetite of the member states and the international community to actually do this" (Interview, 201605); "I would say in reality when you look at the money, which is ultimately what matters, a lot of it is so underfunded" (Interview, 201901). The centrality of resources (including political will) is of such significance in the story of WPS shortcomings that it is captured in the most recent Presidential Statement on the agenda:

> The Council recognizes the launch of the Global Acceleration Instrument (GAI) on women's engagement in peace and security and humanitarian affairs, in addition to existing complementary mechanisms, as one avenue to attract resources, coordinate responses and accelerate implementation, and encourages Member States to consider funding the GAI. (S/PRST/2016, pp. 2–3)

The characterization here certainly positions UN member states in a more powerful position than the Secretary-General's interpellative "we" statements, as UN member states, in this configuration, are endowed with the capability to invest, or not invest, in the success of the agenda—and thus the capacity to realize, or not, the agenda's potential.[1]

Consistently within both these dimensions of characterization is the representation of "civil society" as the locus of effective WPS work: civil society actors are characterized in this *fabula* as diligent and determined implementers of the WPS agenda, whose efforts are curtailed by the lack of resources and will. "[C]oncrete support" is needed from UN entities and member states to ensure that the efforts of women in conflict and post-conflict environments can be translated into lasting change. The statement at the 2012 Open Debate by Bineta Diop, representative of the NGO Working Group on WPS and president and founder of Femmes Africa Solidarité, exemplifies this narrative:

> Women whose communities and lives are affected by conflict demand that the Security Council, with its mandate for maintaining international peace and security, and all Member States and United Nations actors support them and champion women's human rights. From the women in Sri Lanka seeking to rebuild their lives, to the women in Afghanistan demanding a voice in shaping their country's future; from the women seeking protection and medical care in the Kivus, to the women driven from their homes by violence in Colombia; from the women in Sierra Leone, Bosnia and Herzegovina and the Sudan still seeking justice, to the human rights defenders in Iraq and the women disarmament activists in Côte d'Ivoire—these women are rightly expecting the Council to turn its words into action. (S/PV.6877 2012, p. 9)

This storytelling invokes a global network of hard-working, forward-looking women doing peace work despite inaction by the organization charged with maintaining peace.

Relatedly, the temporal organization of the *fabula* is consistently future facing. A persistent motif in the story of shortcomings within the WPS agenda is a need for further action in the future. The way that the story of shortcomings is told is usually through a retrospective narrative, with prospective impetus: the past is accounted for (frequently in terms of actions taken that have generated some limited success) and is related to the future of WPS (in which "we" must do more/better to implement the agenda), creating a present that is only ever a stock-taking moment, not a moment for action in itself. Again, in part the structure of the storytelling lends itself to this kind of temporal organization; when the Secretary-General is reporting on WPS activity, the evaluation references actions in the past, and recommendations aim to inform future practice. Erasing the present from the story, however, creates a degree of predictability, and predictable frustration: "[C]oming up every year, in every SGs report, you could almost verbatim say, 'This is a gap area, this is a gap area, this is a gap area, we haven't achieved progress on this, we haven't achieved progress on this'" (Interview, 201905). The discourses and logics that hold together this story, which represents the WPS agenda as always success deferred, relate not only to the normative desire to see a better future for the agenda than is recorded in its histories or than exists in its present, but also to the emergence of the agenda as a complete and therefore implementable set of policy imperatives.

The *fabula* of WPS shortcomings, as outlined here, brings to mind Langston Hughes's poem "Harlem," in which he asks, "What happens to a dream deferred? . . . Maybe it just sags / like a heavy load. / *Or does it explode?*" (Hughes 1994, 426). The agenda is constituted as a weight borne by the global network of women in civil society working toward gender-equitable peace, as an additional load on the overtaxed resources of both the UN system and its constituent member states. The process of deferral evokes another poet, Robert Frost, who wrote about having "promises to keep / And miles to go before I sleep" (Frost [1923] 1979, 225). Frost's melancholy resignation about the journey not yet complete resonates powerfully with the story of WPS shortcomings, its successes yet to come. And as Nadine Puechguirbal notes wryly, " 'We still have a long way to go' is the catchphrase used by patriarchy to gain time, justify its opposition to change and lull feminist analysers into believing that real progresses are made" (Puechguirbal 2012, 15). It seems churlish indeed to refuse to celebrate the modest achievements of member states and of the UN itself, documented in the previous chapter, when they are *by their own admission* modest, and when *by their own admission* "we"— that assumptive, presumptive "we"—"still have a long way to go": churlish, unreasonable, idealistic, even radical to demand not just incremental gains and little wins (in accordance with a logic of possibility) but transformational change (constructed in accordance with a logic of impossibility). Logics of (im)possibility are prominent here.

Discursive constructions of failure

Many discourses are held in particular arrangements to assemble the narrative of WPS shortcomings. I draw out three that are of particular significance in the story just recounted, which is a story of a failure of funding and of not finding the will to pursue full implementation of the agenda as it is currently conceived. It is also a story of demands—even dreams—deferred to the future, which I suggest is constituted through logics of (im)possibility. The structures of knowledge and practice that emerge through these discourses, and their attendant logics, produce WPS simultaneously as both a knowable policy agenda with specific but obvious challenges hindering full implementation and an idealist, even radical, dream of systemic change. This plurality echoes and reinforces the plurality identified in the previous chapter between the manageable and the messy in narratives of success, reproducing logics of (in)coherence, and reinforces visible logics of (im)possibility structuring the futures of the WPS agenda at UN HQ.

Funding and political will: WPS in the "national interest"

In the majority of the interviews I conducted over the course of this project, the conversation turned to resourcing at some point: "The lack of funding is also a barrier, sustainable funding" (Interview, 201402). Peace work is notoriously underfunded in comparison with spending on security and defense, so much so that the UN Office for Disarmament Affairs recently produced a factsheet titled "The World Is Over-armed, and Peace is Underfunded" (Archer 2013, 26). A commitment to funding peace work is embedded in the architecture of the WPS agenda; three WPS resolutions mention funding not only in their preambular statements but also in the operative paragraphs that mandate action.[2] The Council

"[u]rges Member States, United Nations bodies, donors and civil society to ensure that women's empowerment is taken into account during post-conflict needs assessments and planning, and factored into subsequent funding disbursements and programme activities" (S/RES/1889, para. 9);

"[e]ncourages concerned Member States to develop dedicated funding mechanisms to support the work and enhance capacities of organizations that support women's leadership development and full participation in all levels of decision-making, regarding the implementation of resolution 1325 (2000), inter alia through increasing contributions to local civil society" (S/RES/2122, para. 7b); and "[e]ncourages Member States to increase their funding on women, peace and security including through more aid in conflict and post-conflict situations for programmes that further gender equality and women's empowerment, as well as through support to civil society" (S/RES/2242, para. 3).

The placement of language on funding in the resolutions varies over time, such that the issue seems to be afforded greater and greater priority. The textual positioning of various elements within the resolutions is subject to protracted and often contentious negotiation, so to see the articulation of funding as a WPS priority move from paragraph 9 to paragraph 3 over time suggests that the issue is increasing in significance.

Funding is also frequently identified as an area of concern in the Secretary-General's reports (see, among many other examples, S/2006/770, para. 31; S/2009/362, para. 51; S/2015/203, para. 101; S/2017/861, para. 110). The articulation of this particular explanation for failure is generally reliant on the institutional position of the Secretary-General and the status of the office, as concerns about funding are often expressed in powerful normative language, wherein the agenda is described as "woefully underfunded," for example (S/2006/770, para. 31), or else the report lists multiple challenges to the agenda's realization, including "incoherence, inadequate funding of gender-related projects, fragmentation and insufficient institutional capacity for over-sight and accountability for system performance as well as low capacity for gender mainstreaming" (S/2007/567, para. 34). The privileged position of the Secretary-General and the power he has to monitor and evaluate—and find lacking—the various WPS actors is reinforced through the use of modal verbs; the 2017 report demands, for example, that "Member States and United Nations entities *must* invest in locally driven solutions and increase collaboration, funding and direct support to civil society organizations" (S/2017/861, para. 110; emphasis added).

The materiality of funding (or its absence) is part of the ease with which it is invoked as an explanatory factor in the narration of the agenda's shortcomings. As with quantitative indicators of success, discussed in the previous chapter, the dollar amount of funding disbursed to WPS initiatives is easy to measure, easy to count/account for, and therefore easy to identify as a rationale for success or failure, depending on whether the dollar amount is increasing or decreasing (on funding in the WPS agenda see, for example, Koester et al. 2016; Esplen and O'Neill 2017; Skjelsbæk and Tryggestad 2019). Where funding is only being provided for a small (and shrinking) set of activities, success cannot reasonably be expected: "[W]e have all these wonderful analyses of the importance of gender-responsive humanitarian service provision and it's 2% funded, 3% funded," as one research partici-pant explained (Interview, 201903); the implication here is that the programs cannot be counted as a success with a 97%–98% funding deficit.

Research on WPS implementation similarly reproduces a narrative of failure that concretizes "funding and political will" as the primary explana-tory factors:

> Lack of financial resources coupled with insufficient prioritization and po-
> litical commitment by decision-makers—from national governments or
> the UN alike—are commonly named the key factors for the disappointing
> implementation of the women, peace and security agenda. (Douglas and
> Mazzacurati 2017, 227)

Here, funding is attached to political will such that it becomes visible as a
dimension of political will. According to this logic, adequate political commitment is a necessary, even sufficient, condition for the disbursement of adequate funding. The agenda struggles in—in fact, its shortcomings can be
attributed directly to—the absence of either: "[T]rue political will, and institutional commitment in the form of human and budgetary resources, have
been in short supply" (Cohn 2017, 4–5).

Most of the people working on and around the WPS agenda with whom
I spoke in the course of this research commented on the shortcomings of
the agenda in terms of its lack of resourcing and/or political will: "[T]hat is
a fundamental challenge of the agenda. And until we've cracked that, everything else [can wait]—the proliferation of the resolutions, the localisation
and so forth, but until member states are actually willing to put this as a priority in their foreign policies" (Interview, 201910). This statement, offered by
one research participant, could just as easily be attributed to a dozen more.
We frequently discussed the need for "more concrete financing and political
will" (Interview, 201401) and how the agenda is "qualified by what's politically convenient and what's not politically convenient or what's politically
*in*convenient" (Interview, 201903). "It's not about not knowing, or not understanding, it's about the political will being there to actually do something
about it" (Interview, 201905).

I argue here, however, that it is *also* about "not knowing, or not understanding," or rather—and more specifically—it is about *how* the WPS agenda
is known and understood, and that knowledge/understanding is brought together in part through these claims about political will. The material failures
of implementation are attributed to a lack of resources and/or a lack of political will by the actor(s) in question to take up the WPS agenda in earnest.
I propose that these failure stories—or "failure rationales"—are problematic,
as "political will" is too general an explanatory factor to be politically or analytically very useful. The attribution of failure or success to political will also
tends to be somewhat tautological: there is a lack of political will, which leads
to failures of implementation, which are taken as evidence of a lack of political

will. Thus, the identification of "political will" as an explanatory factor tends to be presumed rather than empirically verified, as the dimensions of political will are more easily captured in other, related concepts (such as the investment of material resources, normative support for a particular issue in a given forum, and so on). As Andrea Spehar argues, "Any evidence of political will or lack thereof as described in the literature is typically indirect, speculative and retrospective" (2018, 236). "Political will," in short, is itself a discursive construct always already embedded within a specific discursive terrain.

Jutta Weldes created the intellectual space for this argument through her elaboration of the social construction of the "national interest" (see Weldes 1996a, 1996b). Weldes makes two interrelated arguments about the concept of the "national interest" that are relevant to the concept of "political will" as it is deployed here. First, "national interest" is a concept worthy of interrogation and continued analytical concern because of the political salience it has in "real world" political interactions (Weldes 1996a, 276). Second, the "'national interest' . . . is created as a meaningful object, out of shared meanings through which the world, particularly the international system and the place of the state in it, is understood" (Weldes 1996a, 277). That is to say, the "national interest" has no objective, a priori, meaning outside of the discursive conditions of its emergence. The implications of this argument for the conferral of legitimacy on a particular set of state actions undertaken in the name of the "national interest" are profound, in that the legitimacy of national interests "is conferred in the process of their construction" rather than being derived or deduced from an external, preexisting, and separate reality (Weldes 1996a, 303).

Weldes's treatment of the "national interest" inspires a similar engagement with the concept of "political will" as it is deployed in the discourses of WPS implementation. "Political will"—or more properly its absence—is a condition of the agenda's failure, and yet also of its success (see S/2015/203, para. 9; S/2018/250, para. 6): "[Y]ou have the group of friends of Women, Peace and Security, which now says there's 57 member states. You've got all these proliferations of women mediator networks. You've got a lot of activity. But when push comes to shove, I don't see member states using their political leverage to insist on inclusive processes" (Interview, 201910). In this way, political will is constructed as an intervening variable rather than integral to the inception of the agenda and its continuation and development over the past two decades. As Weldes argued in relation to the concept of the "national interest," "political will" does not preexist the discursive formations through which it becomes known, nor is it formed through interaction and then endowed with specific qualities; political will is at once an alibi for resistance to the agenda and an alibi for limited engagement, in accordance with a logic of impossibility. It is an empty signifier, a discursive placeholder that communicates everything and therefore nothing about the specifics of how the WPS agenda is stifled and comes up short (Laclau 2006, 107).

The discursive centering of "political will" as a/the explanatory factor in stories of shortcomings has two further elements of significance. First, the presupposition in all configurations of this discourse about resourcing and political will is that the agenda is decided (reinforcing a logic of coherence): the provisions and principles are agreed upon and achievement of success is now contingent solely on support, both material and ideological. This closes down discursive space to continue deliberation about what the agenda is or could be. Further, this discourse puts the success of the agenda in the hands of the formal (state) political actors; it is never the civil society actors, or women's organizations, who are described as lacking political will. This reinforces plural logics of (dis)location. Different degrees of political capital are seen to accrue to state actors in particular through WPS actions; the WPS anniversary effect discussed in the previous chapter creates the environment for member states and UN entities to parade their WPS credentials once a year. "In New York it's politically correct to throw support for the WPS or give a nice statement on WPS even if that goes no further than a statement" (Interview, 201910). Supporting and leading WPS initiatives also garners political capital, as shown in the Secretary-General's reports that highlight the achievements of particular UN member states, but erasing resistance under the signifier of "lacking political will" does not erode political capital. There are no consequences for inaction or outright resistance in the discourse of political will.

A lack of experts and expertise

In addition to, though enjoying much less prominence than, the discourse that lays blame for the shortcomings of the WPS agenda on the absence of funding and political will for its successful implementation, there is a discourse that attaches responsibility to the lack of (institutional and individual) experts/expertise. This discourse presents uneven expertise across the UN system and a concomitant need for training as a rationale for the agenda's shortcomings and also constructs an organizational structure at UN HQ that is not conducive to fostering or sustaining WPS expertise: individuals expend energy learning the system, learning how to navigate gaps and institutional hierarchies, and breaking down the siloes that inhibit effective collaboration and communication on WPS issues. Though subtle, this discourse is present not only in the interview data co-produced for this project but also in the Secretary-General's reports and the transcripts of the annual Open Debates on the theme of WPS. Early in the life of the agenda, the 2004 Secretary-General's report, for example, noted that "[g]reater coordination among United Nations entities, non-governmental organizations (NGOs) and refugee and displaced women's groups is needed" (S/2004/814, para. 46).

The 2006 Secretary-General's report is the first to articulate the WPS agenda *as* an agenda; it reports against the System-Wide Action Plan, mandated in the 2005 Presidential Statement (S/PRST/2005/52), and the first substantive category of evaluation (read: shortcoming) relates to capacity across the UN system:

> "A number of entities reported inadequate understanding by their staff of such concepts as gender analysis and mainstreaming" (S/2006/770, para. 22).

> "[M]any of the gender advisers were appointed at a junior level, precluding them from access to senior officials" (S/2006/770, para. 24).

> "[O]verall the available gender expertise throughout the system was often excluded from mainstream intra and inter-organizational decision-making processes" (S/2006/770, para. 25).

The political economy of WPS is implicated even in this discourse, which interrelates gender expertise (and funding/support thereof) with gender equality (and political commitment thereto): "a shrinking of capacity and resources" (Interview, 201602). In addition to the explicit criticism of inadequate funding commitments, there is evident here a criticism of the inadequate prioritization of gender expertise: "I am concerned that the drive for cost effectiveness in peace operations too often leads to decreased financial support for gender equality and women and peace and security capacity, including cuts in dedicated gender posts and reduction of their seniority levels, as seen in MINUSCA, UNMIL and the United Nations Mission for Justice

Support in Haiti" (S/2017/861, para. 81). Similarly, reduced numbers of gender experts within the UN system means that those remaining are isolated, which has a deleterious impact on the ability to implement the agenda effectively; the discourse situates existing experts in "siloes" (S/2015/716, para. 188; Interview, 201401; Interview, 201601). "While the UN has made important strides in strengthening its gender architecture and expertise, and in mainstreaming a gender perspective into various aspects of its work on peace and security, the evidence suggests that this has been achieved more in word than in deed" (Labonte and Curry 2016, 314). One research participant commented somewhat plaintively, "I feel we're just too few. . . . It's a lot of work. And not a lot. . . . As I said, we're not many people" (Interview, 201902).

The presupposition here is that having the right experts in the right place, able to inform or infuse policy and practice with the right expertise, would increase the likelihood of successful implementation. Several of the individuals I spoke to, however, suggested much broader institutional barriers to success: "Let's train women, let's build more capacity. Actually . . . it's not the women whose capacity needs to be built, it's the gatekeepers and the mediation experts who need to be trained on designing inclusive processes" (Interview, 201909). Moreover, the "siloes" extend to programs and missions beyond UN HQ, where each entity might provide (a double- or triple-hatted)[3] "gender expert" without sufficient coordination:

> [T]here are human rights WPAs, there are DPKO WPAs and there are—I can't remember how they call them, if they call them gender WPAs or Office of the SRSG WPAs. So they all get . . . like thrown in from these different institutional entities and they have them determined this way because all the different entities wanted to have dominion over who got to control the WPAs. This took four years for them to figure out and the problem is that they haven't managed to get them in place, and they haven't managed to deploy them, and they haven't managed to recruit them, and they haven't managed to—and this again is one of the challenges with not having a senior gender adviser. (Interview, 201302)

Discourse on the "lack of experts/expertise" obscures the institutional deficiencies in planning and coordinating for effective construction, retention, and dissemination of gender knowledge across the organizations and reproduces a logic of incoherence and impossibility. The claim that the organization "lacks expertise" again functions as an alibi for its failing to prioritize the nurturing of gender expertise, as well as constructing a few vulnerable "gender experts" who are individualized and implicated in the shortcomings and failures of the agenda through this discourse.

The scope of the agenda

The WPS agenda is constructed here, through various discursive practices, as vast in scope and undecided/undecidable; WPS emerges here as a policy agenda of a magnitude and complexity that cannot reasonably be success-fully implemented across a lifetime of peace work even with all of the nec-essary funding, political will, and expertise. It is impossible, and incoherent. I focus on three dimensions of this discourse here. First, there is the articula-tion of the WPS agenda with the idea either of the agenda being fundamental or there being elements of the agenda that are fundamental to it. Second, the difficulties in clarifying or decomplexifying the agenda captured in the dis-cussion of its fundamentals represent a different kind of failure that is none-theless important: a kind of conceptual failure, related to but different from the failures of experts/expertise previously outlined. Third, and finally, this discourse captures the relentlessly repetitive nature of WPS accounting, sit-uating failure as a kind of iterative practice that is regularly renewed. This speaks not only to the common cadence of failure reporting but also to the more prosaic processes of institutional forgetting that seem to characterize WPS work. I discuss each of these dimensions in turn here.

The word "fundamental" derives from the Latin *fundamentum*, meaning "foundation." The concept of foundation is manifest in this discourse of WPS shortcomings, both in the context of the component parts of the agenda and in relation to the agenda being a component part of a broader set of issues or phenomena. In the case of the former, there is a presupposition that the component parts of the agenda are already agreed or determined; this is visible, for example, when a research participant comments, "We still have huge challenges with what should be the absolute fundamental components of the WPS agenda" (Interview, 201910). This representation of challenges presumes that the "fundamental components of the WPS agenda" are known to both speaker and listener, and perhaps more widely. This representation, and attendant presuppositional moves, feature quite prominently in the in-terview data, which referenced "the core and fundamentals of the Women Peace and Security agenda" (Interview, 201403), proposing that the agenda is "fundamentally a gender perspective on peace and security" (Interview, 201909). It is not my purpose here to debate what the "fundamental components" of the agenda are, nor what the agenda "fundamentally" *is*, but rather to show how the *idea* that there is a "fundamental" agenda is used to explain shortcomings, in that WPS actors have missed the point on the fundamentals, the foundations, and thus failed to capture its potential. The agenda's presumed coherence is the underpinning logic of its limitations.

In the context of the agenda's "fundamental" significance, a similar kind of discursive dynamic is evident; where, for example, the WPS is failing because "the role of women in peace processes generally continues to be viewed as a side issue rather than as fundamental to the development of viable democratic institutions and the establishment of sustainable peace" (S/2006/770, para. 47), it is the fault of those who fail to *see* WPS correctly—as "fundamental to building peace and security" (S/PV.6642 2011, p. 3). The Secretary-General reproduces this discourse in both reports and statements at the WPS Open Debates, commenting, for example, "This agenda is not an optional extra, or a favour to women and girls. It is fundamental to building sustainable peace and ending the conflicts that are causing so much pain and damage around the world" (S/PV.7793 2016, p. 3). Although this discourse ascribes great significance to the WPS agenda—as its implementation is positioned as a necessary condition for the achievement of lasting peace in the world—it also opens discursive space to articulate the agenda as an "optional extra" or "side issue." Relatedly, the repeated invocation of the agenda's "fundamental components" can function to alienate even those who are sympathetic to the agenda but who might articulate it differently, according to the plural logics of (in)coherence and (im)possibility. The use of the concept of foundations or fundaments at once opens up and closes down the discourse about failure, positioning those who wrongly envision or misunderstand the agenda and its significance as culpable for its failures while refusing the possibility that the agenda might yet be undecided, its significance unsure. The scope of change thus needed to effect successful implementation is nothing short of rethinking the world: "We cannot afford to have more than half of the world's population continue to be excluded from the strategies of peace and security. To engage those resources requires a fundamental shift in our thinking" (S/ PV.6005 2008, p. 4).

Relatedly, there is another dimension of this discourse that reinforces and reproduces the logic of coherence and certainty identified here. This is a discourse that attributes failure to conceptual confusion. Per the International

Rescue Committee employee quoted in Nina Hall and Jacqui True's analysis of work on violence against women in Timor Leste, this discourse alludes to the incoherence in, and lack of clarity about doing, gender work; she recalls that when she began working on sexual and gender-based violence she thought, "I don't even know what gender is" (Milena Vilanova quoted in Hall and True 2009, 164).[4] Many research participants commented on this conceptual confusion, noting, for example, "There's a big conceptual barrier around gender for sure . . . What is gender? Does it mean we're working on women or does it mean that we're working on all genders? Or sexuality? So that's a big conceptual sticking point for feminist activists and of course for the authorities responsible for making this happen" (Interview, 201906).

Conceptual confusion as a cause of failure is reinforced through the articulation of a bifurcation in visions of the WPS agenda, where some WPS actors reproduce an understanding of the agenda as being "about" women— and particular kinds of (victimized) women, more specifically—while others focus on gender and power. Even within the construction of the agenda as a set of policy initiatives about women, there is contestation: "I think the comfort zone is women as victims, that everyone is happy to say this is really terrible we need to do something we need to protect we need to, no one will say no, right? Women as political actors, and in leadership positions are where things get a little more complicated" (Interview, 201603). As in the narrative of success recounted in the previous chapter, this configuration of discourse functions to fix the agenda as narrowly and specifically to do with sexual violence. One research participant said bluntly, "We have been concerned in an ongoing way about a restriction of the Women, Peace and Security agenda to the focus on sexual violence" (Interview, 201401). It is proposed by some using this discourse that filling the conceptual gaps in the architecture of the agenda will enhance its success; for example, Zainab Bangura, Special Representative of the Secretary-General on Sexual Violence in Conflict, commented in 2016 that it is increasingly evident "what is missing in the normative framework of resolutions that are our conceptual and operational guide" (S/PV.7704 2016, p. 5). This assumes, however, that there is a singular logic governing the construction of women, the conceptualization of gender(ed power), and the proper policy focus of taking a gender lens to matters of international peace and security, which I am demonstrating here is not the case.[5] A critical interrogation of gendered power is represented as too much of a stretch for many working in areas that intersect with the agenda: "It's axiomatic for people that work in this space, but for people that are not used to bringing a critical gender lens to their conversations or their day-to-day work practices, it's challenging" (Interview, 201605).

These two dimensions of this discourse, which constructs the WPS agenda as simultaneously both settled in its significance (coherent) and conceptually contested (incoherent), reinforce and are reinforced by the third and final dimension that I interrogate here. This dimension features the frustrations evident not only in having to recount narratives of failure, but also in having to relitigate aspects of the agenda over and over again.[6] At the time of writing, this issue is felt particularly keenly, as the negotiations over and adoption of UNSCR 2467, the most recent WPS resolution, revealed cataclysmic schisms in the WPS community. The resolution represents a "compromise"—insisted upon by the US government—on language about sexual and reproductive health rights that had already been negotiated and agreed upon by the Council, enshrined in previous WPS resolutions. Building on text from the preamble of resolution 1889, operative paragraph 19 of resolution 2106 (2013) gives some substance to the Council's provision in this sphere:

> Recognizing the importance of providing timely assistance to survivors of sexual violence, urges United Nations entities and donors to provide non-discriminatory and comprehensive health services, including sexual and reproductive health, psychosocial, legal, and livelihood support and other multi-sectoral services for survivors of sexual violence. (S/RES/2016, para. 19)

Although the draft text of resolution 2467 included the fairly minimal acknowledgment of the need to provide "non-discriminatory and comprehensive health services, in line with Resolution 2016," the final text of the resolution makes no direct reference at all to sexual and reproductive health. Instead, the preamble of the resolution only emphasizes "the need for survivors of sexual violence to receive non-discriminatory access to services such as medical and psychosocial care" (S/RES/2467, preamble).

It is not only the substance of the resolutions that is being renegotiated—and even undone—but also the agenda's achievements. This story of shortcomings articulates such profound limitations around institutional learning that the agenda *cannot* be realized, in accordance with a logic of impossibility: "[W]hy is it that we're still scrambling every time there's a chance to influence a reconciliation or a conflict resolution process? Why is it that we always start from zero? Because we really have changed nothing" (Interview,

201906). It may be the "anniversary effect," encouraging people to reflect on nearly two decades of WPS work in our conversations, but the logic of impossibility, manifest in invocations of often thankless and repetitive work, of revisiting the same debates and failing to take forward successes, is powerful in this discourse:

> "[Y]ou know when they said absence of sufficient policy, lack of mission funding, lack of support, we should do more outreach to women leaders. We've been saying that since the very beginning" (Interview, 201601).

> "[I]n a lot of ways, we're starting from zero again. Where we're forgetting like the now almost 19 years of Women, Peace and Security agenda and going back to the basics of like, just add women to these processes" (Interview, 201901).

> "We're heading into 20 years of Women, Peace and Security and whether its CAR [the Central African Republic], Syria, Yemen, Afghanistan, these processes do not have women at the table. There's something fundamentally missing, I think, in our approach on the last 20 years. That we seem to reinvent the wheel with every process. And we seem to start from scratch with every process" (Interview, 201909).

The way in which WPS actors report endless iterations of "going back" to "the very beginning," "starting from zero again" or "start[ing] from scratch," and "reinvent[ing] the wheel" gives this discourse a circularity, constituting a closed loop of failure from a hopeful—even transformative—foundation through unlearning or inadequate learning to the end/new beginning, a place of increasing frustration. "It's on many fronts that . . . those battles are really being fought. Extremely frustrating, it's extremely frustrating" (Interview, 201302).

Concluding thoughts on failure

This chapter has identified and interrogated the stories of failure that are recounted about the WPS agenda. The narrative offers a clear and consistent rationale for implementation gaps, notably a lack of resourcing and political will. There is no doubt that effective implementation of the WPS agenda requires resources and political will, but other failures are prominent also, including the absence of agreement on what the WPS agenda is, what it means, what should be prioritized, and who should lead and enact WPS. The "huge challenges" identified in the stories of shortcomings remain in part because of the very different visions of what WPS is, who should "do" it, and how it should be done. I identify this in a discourse of conceptual failure, underpinned by logics of (in)coherence. The discursive—and pragmatic— necessity of coherence drives the evaluation of failure (and indeed success) and both informs and reproduces the way in which WPS emerges as a knowable policy agenda. As is the case in the previous chapter, it is evident from the narrative and discourse analysis presented here that these formations— these stories of success and failure—are generative of, and generated by, logics of (im)possibility and (in)coherence.

In terms of the characterization and temporal organization of the failure narratives assembled here, the articulation of shortcomings in terms of funding and political will precludes discussion of some of these wider issues and depoliticizes the highly political processes of forwarding or withdrawing support for the agenda. Configuring the agenda as settled, if ambitious in scope, suggests that states and other actors within the UN system just need to pledge and enact support in order to realize success. This reinforces states and UN actors as power holders within the implementation of the agenda, as well as reproducing the UN Secretary-General as the ultimate arbiter of what *counts* as success and failure. The reports of the Secretary-General, with their repetitive structure and familiar cadence that becomes rhythmic over time, offer an account of the organization's shortcomings, both as an institution and as (more than) the sum of its parts; the recounting of these stories is reliant on the shorthand of "resources and political will" as primary explanations for failure; on the projection of success into the future; and on the presupposition that the agenda is a certain, complete *thing*, a set of principles and provisions that can simply be used as a guide or a tool to effect change in the world. The simplicity of this narrative of failure is appealing, but obscurant, allowing for the erasure of power and political priorities in the present of the agenda. It might thus be productive to think about telling more complicated stories that sit with, rather than defer or shy away from, the tensions, divides, and difficulties that are constitutive of the agenda and efforts toward its implementation. I turn to this discussion in the chapter that follows.

6

Narratives of Tensions and Pressures

The WPS agenda is usually described in terms of four "pillars" of activity: the participation of women in peace and security governance; the prevention of violence and conflict; the protection of women's rights and bodies; and gender-sensitive relief and recovery programming. Over time, however, the emphasis given to each of these pillars has varied, and different actors have supported different initiatives under each pillar, with different political effects. The story of tension evident in the data I have collected or co-produced is primarily articulated in terms of imbalance across the various pillars (which in itself is interesting, as it presupposes the virtue or desirability of balance), which resonates with logics of (in)coherence. This story is thus in part comprised of discourse about whether the agenda is settled, or not, related to—though subtly different from—the discourse of completeness discussed in Chapter 3.

Further, tensions and pressure points are politically and strategically deployed as rationales for (limited) engagement across the agenda as a whole by certain actors, in accordance with logics of (im)possibility. As discussed in the previous chapter, the agenda is constituted as unwieldy in scope, too wide ranging to permit successful implementation. The logics of (in)coherence and (im)possibility create particular constraints around the agenda, which is further reinforced through the logics of the agenda's (dis)locations. I discuss a discourse here that relates to spatial (dis)connections that animate and organize the agenda, frequently captured in the discursive construction of localization versus national implementation versus transnational advocacy. These (dis)connections function to diffuse the agenda across contexts, such that it emerges as not only impossibly vast in scope but also impossible to anchor spatially. The WPS agenda is everything, and everywhere, which permits WPS actors to be selective in their WPS practices—even demands such selectivity.

The final discourse relates to the power of the Security Council. This discourse reproduces a number of themes from previous chapters: the articulation of a disjuncture between the agenda "on paper" and the agenda "in

Narrating the Women, Peace and Security Agenda. Laura J. Shepherd, Oxford University Press (2021). © Oxford University Press. DOI: 10.1093/oso/9780197557242.003.0006

practice," discussed in Chapter 3; and the conceit that the agenda is settled, according to an ambivalent logic of practice and logics of (in)coherence. There is also a discourse about the (lack of) desire for more resolutions, to fill out and finalize the architecture. This discourse suggests that *if only* the right words for the new resolutions could be found, *then* the WPS agenda might live up to its promise. Further, and although the same discourses articulate "resolution fatigue," the representation of WPS in these discourses is again of a policy agenda that is (in)definitely (in)complete; the juxtaposition of these two realities is characteristic of the narration of the agenda as a whole, as I have shown throughout.

Identifying the *fabula*

> Also, we need to be careful about putting too much emphasis on one as-
> pect of the agenda. It's all there in the resolutions; we just need to work
> on implementation. And of course, we're working within the limits of
> the UN system; the Council really only wants oversight of things re-
> lated to peace and security.

The stories of tensions in the WPS agenda are usually told in terms of im-balance across the various (presumed settled) pillars of the agenda, per the narrative outlined in Chapter 3, which constructs a tension between partic-ipation (of women in peace processes) and prevention (of sexual violence) in the process of constituting these issues *as* the agenda. The narration of tensions and imbalance is contingent on the acceptance of the agenda as a coherent set of pillars and associated activities, and this acceptance is evident across all of the storytelling sites I investigated, in comments such as that offered by one research participant early in the project: "[A] lot of times at the UN, there's this focus on creating new language when in actuality a lot of these concepts have already been mapped out and we don't need to reinvent everything. We just need to move forward on what we've got" (Interview, 201401). The idea that "these concepts have already been mapped out" is a necessary precondition for the articulation of tensions. As shown in the pre-vious chapter, there is ongoing contestation over what the WPS agenda can/should be, but in order to discuss competing ideas about what should be pri-oritized, it is necessary to presuppose a settled set of issues that can then be rendered priorities.

Part of the way this story of tension is told is through research literature that identifies the WPS resolutions in terms of their focus on participation or prevention of sexual violence (see, for example, Otto 2010; Kirby and Shepherd 2016; Heathcote 2018); the latter is also identified as protection (see Shepherd 2019, 100), to distinguish the prevention of sexual violence from *conflict* prevention. Suggesting that five out of the nine WPS resolutions focus on prevention,[1] without qualification, gives a misleading impression of the emphasis within the resolutions, as *conflict* prevention is undoubtedly the "weakest 'p' in the pod" of the WPS agenda pillars (Basu and Confortini 2017). For the purposes of identifying this *fabula*, it is not necessary to reach a definitive conclusion on whether the issue is *really* the prevention of sexual violence or the protection of women from sexual violence; the disproportionate emphasis on sexual violence is the concern that dominates this narrative of imbalance. For example, recounting the history of the agenda in 2013—a year that saw the adoption of both UNSCR 2016, on sexual violence, and UNSCR 2122, a much broader-based resolution—one research participant explained:

> [O]ne of the concerns [was] about an additional resolution on participation, which is something that we feel very strongly about, which is something that we actually said—that if you do a resolution on sexual violence and conflict—we said this to the P3,[2] that if you do a resolution on sexual violence and conflict you're going to unbalance the agenda and you have to do resolutions on the other elements of the agenda, you have to, you can't do one only on sexual violence and conflict and leave it at that. (Interview, 201302)

The concern about imbalance reported here was reiterated repeatedly throughout the interviews I conducted.

Underpinning the story of (im)balance are opposing constructions of female subjectivity that position women in relation to peace and security in radically different ways:

> I think that's where it started with WPS, we said, "Okay. Women are victims of conflict, and they're victims of violence. We will accept that and we need to stop that. It's protection focused, and then it moved a little bit more into the participation side where, okay, now we need women at the table. Let's look at these peace processes." (Interview, 201901)

[Y]ou always have the tendency of women need protection, and women, you know? It's always the discussion around women being vulnerable, you know is one that everyone's happy to have about women, you know, I think that needing empowerment but being empowered already for many of women just needing the space, the access and the funding is you know can be much more tricky. (Interview, 201907)

The word "victim" was not used in UNSCR 1325; it entered the discourse of the agenda in the Presidential Statement of 2002 (S/PRST/2002/32, p. 2) and after that point was firmly fixed in the articulations of the agenda's focus on the impact of conflict on women in particular. The Council expressed concern, for example, "that civilians, particularly women and children, continue to account for the vast majority of victims of acts of violence" (S/PRST/2007/40, p. 2), and the Secretary-General's reports similarly associate women with victimhood, from the outset (S/2002/1154, para. 6). The trope of woman-as-victim is powerful within WPS discourse and is integral to this story of imbalance and tension, as this trope is juxtaposed with woman-as-agent-of-change (see also Shepherd 2016c); positioning these constructs as the subjects of "women, peace and security" permits the narration of the agenda in terms of how these different constructs (these differently imagined women) are served (Shepherd 2011; Muehlenhof 2017; Martín De Almagro 2018a).

The characterization within this *fabula* of imbalance rests power securely with the UN Security Council and, to a lesser extent, the UN system more broadly. The story of imbalance and tension is primarily articulated through contestation over the substance of Security Council resolutions and over the need for more resolutions to further the agenda. Obviously the Security Council is the institutional site of power in the production of resolutions. Through the narration of this story of the agenda being pulled in opposite directions by the adoption of resolutions addressing elements of conflict-related sexual violence versus the adoption of resolutions that emphasize women's representation and agency in peace and security domains, the primacy of the Council is reaffirmed: "[C]learly [there was] a growing need, if not, an urgent need, to move forward in the Council on this and that, that was necessary symbolically for the Council to send a message that it actually takes the participation and agency element seriously and on a very practical level" (Interview, 201403). The Council is the central character in this story of tension and imbalance, with advocates from civil society and across the UN system again disempowered, positioned as supplicants: "[W]e really pushed strongly on this and said please for the love of goodness make it strongly on women's participation, we said we believe strongly that sexual violence and conflict is because of a failure to implement the women peace and security agenda as a whole, please don't imbalance the agenda further" (Interview, 201302).

The Secretary-General's reports reinforce this characterization. For example, the Council is positioned as the keeper of the agenda through the narration of the "strong advocacy role" it played "in the absence of a clear monitoring mechanism for implementation of resolution 1325" (S/2009/465, para. 57). There is a paragraph in the 2010 Secretary-General's report that is compelling evidence of the characterization of the Council as the protagonist in the development of the agenda, and it is worth quoting at length:

> During its open debate on women and peace and security, held on 27 April 2010, the Security Council took note of the indicators contained in the report of the Secretary-General and requested him to continue to consult with the Council, taking into account the views expressed by other relevant stakeholders, including broader membership, to develop the indicators further and to include in the present report a comprehensive set of indicators as well as a programme of work containing roles and responsibilities vis-à-vis the indicators within the United Nations system and a time frame to render the indicators operational. (S/2010/498, para. 112)

This is a story of the most privileged body within the UN system rejecting the indicators and recommendations of the Secretary-General's report and "request[ing] him to continue to consult with the Council" about how to monitor the implementation of the agenda. The tensions in the agenda are embedded in the resolutions, and through these representations, the Council is afforded near-absolute authority over how the agenda is to be developed and monitored.

The temporal dimension of the story of tensions runs counter to the historicism of the success stories and the futurism of the failure narratives. The temporal ordering of these tales is organized in and through a motif of presentism: as it is, so has it always been and will always be. With elements of the repetitive and circular motif of the narratives of shortcomings identified in the previous chapter, this is a flatter and more elliptical temporality. The narration of tensions relies on a temporal anchoring of the agenda and its coherence in its moment of inception. The use of the word "always" is significant here: "There's always going to be a key role for the Security Council" (Interview, 201910); "there's always going to be that political tension" (Interview, 201403); "the agenda as it stands, normatively, is a very diverse, complex and broad-reaching agenda. But the emphasis or the low-hanging fruit for most states is always to go to protection issues" (Interview, 201912). "Always" is a powerful temporal signifier, and it simultaneously reinforces both (a particular version of) the *reality* within which the agenda operates and the fixity or stability of the agenda, through the constitution of the impossibility of change. *This* (arrangement or configuration of power) is how *it* (the agenda that "we" accept to be the subject of "our" story) is *always* going to be (so adjust your expectations accordingly).

There are many complicated discursive moves to trace within this story of tensions and pressure, relating not only to the constitution of the Security Council's supreme authority but also to the spatial (dis)location of the agenda and how this discourse interrelates with the discourse of Council power. The expansion and constriction of the formal architecture of the agenda at the UN remains a matter of how the agenda is narrated, and again in the narration of tensions and pressures within the agenda there are moments of resistance to the Council's conservativism, evidencing the logics of (dis)location I identify. In the section that follows I examine these logics in more detail, through analysis of the discourses that are held within this story, and I also foreshadow some of the silences and absences that I revisit in the following chapter.

Discursive constructions of tensions and pressures

As outlined, one of the significant facets of the constitution of WPS at UN HQ is the story of tensions. There is a growing body of work that examines tensions in the WPS agenda (see, for example, Lee-Koo 2014; Kirby 2015; George and Shepherd 2016), not only in regard to the divided focus of the agenda on the prevention of sexual violence versus the participation of women in peace processes, but also in regard to other tensions, including the proper parameters of the agenda, its (dis)connections, the power and authority of WPS actors in effecting changes within (and to) the agenda, and a tension between "paper" and "practice", which I discuss briefly in

Chapter 3. The discursive construction of these tensions is politically salient, as the discourses that are held in array to constitute the narrative of tension have particular productive effects and functions, most specifically related to the perpetuation of logics of (dis)location and an ambivalent logic practice that together delimit boundaries around the agenda that inform and shape its imaginable futures. In this section, I address each of these discourses in turn.

The unsettled agenda

Although the conventional narrative of the WPS agenda suggests neat division into four "pillars" deriving from UNSCR 1325 (prevention, participation, protection, and relief and recovery), this consolidation was in fact a rather later development. The first System-Wide Action Plan for implementation of WPS at the UN identifies twelve areas of action (S/2005/636, p. 3), which were narrowed to five thematic areas (the four pillars, plus a normative dimension) in the second System-Wide Action Plan in 2007 (S/2007/567, para. 42):

(a) *Prevention*: mainstream a gender perspective into all conflict prevention activities and strategies, develop effective gender-sensitive early warning mechanisms and institutions, and strengthen efforts to prevent violence against women, including various forms of gender-based violence.

(b) *Participation*: promote and support women's active and meaningful participation in all peace processes as well as their representation in formal and informal decision-making at all levels; improve partnership and networking with local and international women's rights groups and organizations; recruit and appoint women to senior positions in the United Nations, including Special Representatives of the Secretary-General, and in peacekeeping forces, including military, police, and civilian personnel.

(c) *Protection*: strengthen and amplify efforts to secure the safety, physical or mental health, well-being, economic security, and/or dignity of women and girls; promote and safeguard human rights of women and mainstream a gender perspective into the legal and institutional reforms.

(d) *Relief and recovery*: promote women's equal access to aid distribution mechanisms and services, including those dealing with the specific needs of women and girls in all relief recovery efforts.

(e) *Normative*: develop policy frameworks; ensure effective coordination and awareness raising to advance the implementation of resolution 1325 (2000).

Clearly the duality of *both* prevention ("conflict prevention" and "prevent[ing] violence against women") *and* protection (of safety/dignity and human rights) is articulated in the discourse of the agenda at this early stage. This "pillar" structure was reproduced and embedded in later reports of the Secretary-General and taken up widely in the research and policy community beyond. The five areas were reported on across four pillars in 2010, as the normative pillar was deemed to be "cross-cutting" and was therefore incorporated into reporting on the other four pillars rather than being reported on separately (S/2010/173). This process of narrowing and focusing on prevention, protection, participation, and relief and recovery simultaneously includes the "pillars" within the boundaries of the WPS agenda, broad as they are.

It is thus unsurprising that UN member states do not necessarily agree on the meaning of these pillars in practice, or that research participants referenced the conceptual duality of the core focus areas of the WPS agenda. Some invoke the "protection" pillar with reference to sexual violence; for example arguing that "[s]o much has happened on the protection pillar around conflict-related sexual violence which was extremely important to happen and of course remains an extremely disturbing phenomena" (Interview, 201603). Protection is constituted in this discourse as a politically expedient element of the WPS agenda behind which to mobilize, because it hinges on the construction of women-as-victims previously mentioned, which in turn is faithful to a conventional configuration of a binary gender order that opposes women (weak, passive, and in need of protection) against men (strong, active, protectors): "[P]rotection for sure. Everybody's ferociously committed to that" (Interview, 201906); "[b]y and large, people [are] supportive of the protection agenda, I mean, member states are very supportive of the protection agenda" (Interview, 201905). Some, conversely, discuss action against sexual violence in terms of prevention: "I think we're also not that well-versed in the other pillars. I think we know more about prevention and participation" (Interview, 201904). Prevention is also affixed to sexual violence in several Secretary-General's reports (for example, S/2010/173; S/2010/498; S/2014/181). Yet others—in interviews and documentary text—relate prevention to conflict more broadly: "If you want to start talking about prevention you need to completely break the current pattern and system and structure, the way we've been conducting business and especially in political mission or peacekeeping operations" (Interview, 201601; see also S/2011/598; S/2015/716).

From a discourse-theoretical perspective, it is to be expected that there are no singular and stable meanings that can be relied upon in discourse about WPS. Prevention can be associated with both sexual violence and conflict. Protection can refer to both bodies and rights. The mutability and fluidity of these concepts, however, has problematic effects because these different articulations demand very different kinds of action. If conflict prevention drives the agenda, then different solutions and strategies are thinkable, whereas if preventing sexual violence is the focus, those solutions and strategies will be less appropriate and will no doubt get less political traction. This dynamic can be captured in the tension articulated by one research participant: "[T]he constant, and yet so little addressed, tension between feminist and often peace approaches, to the Women, Peace and Security agenda and the approaches that are far more focused on getting women into peacekeeping, getting women's equal presence in military structures, whether as civilian or as active agents in military structures" (Interview, 201403). This articulation precludes the possibility that the UN might be, or might minimally accept, a feminist or peace organization; the UN system emerges here as concerned, as in previous chapters, with the presence of women in processes that it can control and count.[3]

Discourse about the substance of the agenda also (re)produces a tension between expansionist and conservative dynamics. Resolution 2242 notably incorporated a number of emergent security challenges into the formal architecture of the agenda, including "rising violent extremism, which can be conducive to terrorism, the increased numbers of refugees and internally displaced persons, the impacts of climate change and the global nature of health pandemics" (S/RES/2242, preamble). Sexual violence against men and boys entered the discourse of the agenda as a WPS issue in a 2012 Presidential Statement (S/PRST/2012/3, p. 1), while "arbitrary detention, intimidation and harassment of lesbian, gay, bisexual and transgender persons" was articulated in the discourse in 2014 (S/2014/693, p. 9). The expansion of the agenda is lauded by some as a positive development:

> We would propose a much more rigorous gender analysis, and more expansive gender analysis to say, "Of course we shouldn't just be focusing on women and girls. We want the agenda to be more inclusive." And if you're talking about men and boys, this is an opportunity really to start talking about the relationship between masculinity and militarization. It's also an opportunity to think in other gender issues, like LGBTQI communities and how they're vulnerable in situations of conflict, and so on and so forth. (Interview, 201912)

Others, by contrast, state simply that "there's too much fragmentation of the women, peace and security agenda" (Interview, 201601). These opposing discursive dynamics are predicated on logics of (in)coherence, constructing WPS as a knowable policy agenda to which issues can be added either to the benefit or the detriment of its success. Thus, discourse about the different emphasis on the canonical pillars, or the possible inclusion of "emerging issues," is another area of contestation.

(Dis)connections

Another vector of tension, this more of a series of twists that is challenging to navigate, relates to the spatial (dis)connections that animate and organize the agenda: localization versus national implementation versus transnational advocacy. The spatiality of the WPS agenda is often either obscured completely, through the erasure of space and place in research and policy narratives, or theorized as part of processes of "diffusion" (see, for example, Aharoni 2014; Basini and Ryan 2016; Højlund Madsen 2018; Martín de Almagro 2018b). Discourses of (dis)connection, however, perform a significant political function: locating WPS across all of these spaces, it's everything and everywhere, further reinforcing the logics of (dis)location and (im)possibility that I identify in this narrative. WPS is not only spatially and temporally (dis)located in this narrative but also displaced, anchored within the Security Council but also projected to the "grassroots." Women from civil society organizations, for example, reportedly locate the agenda explicitly at UN HQ: "The resolution is unknown to women at the grassroots level" (S/PV.5294, p. 13); "one said, don't leave your resolutions in the drawer—they're your resolutions, they're not our resolutions" (Interview, 201401).

The discourse of placement and connection at UN HQ, however, is powerful, linking these spaces through determined effort and shared commitment to the vision of the WPS agenda:

> [A]ll of this is brought together by a common focus on translating the Security Council resolutions, there are now seven of them, on women peace and security into realistic options on the ground. So essentially the work is about matching all the talking that's happening in the United Nations, and there is a lot of that, with actual work on the ground. (Interview, 201402)

The trope of "actual work on the ground" plays a strong signifying role in this discourse, aligned with the concept of "grassroots," which has even now emerged into the formal architecture of the agenda, with UNSCR 2467 recognizing "the importance of supporting, and promoting civil society, especially local, grassroots, women-led organizations, and religious and community leaders, girls- and youth-led organizations, for all prevention and response efforts" (S/RES/2467, para. 19). This reinforces the locationary/locutionary impulse of the story of tensions told through space in the Secretary-General's reports, which have consistently reproduced the "grassroots" as the zone of authentic peace work: "All international actors involved in peace processes should be familiar with the extent of women's peace-related activism at grassroots level" (S/2002/1154, para. 32). "Grassroots" is interchangeable in this discourse with "the local" as a spatial signifier; this space is constructed as the space of need, the space of urgent action (Herblinger and Simons 2015; Mac Ginty 2015; Shepherd 2017).

What is at stake here is not so much the existence of these spaces, nor of the myriad relations between them, but the way in which these (dis)connections do political work in the narration of the agenda. First, there is a suggestion that the WPS agenda must be *applied* to this space, rather than growing in and deriving from this space: "[I]n order to make sense of these resolutions in places, in local communities, where they matter, we need to bring on board the local actors" (Interview, 201402). This is resonant of the imperialism of knowledge production discussed briefly in Chapter 1 (see Basu 2016a; Shepherd 2017, 125–128, 140–157). The tension here is articulated in terms of "bridging" the (separate) spaces: "[H]ow [do] you bridge the gap between the Security Council at the political level and really the implementation of that agenda concretely on the ground with concrete results that make a difference in the life of women[?]" (Interview, 201601); "[H]ow do we make the linkages between what is said in the Council and what is action in capital?" (Interview, 201909). Similarly, the 2018 Secretary-General's report comments on the "need for stronger linkages between women-led mediation at the grass-roots and local levels and processes at the national and global levels" (S/2018/900, para. 40). Second, there is a growing sense of disparity between the "grassroots" and the Headquarters: "[T]he policy level and the normative level have gone so far ahead and eclipse what was happening at the country level so much" (Interview, 201602). The disparity in knowledge and capacity is implied when the discourse reinforces the difference between these two domains, suggesting, for example, that "[c]ivil society is often in the best position to share local concerns with national leaders, bringing the perspectives of women and girls at the grass-roots level to the national, regional and global levels and to deliver services" (S/2015/716, para. 124). Third, the local-international (dis)connection obscures the mediation of these two domains through the politics of national representation that is inherent within the formation and operation of the UN, which is an intergovernmental organization. WPS actors are finding ways to work with, and around, national governments that are seen as obstructionist, while simultaneously national governments send representatives to New York to propose and draft new resolutions that belong in and to the Security Council. Thus, these discourses reproduce logics of (dis)location and (im)possibility that structure the narration of the WPS agenda.

The power of the Security Council

The slippage between the Security Council and UN member states—between the UN and UN member states—is an interesting way of avoiding accountability and the allocation of responsibility even as discourse about Security Council preeminence is reproduced in the narratives of tension in the agenda. Building on the discourse of (dis)connection, this discourse centers on the UN Security Council as a source of tension as well as site of activity; these discourses articulate Council conservativism and dominance/control. One obvious vector of this dominance is structural; the WPS agenda is formalized in the resolutions that are adopted by the Council. The Council remains "actively seized of the matter" of WPS; this is the language used in the concluding paragraph of every WPS resolution. The "seizing" of the Council in relation to matters WPS is reinforced through the Secretary-General's reports, where, for example, the scope of the report is determined to include

> information on the impact of armed conflict on women and girls in situations of which the Security Council is seized; on the obstacles and challenges to strengthening women's participation in conflict prevention, conflict resolution and peacebuilding, and recommendations to address those issues. (S/2009/465, para. 1)

The framing of this report derives from the Presidential Statement of 29 October 2008, at which time China held the presidency (S/PRST/2008/39). The specificity of the request limited the information required to advice on "the impact of armed conflict on women and girls in situations of which the Security Council is seized." Any other impact—deemed *not* to be directly related to armed conflict—on any other persons—deemed not to be women and girls—in situations of which the Security Council is *not* seized is automatically out of scope.[4] This relates, but is not reducible, to the question of the issues that should and should not be included in the agenda. What is at stake here is the power of the Council to determine not only the issues at stake but also how and under what circumstances those issues should be monitored.

Unsurprisingly, this discourse was prominent among those to whom I spoke in the course of this research.[5] The Council—almost always just referenced as "the Council"—is represented in this discourse as a monolith of power and authority:

> "[V]ery much in the Security Council, convincing members that security of women actually had an influence on international peace and security was a massive coup, and that took a huge amount of time, and effort, and advocacy to get to that point where they recognized that" (Interview, 201905).

> "I was told very clearly by many, many people, you cannot push the Council to do anything further on Women, Peace and Security. Don't try new resolutions. They won't work. The Council is not interested, it can't happen" (Interview, 201906).

> "I also see a lot of academics writing about WPS critically that when I read their work, I feel like their problem is not with WPS, it's with the Security

Council, is almost a fundamental disagreement with a mechanism that is inherently unequal, and has the Permanent Five. It doesn't have that much relationship to how WPS is narrowed down by the Security Council structures" (Interview, 201908).

"The Council" is also represented as comprised of self-interested states, largely uninvested in the agenda unless there is a direct and compelling motivation to invest, driven by "national interest, political interest, economic interest" (Interview, 201912). "The Council has heard the desperate cries of women many times, without really hearing them" (S/PV.7533 2015, p. 7).

Within the Council, of course, there are bad actors, "conservative and hostile states" (Interview, 201912), opposing, resisting, or undermining the agenda. For advocates, this means learning "where you could push and where you couldn't and how. And, of course, it depends on who's on the Council in any particular year because the E10 [the ten elected members] are very important" (Interview, 201906). "There's a strong pushback from countries who think everything should be state-run. . . . Russia and China. When we negotiated our last . . . or when member states negotiated the last resolution on mediation in the General Assembly, they were opposed [to] pretty much anything that [has] to do with women" (Interview, 201904). The institutional structures that support and hold up the WPS agenda are, of course, deeply implicated in how the agenda unfolds, but of critical significance here is the centrality afforded to the Council, and member state complicity, in the narration of the agenda, in the stories that are told. The Council is simultaneously an enabling and disabling space of WPS activity; it is the author of the resolutions and also "one of the most top-down and incrementalist bodies we have" (Interview, 201912), within which masculine realpolitik dominates, which believes " 'boys will be boys', which I've heard Security Council members say in 2007" (Interview, 201906), and women should be protected by national governments. Even the Secretary-General's reports occasionally refer explicitly to the Council's conservativism and the need for member states to "take ownership" of the agenda: "Various factors constrain the ability of the Security Council to take action on information pertinent to resolution 1325 (2000), including the fact that securing lasting peace and security requires commitment and ownership of decisions by Member States as well as all parties to armed conflict" (S/2010/498, para. 81); "data show that the information flow to the Security Council and the Council's response to women and peace and security concerns continue to be uneven" (S/2012/732, para. 11).

One way in which this discourse produces tension is through the question of accountability. The Council is charged with authority over the agenda and also with monitoring its implementation. "The support of Council members is needed to ensure the strong, high-level leadership, the coherent and systematic approach towards implementation, and the concrete monitoring mechanism to address the gaps in the system that those [WPS] resolutions necessitate" (S/PV.6196 2009, p. 7). Efforts to direct the Council and force accountability feature prominently in this discourse, shot through with differential power dynamics; some WPS actors spoke of "trying to drag the Security Council and its work into this sort of feminist progressive responses, . . . we feel strongly that it . . . should be responsive to" (Interview, 201302), while others stated bluntly that "the Council itself needed to hold itself to task" (Interview, 201403). This discourse also diminishes the authority afforded to the Secretary-General, as his reports—read as efforts to hold the Council to account—are "pursuant to" the pronouncements of the Council in some way. The Secretary-General is a powerful entity, but the Office cannot overcome the structural constraints of the organization, in this tale of tension.

"All these resolutions and the bodies keep piling up . . . ": Resolution fatigue

As mentioned previously, one of the prominent sets of logics in the story of tensions and pressures in the WPS agenda is identified as logics of (in)coherence, which describes the agenda as (un)settled, captured in the resolutions (and obviously dependent on a static and singular reading of the meaning of the resolutions), but simultaneously open to expansion. The defining feature of this element of the story is its constitution through a discourse of "resolution fatigue" (Interview, 201403). "I think there is resolution fatigue. . . . I don't think we need another big report . . . to tell us that you know, when you have women included it's better for everyone because I think it's been pretty well demonstrated. The problem is . . . how we make it happen" (Interview, 201907). This discourse is organized according to logics of (in)coherence and also an ambivalent logic of practice. The idea of "resolution fatigue" is premised on the agenda's existence as a complete and settled policy architecture, always already coherent, which constitutes "the problem," per the comments of the research participant quoted here, as an inability to implement the agenda *in practice*.[6]

The ambivalent logic of practice is powerfully present in the discourse of resolution fatigue, deployed in particular by civil society representatives at the Open Debates. In 2008, for example, Sarah Taylor, coordinator of the NGO Working Group on Women, Peace and Security, noted, "Eight years since the adoption of resolution 1325 (2000), there has been a great deal more talk about the protection and promotion of women's human rights in conflict-affected situations. . . . It is now necessary to move from words to action" (S/PV.6005 2008, p. 8). In 2010, Thelma Awori of the Civil Society Advisory Group to the United Nations on Women, Peace and Security used remarkably similar language in her statement to the Council: "It is time for action, not words" (S/PV.6411 2010, p. 11). "Action" is afforded value in this construction, according to a logic of practice that elevates doing over thinking/writing. The significance of the resolutions—manifestations of thinking/writing rather than doing—is diminished through this discourse. Such comments were reinforced by many of the people I spoke to during the interviews I conducted. The distinction between the agenda "on paper" and "in practice" resurfaces in this discourse of resolution fatigue, with participants noting, for example, "I think we have everything we need on paper at the policy level" (Interview, 201601), and arguing strongly: "We don't need another resolution. We got the eight resolutions on this agenda that we need. And actually what we need is implementation" (Interview, 201909). Many expressed concern that the anniversary effect is going to create the conditions for another resolution and, following on from the negotiations and adoption of resolution 2467, WPS advocates are—understandably—concerned about the potential disbenefits of working toward another resolution in the current political climate: "[T]his resolution process should show you that this is a very dangerous environment in which to be negotiating. So think very hard before you decide you want another legacy resolution in 2020, because you know this conversation's going to come up again" (Interview, 201912).

The concern about the rolling back of the agenda, however, is a recent twist in the ongoing tale of tension, which has been consistently told through the discourse of resolution fatigue almost since the inception of the agenda. Part of the narrative of the WPS agenda is a constitutive tension over whether even resolution 1820 was necessary in order to achieve the aims and objectives of the agenda, as outlined in the origin stories. Relatedly, Sam Cook reports that critics argued that Resolution 1325 provided a broad and fairly comprehensive framework for a range of issues and singling out one issue was both arbitrary and perhaps even dangerous. Some believed that this focus would take away from the powerful breadth and depth of Resolution 1325. They argued that it would diminish the importance of Resolution 1325 by reducing the women, peace, and security agenda to issues of sexual violence and victimhood again. (Cook 2009, 127)[7]

Anne Marie Goetz, then chief adviser for the Governance, Peace and Security program at the United Nations Development Fund for Women (UNIFEM), alludes implicitly to such tension in her account of the adoption of UNSCR 1820: "1820 is addressing a very specific piece of 1325, which is the issue of sexual violence and the need to prevent it. 1325 does not fully address the gendered nature of the conduct of belligerent actions, and that's what 1820 does. . . . 1820 takes a piece of 1325 and elaborates on it. It also goes beyond 1325" (in interview with Ali Atef; Atef 2008, 74). Goetz and Cook, both of whom were working in the WPS world in New York at the time of the adoption of UNSCR 1820, acknowledge in these writings the tension that is part of the agenda in their discussion of its expansion through additional resolutions, and this tension has absolutely not resolved over time. Moreover, the tension is constructed through the logic of practice manifest in discourse about resolution fatigue, as affirmed by people I spoke to in the course of this research: "It isn't necessarily meaningful to just have another resolution" (Interview, 201401); "you can have everything on paper, and it's not going to make any difference" (Interview, 201605).

There is no consensus about what the resolutions are or what they do. One research participant, in a counter-discourse to the prominent formation of resolution fatigue, commented:

I would like to see a resolution promoting, strengthening, the recognition of the role of women human rights defenders for instance. There are areas where I think the agenda could move forward progressively and could then also really help the local efforts of women peacebuilders. Because we know that 1325 and 2242 are used in-country by local activists. We know it. And we always used to ask our colleagues who would come from conflict and crisis-affected countries, "How do you use 1325?" And it's a crucial tool for them, which is why it's important that the resolutions do go in the right direction. (Interview, 201910)

This articulation presupposes that there is a "right direction" in which the resolutions can move, which reproduces a logic of coherence. This construction also reinforces the subject-positions of authoritative (either conservative or expansionist) state/UN actors in opposition to civil society actors, whose "in-country," "local" (read: authentic) experience may not translate to visible/recognizable expertise or authority. "I think there's well-meaning like-minded amongst the member states, who think that a resolution is the right thing to do. And not necessarily always listening to the constituency who has been walking this agenda for twenty years" (Interview, 201909). This of course is imbricated with the logic of (dis)location, which in turn informs the discourses of (dis)connection and resolution fatigue that form part of how the story of tension within the agenda is told. These constructions reproduce and reinforce the spatial, and hierarchical, distinctions between resolutions and actions, paper and practice, policy and implementation, formal and informal spheres of political activity. All these binaries inform the discourse on resolution fatigue and other discourses discussed here, and all of these binaries are gendered in ways that inform and influence the narration of the agenda as caught in tension. The story of the agenda in tension is a story of an (in)definitely (in)complete agenda, the agents of which are (dis) located spatially in ways that render coherence and consistency across the agenda (im)possible.

Concluding thoughts on tensions and pressures

The narrative of tensions and pressures in the WPS agenda in part focuses on the tensions between the different "pillars" of the agenda and further highlights tensions between status quo and expansionist discursive moves in relation to the proper remit of the agenda, according to logics of (in)coherence and (im)possibility. This story is constituted in discourses of the agenda's priorities, (dis)connections, Security Council conservatism and state resistance, and resolution fatigue. As shown, the plural logics that underpin the discourses, and thus narratives, of the WPS agenda refuse reconciliation or resolution to singular clarity. Narrating the pressures and tensions of the WPS agenda through the construction of "balance" across the predetermined "pillars" assumes that these pillars derive from the resolutions themselves, though they are as much a political construct as any other way of conceiving the agenda's provisions and principles. This story, however, appeals to a sense of orderliness and structure: an agenda in balance should not be unbalanced or upset. This in turn leads to, and is informed by, contestation over whether the agenda should be maintained "as is," limited to and by the issues detailed in the formal policy architecture (which itself presupposes that there might be agreement on what those issues are and how they can be adequately addressed), or whether the agenda should be expanded, potentially though not necessarily through new resolutions. These configurations are held by logics of (in)coherence.

A logic of coherence constructs an agenda that is knowable and manageable, through the presupposition that effective implementation relies on a settled and agreed upon set of policy principles to implement. Surfaced in the discourses, however, are significant logics of incoherence and impulses of decoherence. Further, the tensions and pressure points are narrated such that they constitute an alibi for resistance and backlash by certain actors, in particular the Security Council and some among the five permanent members: "[T]he Council [is] always trying to limit its agenda because it's damn busy, and all this is very expensive" (Interview, 201906); "[t]here's a strong pushback from countries who think everything should be state-run. . . . Russia and China. . . . [W]hen member states negotiated the last resolution on mediation in the General Assembly, they were opposed pretty much" (Interview, 201904). Logics of (dis)location structure this discourse: the agenda is both situated within the Council and at the "grassroots." Similarly, an ambivalent logic of practice attaches value to the agenda-in-practice (positioned as superior to the agenda-on-paper) while simultaneously positioning the Council (location of the agenda-on-paper) as the preeminent authoritative WPS actor. As in the discourse of the anniversary effect, discussed in Chapter 4, the discourse of Security Council preeminence, which is part of the story of tension, recognizes disparities between member states, which in turn undermines the illusion of consensus around the agenda and thus its coherence.

7

Silences, Secrets, and Sensibilities

This chapter explores representations of silence, and perceived absences, in the WPS stories I analyze. There are specific silences and absences that have a formative effect on the political affordances generated by the WPS agenda; the "common sense" of WPS is that these dimensions should be left unspoken lest they provide cynics and skeptics with critical ammunition to undermine the agenda. Examining these silences and absences as constitutive of the WPS agenda, and therefore as implicated in both its failures and its successes, reinforces the plurality and polyvalences of WPS as it emerges as a knowable policy agenda through its narration. The suppressed frustrations and the barely detectable influences and influencers are as much part of the formation of the WPS agenda as the indicators, audits, and action plans. In this chapter, I surface some of these silences and secrets and describe the sensibilities that emerge through the storytelling.

The first discourse I identify is about "bad data." Although—as shown in Chapter 4—there are frequent representations of data in narratives of the WPS agenda that attach primary value to (quantitative) data, this discourse relates specifically to the quality of data relied upon in accounts of the WPS agenda. Underpinned by logics of (im)possibility and (in)coherence, this discourse of "bad data" both sustains the ideal of a coherent and possible agenda and undermines this ideal. I go on to explore the story of silences in the agenda through the characterization of WPS experts/"knowers" and "doers," a formulation developed by Sam Cook (2019), in a discourse about individual influence. Here, the ambivalent logic of practice strongly informs the discourse, as do logics of (dis)location. The experts/knowers are also doers, but through various discursive practices they are aligned with UN HQ as a site of power, with the authority of the Security Council, and with the thinking/writing of the agenda into being. The experts/knowers are also keepers of the agenda's secrets, holders of the silence around the quality of data that is fetishized as evidence of the agenda's success, and invisible architects of many of the political opportunities that have effected significant change. The palimpsest of the agenda, described or tacitly acknowledged in

Narrating the Women, Peace and Security Agenda. Laura J. Shepherd, Oxford University Press (2021). © Oxford University Press. DOI: 10.1093/oso/9780197557242.003.0007

the data I examine here, reinforces both discourses of silence and (expert) sensibility; the agenda, in all its complexity, is seen by/visible to only a few (experts/knowers, rarely doers).

The narratives of silence, in conjunction with the specific sensibility of WPS, again reinforce logics of (im)possibility in the narration of the WPS agenda. In line with the representation of the agenda as (un)certain and (in) complete, a motif to which I keep returning, the unknown futures of the agenda affect how WPS actors engage with the agenda in the present. There are two strands to this discourse. First, a discourse about intuition reproduces the subjects of experts/knowers and holds the agenda tightly within the UN system (even exclusively within small pockets of the institution). Second, within that same system, a discourse about the ambitions of the agenda and the individuals who sustain it impose constraints on the imaginable futures of the agenda. It cannot take up too much space, be too visible or demanding; this is a particularly feminized sensibility, I think, and one that intersects also with other feelings coded female, such as being grateful for the opportunities thus far afforded, being cautious not to upset the system, and being restrained in advocacy and other forms of engagement.

Identifying the *fabula*

> But we can influence the process sometimes. We all know each other, and we know who to call if we need to get that piece of paper on someone's desk before that meeting. Often, I've just been lucky, I've been in the right room at the right time. But you know, we can't really talk about that.

This is a story of known and unknown dimensions of the agenda, of overt frustrations and barely detectable influences and influencers, of the "true" WPS agenda and the "real" stories of change. This is a story told in ellipses, in pauses in conversation, in references to the things—and the people—that are not referenced: "One thing I wanted to flag is how interesting I find it that some words are very clear red flags in our side of the UN, like patriarchy, feminism. There's a lot of words that we know that our counterparts . . . definitely cannot use" (Interview, 201904). But this story is also told in embodied ways: in sighs and raised eyebrows, in wry smiles and resigned shrugs. These are harder to capture and analyze, but infuse the story of silences as it emerged through the conversations I had and the documents I read in preparation for writing this book. This is a story of the WPS agenda as "unseen": "[W]hen you're enmeshed in the work here and you're doing that work and identifying it, the sort of broader narrative of the work that you're doing gets lost and remains unseen" (Interview, 201903); "a lot of it is very secret, it's very hard to understand. But it's also very high profile and it's associated with the biggest personalities, with the most urgent crises, with the biggest heroism" (Interview, 201906).

It seems counterintuitive to suggest that silence is a key part of the story, but it is a story *about* silences, and about sensibility: how people feel about the work that they do, and the dispositions they develop over time, as they serve the agenda. Sensibility can be defined as a particular sensitivity toward, or emotional response to, an issue or the emotional content of an event or phenomenon. The emotional dimension of WPS storytelling is rarely analyzed (though for notable contributions to the study of the politics of emotion in WPS work, see Gibbings 2011; Cook 2016; Waldron and Baines 2019), even while it runs through the stories that are told about the agenda. Anne Marie Goetz, for example, comments in conversation with Natalie Florea Hudson that effective advocacy has "an emotional element. Policymakers have to *feel* different in order to *act* differently" (Hudson and Goetz 2014, 341–342). The aim is to make policy makers feel different, which means doing "emotion work" (Moisander, Hirsto and Fahy 2016, 963); thus, the advocates must evoke an affective connection, a sympathetic sensibility.

The division of emotional labor presumed within the story of silences in the agenda locates the emotional connection to the agenda and its "lived realities" within civil society and, to a lesser extent, across the UN, only in entities other than the Security Council. By performing emotion in service of advocacy for the agenda in front of the Security Council at the annual Open Debates, "the 'experience' of the figure of the woman-in-conflict becomes determinative of the "needs and interests" of historically situated living women in various places" (Cook 2016, 365). The emotions are carefully curated, however; only "motivational and inspiring" stories are allowed (Gibbings 2011, 526).[1] This *fabula* reinforces the construction of the UN and its constituent representatives—notably but not exclusively the member state delegates at the Open Debates each year—as rational actors, with all of the attendant gendered associations that connect rationality with particular, masculinized, bodies and behaviors.

The characterization within this story of silence divides WPS actors into experts/"knowers" and "doers" (see Cook 2019). The experts *know* the agenda, while the "doers" bring the agenda to life. It was reported to me that "the professionalization of the field has been huge in the last 10 years" (Interview, 201604); I propose that "professionalization" here stands in for institutionalization, the creation of a WPS "enterprise" inside and outside the UN, what I have referred to elsewhere as "a knowledge economy of expertise" that "has flourished in the field of Women, Peace and Security" (Shepherd 2018, 54). "Professionals" are experts/knowers within this telling of the agenda. There is a hierarchy of knowledge here that presents and produces subjects differentially positioned according to their placement/location geographically and their proximity to the UN, which is constructed as both the locus of expertise/knowledge and the locus of inactivity/ineffectual engagement. Knowers and doers of course interact, but in ways that are largely reliant on doers "standing in for," or representing, the field or space of "doing" (see Cook 2016). Knowers interact with each other in ways that are highly personalized: "[C]ommunication ebbs and flows and ebbs and flows depending on what you happen to be working on, at any given time and also your interpersonal relationships" (Interview, 201403). I explore the discourses that make up this story shortly.

The final dimension of the *fabula* that I want to account for here is the temporal ordering, which is complex and wide ranging. The story of WPS silences and sensibilities has multiple temporalities. There is a long historical temporal demarcation, in which history is read as experience and thus features as a marker of expertise to constitute knowers/experts and doers, though the latter are constituted as "experts by experience" in a hierarchical ordering of knowledge subordinate to other forms of expertise.[2] There is a presentism also in this story, in which the "interpersonal relationships" previously mentioned are nurtured in the present: "I think you can't underestimate just how much work it takes to maintain relationships. And a lot of it is relationships" (Interview, 201903). Further, the characters—the experts/knowers and the doers—are situated in the present as the custodians of the agenda, the keepers of its subtle and intricate secrets, who might move on, away from New York, back to "the field" or into the academy and who will pass on their knowledge, if not their relationships, to future custodians. In this way, the future projected in this story is unknown. There is such a lack of certainty around the agenda, such a fear of asking too much and losing precious gains already made, that the future is spoken of in tentative terms only.

"I really don't know where we're going with this WPS," said one participant. "Maybe there is a road map somewhere" (Interview, 201601).

The story of silences, secrets, and sensibility constitutes particular knowing subjects and a knowable object by holding together discourses in formation that reproduce the expert/knowers and doers whose WPS efforts—even as they are "unseen" or hidden—are the engine of progress in the WPS agenda. The narration of this story creates a unified temporality in and of the agenda, linking the histories of WPS activity to an uncertain future by way of a highly individualized and personalized present. In the following section, I explore the discourses that are arranged in this narrative and tease out the associated logics that underpin and reinforce the ways in which this story is told.

Discursive constructions of silences, secrets, and sensibilities

There are four particularly prominent discourses that make up the story of silences, secrets, and sensibility, explored in this section. First, one of the key silences relates to the data marshaled in support of the narrative of success that I excavated in Chapter 3. This is a discourse about how progress is measured and the foundation on which claims to success are built, summarized as a discourse about "bad data." The second discourse is one of individual influence; it (re)produces the experts/knowers and doers as WPS actor-subjects, through various configurations of the relationship between role/position, expertise, and connections. Third, and interrelated with the first two discourses I identity, there is a discourse about intuition that emerges as significant. This discourse reproduces logics of coherence and possibility, constituting both a knowable object and expert/knower subjects; by surfacing the discursive construction of secrecy and sensibility in this context, I show how the agenda is reproduced according to logics of (im)possibility. The fourth and final discourse I examine in this section is about the valence of emotions attached to the WPS agenda. As mentioned previously, doers are constituted as appropriate knowing subjects only if their emotional performance has a positive valence; there can be, as Sheri Lynn Gibbings astutely comments, "no angry women at the United Nations" (Gibbings 2011). Similarly, there are appropriate and inappropriate valences constituted in the discourse of sensibility I explore here. Notably, caution and restraint are positively coded in the emotional landscape of the agenda, which again has implications for how both the subjects and the object of the WPS agenda are constituted in line with logics of (dis)location and an ambivalent logic of practice.

Bad data

There is a strong emphasis on data in the accounts offered of the WPS agenda; as discussed in Chapter 4, those working on and with the WPS agenda are not immune to the seduction of quantification (cf. Merry 2016). Across the whole corpus of WPS documents, including the interview data co-produced for this project, there is a powerful discourse about the utility of data in measuring progress on the agenda. The first WPS resolution articulates this focus on data in the discourses of the agenda in the preamble, "Noting the need to consolidate data on the impact of armed conflict on women and girls" (S/RES/1325, preamble), and three other WPS resolutions articulate a need for more, and better, data in service of the agenda. UNSCR 1889 puts forward the most wide-ranging requirement for more, and better, data, requesting

the Secretary-General to ensure that relevant United Nations bodies, in cooperation with Member States and civil society, collect data on, analyze and systematically assess particular needs of women and girls in post-conflict situations, including, inter alia, information on their needs for physical security and participation in decision-making and post-conflict planning, in order to improve system-wide response to those needs. (S/RES/1889, para. 6)

UNSCR 1960 asks for data on "incidents, trends, and patterns of rape and other forms of sexual violence" (S/RES/1960, para. 8), while UNSCR 2242 requests data on "the drivers of radicalization for women, and the impacts of counter-terrorism strategies on women's human rights and women's organizations" (S/RES/2242, para. 12). Further, three of the Presidential Statements articulate a data deficit, reinforcing the desire for more, and better, data as an issue of critical WPS significance (S/PRST/2007/40, p. 3; S/PRST/2012/3, p. 1; S/PRST/2014/21, p. 3).

With this in mind, demonstrating the clarity of a discourse about data and its centrality in the constitution of the WPS agenda, it may seem paradoxical to suggest there is a silence or aporia in this discourse, but in

relation to the data that currently exist—in particular the statistics that
are frequently cited, repeated, and reported—there is a silence around
the data *quality*. As discussed in previous chapters, the fetishization of
quantitative data is common. It is assumed that what can be counted is
what counts. But there are two vectors of silence that make up this discourse about measuring progress with bad data. First, there is widespread recognition that the statistics that are reported, for example in the
Secretary-General's reports, are likely woefully undercounting incidences
of sexual violence in conflict and conflict-affected settings, in line with
the underreporting of sexual and gender-based violence in other contexts
(Lewis 2009; Manjoo and McRaith 2011; Solangon and Patel 2012). The
reliability of data is addressed occasionally in the Secretary-General's
reports, but these acknowledgments do not break the silence around how
the data that do exist must be heavily weighted with caveats and used with
caution. For example, the 2015 report notes many factors that influence
the collection of reliable data, including

> inadequate coordination between peace and security institutions and na-
> tional statistical systems, lack of political will and understanding of the
> critical role that quality statistics can play in promoting peace through
> targeted interventions, limited statistical capacity in fragile and developing
> settings, safety concerns affecting household survey data collection and ad-
> ministrative record keeping, and confidentiality concerns and statistical
> laws preventing the dissemination of security-related data. (S/2015/716,
> para. 120)

Data-based conclusions about successes of the agenda, however, are
presented *in the same report* as strong evidence of effective implementation
mechanisms: "New evidence, added through research commissioned for the
study, demonstrates clearly that the inclusion of women leads to more sustainable peace and enhanced prevention efforts" (S/2015/716, para. 8). The
discourse about a need for more, and better, data does nothing to undermine the fetishization of quantitative data, the silence about the accuracy of
the numbers that do exist, or the silence about the way in which the numbers are constructed (reliant as they are—as are all quantitative data—on
interpretation).

The second vector of silence relates to this last point. Data are used in
success stories as both baseline and evidence of progress. There is a critical

silence, however, around some of the statistics related to the WPS agenda that have become integral to the story. The fetishization of quantitative data, a dynamic that animates knowledge production at, and far beyond, the UN, influenced and shaped the priorities afforded to specific WPS activities:

> [I]n the run-up to the 10th anniversary, UN Women decided to do a study, and find out how many signatures, how many women negotiators, and so on . . . and no one had documented it, so there was no data available—there was no paper trail—there was no one. There was no way to find out. And what they did was, they actually went in and looked, in many cases, at pictures from signing ceremonies, and tried to document if women had been present. That's by no means an accurate way of doing research, right; that's totally haphazard. There would also be men and women there only for ceremonial purposes, who never was involved in the peace process. So we have stopped relying on this data a long, long time ago, because it's so out-dated, and so inaccurate, (Interview, 201606)

The issue is that the "we" articulated by the research participant quoted here is a small and quite exclusive "we." Those data have taken on a life of their own, far beyond the "we" community invoked here; there is widespread cita-tion of those data, as they have become part of the accepted narrative of the WPS agenda, in line with clear logics of possibility and coherence.

Early on, one research participant recounted, "[I]n order to be able to prove the assertion that the women peace and security agenda was not working the way that we want it to work, we needed some data and some facts" (Interview, 201602). There is thus constructed a silence around the *reliance* on data, the significance afforded to data—the fetishization I have written about repeat-edly throughout this book.

> All of this work on Women, Peace and Security should be done without the data. It doesn't need the data. The one area where data is obvious is roles of women in peace processes and numbers, size of civil society movements. And while it actually, that's not clear, women's engagement in politics of this conflict countries, that's all fairly well known and we should be really just using that. That's the important stuff. And even then, the numbers don't necessarily matter. It's like, what agendas are being promoted? Do we have enough data on what's driving women's participation or not or obstructing them? That we don't have either. (Interview, 201906)

Although the documentary artifacts are literally silent on the normative question of whether the WPS community *should* collect and deploy (more, and better) data in service of the agenda, there were a scant few interviews during which this question arose. Mostly, though, even the interview data presupposed the desirability of (more, and better) data: "I think the normative . . . it's still important and it still stands on its own, but we have really married it with the effectiveness and the operationalizing of the whole terminology" (Interview, 201904). This discursive dynamic speaks to the need to render the WPS agenda manageable and measurable; this discourse is thus organized by a logic of coherence that animates and sustains, through imbrication with other less prominent logics (of scientism, for example), a set of discourses about progress and success—or the lack thereof.

Individual influence

One of the silences that exists around WPS at UN HQ is the fact that the majority of WPS documents—the resolutions; the Presidential Statements, the Secretary-General's reports, and the contributions made by various UN entities to the regular Open Debates—are co-produced. These documents spend months in the drafting and always contain language that is hard fought, with different actors contesting different content at different times. This is most obvious to the broader public audience when there is news and social media coverage of sticking points during the negotiation of a new resolution, as was the case during the negotiation of UNSCR 2467 (for example, see What's in Blue 2019; Ford 2019), but the resolutions are only the most visible form of coauthorship. It is interesting that it is assumed to be widely known that, for example, the Secretary-General's reports are drafted by multiple people and reviewed by many more. What is pertinent here is not so much the multi-author production of the WPS documents, but the way in which the story of the silence around this multi-author production is part of how an in-group (of experts/knowers) is constituted. For example, one research participant commented:

> [I]t's a heady space, right? Like, "the US has a resolution and we were in the room and we can work on it." And it's exciting. And even if you're not doing it for your own enjoyment, there's something in that, in collaborating with

people to make an actual thing, get adopted which is exciting and it sort of keeps the momentum going. (Interview, 201911)

Although these documents—resolutions and other artifacts—are singularly attributed to, for example, the UN Security Council or the Secretary-General, it is important to remember, when considering expertise and the politics of knowledge in relation to the WPS agenda, that they are all the product of many minds, marshaled through attribution to become a single coherent author/authoritative subject.[3]

Within the discourse of expertise that makes up the story of silences, secrets, and sensibility, the UN is constituted as a center of power, through a logic of location; this is reinforced by the idea that "[t]he United Nations must lead by example" (S/2009/362, para. 34). The UN's authority here is reproduced and reinforced through the disaggregation of the UN system into subordinate expert entities engaged in WPS activity. This is particularly evident in the story of the creation of the Office of the Special Representative of the Secretary-General on Sexual Violence in Conflict (SRSG on SViC) and the UN Action network, and the creation of UN Women. At its inception, UN Women is invited by the Security Council "to regularly contribute to its work on women and peace and security," and the Council further "notes the valuable role it will play in supporting women's roles in peacebuilding and the prevention of sexual violence in conflict, including through coordination and coherence in policy and programming for women and girls" (S/PRST/2010/22, p. 1). This is then reported as the recognition of UN Women "as the system lead on women and peace and security by the Security Council" (S/2011/598, para. 60), in a paragraph that also cites UN Women as "a major policy and institutional resource to respond to the Security Council's consistent call for support to Member States on sustained and coordinated efforts to implement its resolutions on women and peace and security" (S/2011/598, para. 60). The expertise of UN Women is reaffirmed in later reports (see, for example, S/2013/525, para. 75c). Similarly, the 2013 Secretary-General's report consolidates expertise on sexual violence in the "United Nations Team of Experts on the Rule of Law and Sexual Violence in Conflict" and "the network of United Nations entities called United Nations Action against Sexual Violence in Conflict" (A/67/792–S/2013/149, para. 1; for reiterations of the expertise of these entities, see S/2014/181; S/2015/203, para. 101; S/2016/361, para. 6; S/2017/249). These articulations construct the UN as a subject with a WPS sensibility, an expert sensibility toward sexual violence in conflict, and in so doing holds expertise within that context and location. Indeed, subtle criticism is leveled at the member states that attempt to perform expertise or knowledge credentials in this particular space. The adoption of the Declaration on Preventing Sexual Violence by the Group of 8 in 2013, for example, and the UK's co-chairing with the SRSG on SViC of a side event on sexual violence in conflict at the 68th session of the UN General Assembly in the same year was somewhat damned with faint praise in the Secretary-General's report of the subsequent year: "These are notable and important advances, but it is crucial that we now focus our collective efforts on converting these political commitments into concrete actions aimed at prevention and the provision of services on the ground" (S/2014/181, para. 10). This appears to reinforce the construction of the UN as expert par excellence.

It is interesting, however, that the reports cited here, in relation to the construction of expert sensibility for the UN on sexual violence, are all sexual violence reports, related to the sexual violence resolutions and mandated in sexual violence resolutions and statements. These reports are usually presented to the Council in the first half of the year, typically in March or April, following on from the first Report of the Secretary-General on Sexual Violence in Conflict, which was presented on 12 January 2012 (A/66/657*–S/2012/33*). The reports presented in the second half of the year, at or around the Open Debate on the theme of WPS, frequently open up the tightly held parameters of expertise a little. The 2015 report, for example, cites "expertise offered by civil society" (S/2015/716, para. 123) and, flowing from the provisions of UNSCR 2242, the (implied) contribution to the agenda made by an "informal expert group on women and peace and security" (S/2017/861, para. 88). UN member states are also rendered more visible as experts/knowers in these reports, with Spain in particular receiving recognition for coordinating the WPS National Focal Points Network, which was launched in 2017: "The Women, Peace and Security National Focal Points Network, launched by 63 Member States last year in an initiative of Spain, had its inaugural meeting in April 2017 in Alicante, Spain (see S/2017/485). The meeting included more than 100 national focal points, government actors and civil society representatives from 61 countries discussing innovative uses of national action plans" (S/2017/861, para. 70). These constructions of expert sensibility further entrench a separation in the agenda between sexual violence and everything else, according to a competing logic of location. The narrow, knowable realm of sexual violence is a tightly held domain of UN expertise, while the broader agenda can permit multiple experts/knowers.

It is generally within this latter space that the individual is constituted as an expert/knower. Invisible in the multi-authored, documented life of the agenda, this individual expert sensibility is constructed through the iterated articulation of "I-selves" and achievements/opportunities taken. Many of the people I spoke to for, and about, this project—some of whom declined to be formally interviewed for fear of inadvertently reproducing this very dynamic—were reflective about this enforced, and reinforced, *dispositif*:

> [W]e make heroes of people, individual heroes of people. Sometimes it's because governments invite the same NGO people again and again, and sometimes it's because we only have a staff of the same people. . . . I think that that is dangerous because it really forgets that all of us who get cited and all of us who get invited are not the actual face of the work that gets done. (Interview, 201911)

Even as a tiny and irrelevant entity in the orbit of the constellation of WPS activity, I personally feel the pull of the seductive idea that I too might possess this sensibility, this expertise that would position me as "one of the main people who gets tapped on the shoulder" (Interview, 201301). The individualization of the agenda introduces a degree of precarity to its unfolding, with this discourse organized again according to logics of (in)coherence. When the agenda rests on the expertise of individuals, the interpersonal connections that they forge and sustain and the specific occupation of key roles by key people become instrumental in the way that the agenda is apprehended and reproduced: "[A]s always with institutions, you have the institutional mandate in positioning and then you have the people who occupy the position within the organizations" (Interview, 201603); "the wrong person in that role in can do more harm than good, and we have seen the wrong person in that role" (Interview, 201302). "On women, peace and security, it comes down to the people and the individuals who would support the mandate" (Interview, 201601). "Sometimes in the UN system very much also depends on personalities involved. You know, who's working on the file? Do you know them well? That makes a lot of difference" (Interview, 201605).

The expert sensibility is thus attached not only to the UN as a collective subject but also to individuals within the UN system—but always, per the logic of location, *within the UN system*. Even where member states are acknowledged as experts/knowers, their contributions are mediated through their articulation with UN activities and knowledge architectures. Almost completely absent from this discourse is the expertise of civil society actors that are afforded such prominence in the origin stories outlined in Chapter 3, which makes visible a plural logic of (dis)location and an ambivalent logic of practice. Constructed as the "doers" of the agenda, this subject-position includes not only the civil society actors located in New York but also the representatives of civil society organizations that brief the Council in the regular Open Debates and—more recently—"in country-specific considerations and relevant thematic areas" (S/RES/2242, para. 5c), supported by UN Women. These subjects are silenced in this particular discourse, leading to this narration of the agenda forming a peculiar vacuum around the location of the agenda beyond New York: "[T]hat's a critical missing piece. . . . [W] e're still talking far too much to ourselves, and not enough to those who are actually implementing the broader peace and security agenda" (Interview, 201909). The implementing/doing subjects are thus located differently than the experts/knowers, in accordance with an ambivalent logic of practice that affords value to implementation/doing while simultaneously ascribing status and expert sensibility to the knowers of the agenda.

Intuition

This discourse in a way brings together the two discourses already mapped out, as it structures the silences of the agenda. It constitutes the parts of the agenda that "we" don't talk about—including but not limited to the quality of the data we have on successes and shortcomings of the agenda, as explained previously—and explicitly acknowledges the silences and secrets that are woven into the fabric of WPS stories. The idea that there is something unsaid, something obscured, is prominent in the narration of the agenda, alluded to by several of the people I spoke to in the course of this research but elusive in form. "Sometimes it's easier to see things if you know that there is something hidden" (Interview, 201606), said one research participant, while another commented on the invisible labor that goes into maintaining the agenda at UN HQ: "[T]hey're working their heads off and it's like, this is not sustainable. So there's also the wellness, and people get burned out and people get sick, and it affects their families, and all these things" (Interview, 201905). Hidden also is the lack of clarity about what the WPS agenda *is*: "I feel really weird calling it an agenda. It's never been. But everybody says that, but what is the agenda?" (Interview, 201906). Further, the effects of the individualization of expertise are perceptible here, in the discourse of what is not often spoken: "this competition, the ego, the backstabbing, the 'information is power so I'm not sharing with you'" (Interview, 201601). The personal gain and the reflection of positive personal qualities in undertaking WPS work are not frequently discussed. By definition, this discourse is not featured or captured in any of the formal artifacts of the agenda, but its emergence through these small openings, these moments of candor in conversation with the people working in this space, show how the secret agenda is the unacknowledged underside of the agenda.

Manifest as a palimpsest in/of the discourse of individual influence, in this discourse of intuition there is also a sense of urgency, of compulsion, that is not often acknowledged as part of the story of WPS. Of course, this language is in the resolutions and reports. All eight of the resolutions contain some version of the verb "to urge," while statements to the Open Debates, from UN entities and civil society representatives alike, frequently comment, for example, on "the urgency of the need to accelerate the implementation of resolution 1325 (2000)" (S/PV.5294 2005, p. 8) or the "urgent need" for "urgent action" (S/PV.6411 2010, p. 7). In 2016, the Secretary-General briefed the Council as follows:

> I urge the Security Council to do everything possible to create the conditions for peace in our world. I will never stop, and we must never stop, in the urgent drive to bring women into their rightful place at the heart of building peace and security. (S/PV.7793 2016, p. 3)

The urgent motivation attached to the agenda also emerges as a form of compulsion in this discourse: "Anyone who gets involved in is often seduced by the compulsive nature of work in this area" (Interview, 201906). The same research participant described the agenda as "prestigious" (Interview, 201906) and commented, "There is a certain heroism in defending this agenda. I have huge admiration for the people who don't have to, and do it" (Interview, 201906). Similarly, they noted that "there's a very well-oiled machinery at the UN which it sucks you in, it's almost irresistible in the sense that all the action is there" (Interview, 201906).

Thus, this discourse intersects with discourse about expertise and connections, reinforcing the logic of location that positions the UN as the locus of WPS activity and authority and simultaneously reproducing WPS experts/knowers through the idea of an intuitive and "prestigious" agenda

seen by/visible to only the chosen few. The final strand of this discursive formation is manifest in the idea that the detail of WPS work is often deliberately obscured, with WPS actors resistant to using—or at least hesitant to
use—certain forms of language in their WPS work. Some of this resistance
is somewhat predictable; one research participant commented that "when
you use terms like 'patriarchy' and 'masculinity' and stuff, first of all, it's very
academic. It's very research-oriented" (Interview, 201904), the implication
being that such language would alienate and exclude the non-academic, non-
research-oriented, expert/knowers of the agenda. Discourse itself is implicated here in the construction of expert/knower subjectivity by the experts/
knowers; the way that some WPS actors use some concepts or arrangements
of language, and even their presentations of self, are seen to affect their
credibility in the WPS space: "My feeling is some radical feminist with like
purple hair, would not fit in the culture of [redacted]. Somebody who's actually going to work with them every day and push gender has to also fit in
to their culture and it's not going to be some anti-nuclear activist person"
(Interview, 201602). Because of this, some research participants admitted—
and it was always somewhat confessional when these silences were narrated
to me—that they don't use the language of WPS in their work: "I think we're
always very keen to never talk about WPS. We always talk about gender. Even
our training, we call it Gender, not WPS training because it's not just about
women's rights" (Interview, 201904). This discourse is organized around
logics of (im)possibility, as well as the ambivalent logic of practice previously
mentioned, for how can WPS be known if it cannot be spoken? Logics of
(dis)location are interwoven with other logics in this discourse, at once positioning the WPS agenda as belonging in and to the Council (and, by association, state and UN actors) and simultaneously situating the agenda in and
with the doers, a constellation of civil society actors denied access to the sites
of power yet themselves the originators of the "real and true," authentic WPS
agenda.

Ambition

This discourse, an integral part of the story of how particular sensibilities
emerge in the WPS agenda, is foundational to the constitution of WPS
subjects as experts/knowers and doers. Experts/knowers are wary of "asking
too much," while doers are "asking a lot." Thus, this discourse constitutes a

sensibility defined by caution, or lack thereof, and tentative engagement at moments of political opportunity (or, in the constitution of the doing subject, forceful invocation of rights and the responsibilities of the UN Security Council to create different opportunities, different realities). Interestingly, a few of the Secretary-General's reports subtly reinforce the idea that the agenda's advocates are asking a lot. For example, in 2009 the report comments that some challenges in implementation

> emanate from the very nature of armed conflict which creates social, economic and political instability and disrupts existing social networks, infrastructure and economic and social activities. *Others relate to the breadth of resolution 1325 (2000), which requires novelty and creativity to address these challenges.* Yet others arise from a weak implementation framework and the absence of clear targets and reliable data. (S/2009/465, para. 60; emphasis added)

Here, the breadth of the agenda itself is identified as the primary obstacle to its successful implementation. Thus, the agenda's advocates are "asking a lot" when they seek full and effective implementation.

The emotionality of the doing subject, embodied in—but not limited to—the women who speak to the Council during the WPS Open Debates, is central to this discourse. Though disciplined, as mentioned above, through the expectation that their testimonials will be "motivational and inspirational" and above all, as mentioned, not angry (Gibbings 2011, 526 passim), these doing subjects are essential to the narration of sensibility within the agenda. Looking back at the recent statements to the Council from representatives of civil society organizations, brought to the Open Debate to speak on behalf of their organizations and also on behalf of the NGO Working Group on Women, Peace and Security, there are patterns evident in the "asking":

> "Across all conflicts and crisis situations, the Security Council *must* also prioritize women and girls' protection. . . . South Sudan is increasingly becoming a living hell for a lot of women and, in my opinion, *this should not be happening on the Council's watch*. If the Government and opposition leaders of South Sudan do not meet the requirements set out in the latest Security Council resolution, then the Security Council *must* impose more targeted sanctions on individuals and a total arms embargo. . . . The Security Council, the Member States, and the United Nations *must* significantly

improve their engagement with women civil society during times of crisis at Headquarters in New York and in missions, including those undertaken by Security Council members." (S/PV.7793 2016, pp. 6–7; emphasis added)

"The Security Council and the international community *must* support the Colombian Government in the process of designing and implementing gender-responsive, community-based security and self-protection systems, in consultation with Afro-descendant and indigenous communities. . . . *It is the responsibility of all actors, including the Security Council, the United Nations system, regional and subregional organizations and, importantly, Member States, to fulfil their obligations."* (S/PV.8079 2017, pp. 8–9)

"If the Council cannot prevent sexual violence in war, then it *must* at least punish it. . . . [I]nstead of abandoning international justice we *must* stand up for it, because justice is not inevitable—it does not just happen and *it does not stand a chance if people in power, including those at this table, do not make it a priority. . . .* This is the Council's Nuremberg moment, *its chance to stand on the right side of history.* The Council *owes* it to Nadia and to the thousands of women and girls who must watch ISIL members shave off their beards and go back to their normal lives, while they, the victims, never can. . . . *It is time for the Council to make justice its priority* so that history can record what happened, so that we can stop it happening again and to truly honour those who, like Nadia, have already suffered too much." (S/PV.8514 2019, pp. 10–11)

Made by different women at different times, these statements were all part of lengthier statements to the Open Debates in 2016, 2017, and 2019 that I have isolated here for the purposes of analysis.

There are similarities in the "asks" that are made of the Council, forms of discursive continuity across different speeches uttered by different WPS actors that nonetheless form a coherent discourse of demands. First and most obviously is the repeated use of the verb "must." "Must" belongs to the class of verb known as "modal auxiliary verbs"; these verbs attach a specific property of obligation to the verb that follows (for example, in the phrase "the Security Council must also prioritize" it is the verb "prioritize" that is modified by the modal auxiliary verb "must") and can be read as commands. While normally within a discursive formation the subject giving commands would be the dominant subject, the repeated and iterative nature of the communication of obligation undermines and lessens the impact of the use of the verb "must." Second, the "asks" reaffirm the Council's preeminence—unsurprising, given that the speakers have been permitted, by invitation only, to address the Council in its own chambers, but nonetheless discursively significant in terms of how the doing subjects are thus positioned. Here, the statement that "this should not be happening on the Council's watch" also employs a modal auxiliary verb ("should") to communicate specific properties: the phrase *should not be happening* implies expectation; were the Council fulfilling expectations, the violence making life "a living hell for a lot of women" could be lessened or cease entirely. This construction puts power in the hands of the Council, while at the same time holding it to account for the peacelessness and violence "happening on the Council's watch." The third and final continuity of interest relates to the construction of accountability that happens through the ascription of power and authority to the Council. The articulation of responsibility offers a clear construction of accountability, as do comments about fulfilling obligations and standing "on the right side of history." The Nuremberg trials held accountable many military, social, and political leaders for crimes committed during the Holocaust and are widely recognized as a turning point in the development of international law because they attributed responsibility to the individuals who had ordered, condoned, or perpetrated such war crimes. The invocation of the Nuremberg trials here functions not only to position the Council as a body of similar significance in the development of international law, but also to ascribe to the Council the same authority to hold war criminals accountable for their actions. The discourse identified here, of "asking a lot," thus reaffirms and reinforces the power and authority of the UN Security Council, through the constitution of the doing subject.

The expert/knowing subject is wary of "asking too much." This motif came through prominently in the interviews I conducted for this research. There is a significant field of feminist research that interrogates and explores the way that women are conditioned to use space—intellectual, physical, corporeal space—in particular ways.[4] The tentative and conditional ways in which the people I spoke to discussed how they interacted with other WPS actors and the agenda more broadly suggests a similar, and similarly gendered, dynamic at play here, such that the agenda—and the actors themselves—cannot be seen as asking for "too much" or occupying "too much" space: "[I]t's a little bit of a catch-22 when you know that there's something that is not good enough, you want to criticise it. But at the same time you don't want to be seen as criticising too much" (Interview, 201601). An associated silence in the agenda is the volume of work (overwork) that falls to the few experts/knowers working on and around WPS at UN HQ. This is similarly gendered, echoing feminist political economists' analysis of the double and triple burden of labor that is widely associated with feminized subjectivity:

> I feel like this thing about women's work being so undervalued and overtaxed applies across the whole Women, Peace, and Security agenda, in all these areas. In the fact that we're covering 50 more files than our counterparts and the fact that we have to, therefore, do things a lot more superficially which then also means that we're less effective, and we're not able to go in and hit the nail on the head the way we would be if we could actually have proper time to think about something or read something before we go into a meeting. (Interview, 201905)

The pressures on "feminist bureaucrats" were also articulated by one research participant, who said: "I don't know how much you have spoken with or looked into how hard it is to be a feminist bureaucrat. I think that that's rough because you get it from all sides" (Interview, 201903). These constructions, of workload, effort, and the need to tone down criticism, to articulate challenges and suggestions for improvement in a neutral, acceptable, palatable way fuse at the nexus of the discourse of "asking too much," specifically *avoiding* asking too much: "I think we've been too complacent and we feel so guilty as feminists sometimes to challenge the system so we are seen as too radical, too critical, too ungrateful" (Interview, 201601). To manage one's emotions, to invest superhuman effort, to *be grateful* is part of how the expert/knower is constituted.

The difference between the expert/knowing subject and the doing subject sketched out here is captured in a fragment of a conversation I had in New York: "If I'd come in as an advocate from the NGO, or UN Women, people would have said, 'You don't understand—we're up against the constraints and challenges'" (Interview, 201606). "Understanding" here, and knowing not to ask too much, is a powerful organizing feature of this discourse. Here I identify again the ambivalent logic of practice, and logics of (dis)location. Practice (in terms of lived experience) is afforded significance and value through the discourse of "asking a lot," but it is not attached to, or constituting positional authority in the construction of, the doing subject. Similarly, logics of (dis)location reinforce the construction of the UN as the space of expert/knowers, where knowledge is produced and feminist bureaucrats are conditioned and disciplined. As one research participant recounted wistfully, when they began their WPS work, there was a place they frequented in their leisure time with other WPS workers: "[I]t was a sort of cheerful, happy place. And there was a juke box and whatever. And then when I went [back], everybody was at this stuffy seriously overpriced place called, The Library or something like that, with the governments and we never went out with. . . . We didn't socialize with government people except for those events. And now it's like the people who are doing Women, Peace and Security are considered as professional and they go out and do those kinds of things" (Interview, 201911).

There is a racialized politics to these discursive mechanisms that must be acknowledged. Restraint is a palimpsest across all of these discourses. The "unrestrained" (though carefully managed and modulated) emotion of the representatives of civil society organizations that brief the Council during Open Debates contrasts with the careful, cautious, measured disposition associated with the expert/knowers. Overwhelmingly, the women brought from conflict-affected settings to brief the Council are women of color; it is particularly pernicious that the positioning of these subjects associates experience (of surviving conflict and violation) and emotion with the bodies of women of color, reinforcing as it does the thread of coloniality that runs through the fabric of the WPS agenda (see Pratt 2013; Shepherd 2016; Martin de Almagro 2018a; Parashar 2019). Elsewhere, I have indicted the WPS agenda for complicity in the "perpetuation of a Eurocentric and hierarchical model of global political affairs, which locates agency, power and authority in the minority world that is always already peaceful (read: civilised, superior) and 'expert' in matters of security and governance" (Shepherd 2016, 4). These discourses, of intuition and ambition, do nothing to undermine this racialized hierarchy.

Concluding thoughts on silences, secrets, and sensibilities

Although it might seem counterintuitive to discuss discourses of silence and secrecy, I have shown here how the oblique (and sometimes explicit) acknowledgment of such tacit—or even hidden—aspects of the agenda are an integral part of how the agenda is known at the UN, and therefore encountered and acted upon. I have opened up the silences around the data and evidence base that underpins many of the prominent knowledge claims that are part of how successes (and shortcomings) of the WPS agenda are narrated. Here, I have shown how there is a contrapuntal discourse at work that actively seeks to silence aspects of measurement in relation to the agenda; this discourse posits that deficiencies should be left unspoken lest they provide cynics and skeptics with critical ammunition to undermine the agenda.

I have shown also how particular sensibilities, or dispositions, are constructed through these same discourses, in such a way as to construct dual subject-positions within WPS discourse: the doing subject and the expert/knowing subject. The latter's positional authority is reinforced through their familiarity with the politics of the institution: their ability to navigate the UN system, to "walk the halls of power" (per Halley 2006, 21), and to contain both their expectations and their emotions functions to reinforce their status as expert/knowers, and this is a dimension of the "professional-ization" of the agenda that is not often discussed. Within these discourses, there is a sense in which doing WPS work—at the UN or elsewhere—is always-already being a problem, demanding a lot (too much), and agitating for systemic change. Logics of (dis)location and the ambivalent logic of practice structures these discourses to support a story of WPS that admits to the influence of the intangible at UN HQ: the interpersonal relationships, the unwritten codes that govern conduct, the whispered or even unspoken knowledge that is held by the expert/knowers in New York. Meanwhile, the juxtaposition of these "feminist bureaucrats" with the doers, the "subjects of practice" (Cook 2016), reinforces, through this dichotomy, the hierarchy of expertise that subordinates lived experience to the power and authority of the UN Security Council.

8

Resisting Narrative Closure

Part of how the WPS agenda is known is through its narration, including within—though not limited to—the stories that I have elaborated and analyzed here. As I have argued throughout this book, WPS emerges as a knowable policy agenda through the stories that are told about it, through the narrative practices that constitute and (re)produce the agenda across disparate sites of practice. I have focused only on the narration of the agenda at the UN HQ in New York and have limited the scope of the study further to narratives captured in formal documentation of the agenda and unstructured interviews conducted between 2013 and 2016 with individuals and teams working on WPS at and around the UN. Having laid out the story of the WPS agenda, examined in five interrelated but distinct sections (each of which is captured in one of the previous five chapters), I have shown what telling stories about the WPS agenda has to tell us, as scholars of world politics.

In this chapter, I offer a brief conclusion to the arguments developed throughout this book. I revisit the questions driving the investigation presented here, recapping the logics I identify and reflecting on the implications of these logics for the imaginable future(s) of the WPS agenda. I also revisit the contribution that the book hopes to make, both to research on global governance and to research on the WPS agenda. I situate the WPS agenda as a form of international policymaking and international policy practice constituted in and through the stories that are told about it and argue that in order to apprehend WPS as a knowable policy agenda, due analytical attention should be paid to the ways in which it is narrated. Through analysis of narrative and discourse, it is possible to identify the logics that organize and (re)produce meaning in particular configurations and that therefore structure the horizons of possibility around WPS as a policy agenda. The plural logics I identify resist efforts to close down or narrow the meaning of WPS as a policy agenda in global politics, and so effective political engagement—the realization of the agenda—depends on sitting with, and finding productive potential in, multiplicity, polysemy, and ambivalence.

Narrating the Women, Peace and Security Agenda. Laura J. Shepherd, Oxford University Press (2021). © Oxford University Press. DOI: 10.1093/oso/9780197557242.003.0008

Narrative, discourse, logics revisited

The questions motivating this research are quite straightforward. At the outset, I asked: What are the narratives of the WPS agenda that are told at and around the UN HQ in New York, site of the UN Security Council and thus architectural "home" of the formal elaboration of the WPS agenda? How do these narratives shape and inform the ways that the agenda is encountered, acted upon, and imagined into the future? The answers to these questions are, however, quite complex. Indeed, complexity is a key part of the answers I have generated through the research presented here.

I articulate a theoretical and conceptual framework in Chapter 2 that enables me to identify the stories of the WPS agenda, specifically isolating the *fabula*, or sequence of events and experiences ordering subjects and objects. I argue that narrative is made up of sticky arrangements of discourse, and that discourse analysis can therefore be used to good effect to examine how narratives tell—or communicate—particular stories. Discourses are, in turn, organized according to particular logics, which create a semblance of stability or fixity within a discourse, such that it—literally—makes sense. There are many logics interwoven in discursive formations, and nothing is predetermined about how specific logics will organize a given discourse. As I conceived of this theoretical and conceptual approach, I found the metaphor of weaving both useful and illustrative: yarn is turned into fabric through the process of working weft threads over and under warp threads, which are held longitudinally within a frame. The design of the fabric is influenced, though not determined, by the spacing and thickness of the warp threads and the way that the weft thread is pulled through them, just as a narrative is shaped, though not determined, by the discourses that comprise it and the logics that organize those discourses. How the warp and weft thread interacts, the coloration and consistency of the threads and complexity of the patterning of their interactions, produces fabrics of different kinds: rugs, shawls, blankets, or brocade to swaddle babies, dress ministers, or drape curtains. All of these fabrics are made up of the interplay of weft and warp threads. Narratives, similarly, are made up of the sticky arrangement of discourses that are structured according to particular logics.

The story of the WPS agenda that I interrogate here has five dimensions. At, and around, UN HQ, the WPS agenda is narrated in stories of the agenda's origins and about the ownership of the agenda. It is narrated in terms of its successes, failures, pressures, and tensions. The agenda is also constituted through the stories of silences, secrets, and sensibilities that are told about it. In the previous chapters, I examine each of these dimensions in turn. This is, in essence, the empirical contribution that I seek to make in this book. Through an analysis of more than ninety documents and the transcripts of twenty-four interviews, together comprising many hundreds of pages of textual data, I identify these stories as being not only present but prominent in the way that the WPS agenda is represented. Further, by treating the textual data as the base material of narratives, I am able to apprehend, in each case, the discourses that comprise each of the narrative elements I presented. The story of ownership and the origins of the WPS agenda is made up of discourses about the agenda's significance; its interconnectedness with other, proximate, policy frameworks; and its completeness. The agenda's success stories are told in and through discourses of the "anniversary effect," which marks time in the agenda and (re)produces the idea that the adoption of the resolutions as a political act is itself an integral part of the agenda's success. A motif of moderation in the story of success is captured in the discourse of "little wins" and discourse about the possibility of leveraging the agenda into further, more significant change. Failure narratives comprise discourses about lack: lack of funding, lack of political will, lack of experts and expertise necessary for effective implementation. Present here also is an important discourse about the scope of the agenda and its magnitude—so vast as to prevent effective implementation from the outset. This resonates with the discourses that make up the stories of tensions and pressures: the magnitude of the agenda is also invoked in the constitutive discourse about how the priorities and emphases of the agenda are both settled/agreed and also not yet settled/agreed. The story of tensions and pressures is also told through discourses of institutional and geographical (dis)connections and the power of the Security Council. A final discourse within this narrative relates concerns about resolution fatigue, which is interconnected with discourse about the (un)settled nature of the agenda. The final narrative structure that I examine tells stories of silences, secrets, and sensibilities, through discourses about data, influence, intuition, and ambition.

Holding these discourses in formation and constituting meaning in and through the discursive practices I examine are four sets of logics: logics of (in)coherence, logics of (im)possibility, logics of (dis)location, and an ambivalent logic of practice. As outlined in the earlier chapters, these logics refuse reconciliation, refuse to privilege one side of the presented binary over the other. The discourses I identify do not produce, in combination and over time, *either* coherence *or* incoherence, *either* possibility *or* impossibility; they produce *both/and*. Hence the intrinsic plurality of the logics I identify. There is a story about WPS that constitutes the agenda as a coherent set of principles and practices, enshrined in UN Security Council resolutions authored by UN member states in consultation with representatives of civil society, of which implementation is possible given the right conditions. But there are also numerous other stories that contest and conflict with this account that show the ambiguity of the agenda's core tenets and trouble that which is taken for granted (Should "prevention" be attached to "conflict," for example, or to "sexual violence in conflict"? Does "protection" refer to rights, or bodies? Are representatives from civil society organizations the authentic progenitors of the agenda, and does this elevate their credibility and authority over the career diplomats representing state interests at the table in the Council chambers?), and these stories are true also. The agenda is coherent, possible, located within the Council and enshrined within the Council's resolutions *and* it is incoherent, impossible, spatially dispersed, and embedded in the practices of multiple actors: advocates, policy makers, practitioners, and those same career diplomats. It is both/and all of these things, and there is value in recognizing this plurality, this complexity, as constitutive of WPS as a policy agenda.

The WPS agenda as a complex governance system

This approach to understanding WPS as a policy agenda has implications beyond WPS. That is, in addition to the empirical contribution outlined here, there is a broader theoretical contribution that I hope to make in this book, related to the interplay of narrative, discourse, and logics and their deployment within a theoretical and conceptual framework as a means to understand complex governance systems. There is also a methodological contribution, as I hope that the way I have encountered the WPS agenda here can be replicated and applied to other variegated and complex systems of global governance.

The WPS agenda is an example of a complex governance system: its principles and priorities are enshrined within multiple protocols, guidelines, plans, and resolutions across international, national, and even local contexts. There are numerous actors involved in the processes and practices of WPS governance, spanning formal and informal political domains, and there are multiple forms of WPS activity, including mechanisms for policy formation, implementation, and monitoring, but not limited to these; WPS activity might also include protest marches, advocacy, and the creation of new forms of WPS knowledge over time. But the WPS agenda is not unique in this complexity. Scholars of international organizations, global governance, and regimes have begun to examine different forms of complex governance systems in order to understand what insights can be gleaned from centering and working with complexity in relation to governance and policy (see, among other notable examples, Hendrick and Nachmias 1992; Lubell 2013; Chandler 2014; Ansell and Geyer 2017).

Complexity in governance has been taken as an object of study in its own right, not to develop explanatory theory but to provide a context or framework for theorizing the interplay of specific contexts, mechanisms, and practices (Blalock 1984 and Checkland 1981, cited in Hendrick and Nachmias 1992, 315). Governance systems have also been analyzed through the lens of complexity (Rosenau 1990; Snyder and Jervis, eds. 1993; Harrison, ed. 2006; Kavalski 2007). Starting from a position of complexity, or an ontology of complexity, if you will, engenders "three assumptions: that there is no necessary proportionality between 'causes' and 'effects'; that the individual and statistical levels of analysis are not equivalent; and that system effects do not result from the simple addition of individual components" (Law and Urry 2004, 401). Taken together, these assumptions intersect to constitute an object of analysis that is not reducible to a single, simple set of interactions. Complex systems are dynamic, decentralized, and unpredictable, and—most crucially—they are always *in process*. I propose here that the narrative approach I develop in my study of the WPS agenda can be applied to other policy agendas and similarly complex governance systems in order to understand both how complexity is produced and what kinds of logics inform that complexity.

There are larger debates about complexity theory in world politics that I am deliberately sidestepping here (though for an excellent summary, see Bousquet and Curtis 2011), as I wish simply to acknowledge here the existence of complex governance systems, each element of which requires appropriate methods of inquiry in order to understand how it is produced and operates in the world. Examples of such complex systems are the governance of public health concerns, global security initiatives such as the Global Counter-Terrorism Coordination Compact, and the governance of human rights protection. In each case, the complexity, the governance processes, and the system itself must all be (re)produced: "[T]he real is produced in thoroughly non-arbitrary ways, in dense and extended sets of relations. It is produced with considerable effort, and it is much easier to produce some realities than others" (Law and Urry 2004, 395–396). Methods of inquiry, therefore, must be fit to interrogate processes of (re)production. The tripartite framework I elaborate here, drawing on both narrative and discourse theory in order to lay out the logics that structure the stories told about a particular policy agenda and apprehending the narration of those stories as a constitutive political practice, could usefully be deployed in such a way.

"It's complicated . . ."

The narratives of the WPS agenda are structured by plural and undecidable logics, which defy attempts at reducing the agenda to a singular "thing." The plurality and multiplicity creates diverse forms of political possibility and also shows how apprehending the emergence of WPS as a knowable policy agenda through its narratives is to situate oneself in relation to the intrinsic ambiguity of its constitution. These logics introduce "a kind of systematic, non-decidable plurality" (Weber 2016, 42) into the discourses that I analyze, which has significant implications for the imagined futures of the agenda, as well as the ways it is encountered, known, and enacted in the present. Surfacing the plurality of these logics means that those working on and around the agenda must necessarily give up on the illusion that the agenda is, or ever can be, conceived of as singular (and thus manageable, coherent, and possible). There is no singular, authentic, "real and true" WPS; there are inevitably competing and often conflicting claims and counterclaims about the agenda's principles and priorities. Some of these are more persuasive than others, and some aspects of the agenda are widely accepted among the WPS epistemic community as having been codified within the agenda's artifacts—but even these cannot be simply ported from, for example, resolution to program delivery site; interpretation and translation is always required. Recognizing the undecidability of these logics not only reaffirms their plurality but also acknowledges the ambiguity of the agenda: its regressive as well as its transformative possibilities, the moments of its silence as well as its potential as a platform for amplifying the voices of those marginalized or dispossessed by security practices that too often ignore insecurity, and its violences as well as its solutions for peace.

There is a seductive attraction in the idea that the WPS agenda has a single, pure authenticity. It is politically, and normatively, appealing to be able to articulate a "right way" to do WPS, a set of policy prescriptions that, once fulfilled, would mark the agenda's full achievement, for example:

> When the Security Council finds it unthinkable to address a crisis without addressing women's rights, when humanitarian responders have full funding for their gender-specific services, when women grass-roots leaders find their work fully funded and politically supported, when it is unimaginable that peace talks be held without women's full engagement, only then will the full potential of resolution 1325 (2000) be realized. (Alaa Murabit, the Voice of Libyan Women, briefing the Council during an Open Debate, S/PV.7533 2015, p. 11).

But seeing the agenda in terms of the plural and undecidable logics that organize its narration is not to give up on its realization; it is to open up possibilities rather than attempt to effect closure. The fluidity of the agenda and the breadth of its coverage render it complex and difficult to grasp, but it can also be freeing and enabling of the kinds of victories that will ultimately sustain the agenda: "[W]hen you're involved, I mean it's definitely something there in the kind of excitement of it all that you can't really step back and say, 'Oh hey, I don't want to do this at all.' You don't really have. . . . It's like you hold on to a place to try and make it the best it can be" (Interview, 201911).

The plural and undecidable logics I identify organize competing narratives about what "really matters" in and to the WPS agenda. These logics, and the discourses that they structure, constitute a series of binaries in the agenda: inside/outside, bureaucrat/feminist; advocate/activist; theory/practice. It was suggested to me, for example, that "there's a danger that WPS has become too institutionalized in some ways, and that institutionalization can lead to emptying it of its original transformative intent and political content" (Interview, 201912). This configuration positions WPS outside of, even in opposition to, the institution (of the UN), which is in turn responsible for blunting and diminishing the agenda's "transformative intent and political content," the latter of which inheres or travels through from the agenda's originators, who, by implication, are external to the institution. The fear of co-optation infuses this discourse, but it is not the case that these binaries line up neatly to produce a compelling and dominant narrative that interpellates individuals into "good" and "bad" subject positions, or that the binaries I identify remain stable over time and in different discursive contexts: the ambivalent logic of practice, in particular, confounds efforts at effecting closure or stability within discourses about how knowledge is produced within the agenda, what kinds of knowledge are valued, and what kinds of knowledge artifacts or embodiments of knowledge count as WPS knowledge. Some people that I spoke with made efforts to sit in, and with, those tensions, to carve out and occupy a space between: "I see lots of reactions about whether an emphasis on numbers is a bad thing or an emphasis on gender equality is a bad thing, or are we focusing too much on sexual violence or are we not focusing enough on sexual violence against men. It's a lot of that and I think it hurts our agenda, because in general, I see slow progress on all of the angles and that they move much more.... They're much more complimentary in a way" (Interview, 201908). The agenda produced through this discourse, and the other discourses I examine here, is a slippery and mutable thing.

The idea that there is a "fundamental" agenda is used to explain shortcomings, suggesting that WPS actors have missed the point on the fundamentals, the foundations, and thus failed to capture the agenda's potential. Its presumed coherence is the underpinning logic of its apparent limitations. But its potentialities lie here too. Bringing the WPS agenda into the world in this way, engaging with it as a complex governance system and positing that WPS emerges as a knowable policy agenda in part through its narration at UN HQ, implies that its complexity can no longer be used as an excuse or rationale for inaction. I have had recounted to me numerous times the experience of being told "It's complicated . . ." when WPS actors are pushed to explain or account for why their implementation actions are falling short, so much so that it has become something of a running joke when talking with friends who also work in this space.[1] It is complicated. The agenda is complicated. And it is hard work.

Uphill, barefoot, in the snow

Simple solutions are appealing, simple systems that govern singular problems even more so. Holding open the space for complexity, for competing and conflicting interpretations, and sustaining the "truth" of multiple interpretations is hard work, both intellectually and in practice. There is a reason social scientists like parsimonious theory and policy makers like one-page briefing papers of no more than three bullet points. But as Cynthia Enloe reminds us, the production of a simple explanation for a complicated social phenomenon requires a lot of effort, and it is important to acknowledge that "[f]or an explanation to be useful, a great deal of human dignity has to be left on the cutting room floor" (1996, 188). Moreover, it is important to acknowledge the effort that goes into operationalizing a complex policy agenda like WPS. The people that I spoke to in the course of this research are each entirely and profoundly committed to the work that they do to bring into being the principles and priorities of the WPS agenda as they see them. I have seen exhaustion, and frustration, and evident irritation, on the faces of the people that I interviewed as they recounted how a latest strategy had been subverted or much-needed funding had been diverted.

SPEAKER 2: And then we get exhausted because we're like, oh we'll fight that and we'll fight this.
SPEAKER 1: And we'll fight that other thing.
SPEAKER 2: Then it's breakfast time and . . .
SPEAKER 1: Then you have to take your kid out to daycare. Feed them, God! Who knew they'd need food? Three times a day plus snacks.
(Interview, 201903)

In arguing that the irreconcilability of these plural, or ambiguous, logics precludes the realization of the agenda as a singular, essential "thing in the world," I do not mean to suggest either that their tireless efforts are somehow misguided or that their efforts are fruitless. There is no "true" WPS agenda that practitioners, activists, and policy makers can apprehend and use as their guide; there is only an intrinsic plurality, a messy and contested space for political interventions of different kinds. Much energy and resource is expended in efforts to reduce or resolve the agenda to a singular, essential "thing"—with singular, essential meaning. This is not a disciplinary or disciplining technique peculiar to the WPS agenda. My interlocutors in this project are caught up in the same power/knowledge systems that produce and organize broader claims about social reality and its singularity.

John Law's work on how social science research reproduces the Euro-American fetishization of an already-existing social world that is "independent and prior to an observer; definite in shape and form; and also singular (there is only one reality)" is instructive here (2004, 145). Much work on governance systems, whether they are taken to be simple or complex, assumes the ability to isolate, monitor, evaluate—in fact, to *know*—the object of analysis as a singular thing and thus to explain cause and effect within that bounded context. It is hard to think of knowing otherwise. When I used to teach social science research methods, I included a section on my experience of conducting research as an undergraduate student in a world before digital databases, online indexes, and search engines. This section concluded with a quote from Dustin Wax's advice for students on producing better research: "Remember, though, that until a few years ago, most of us managed to do research with no Internet at all! With typewriters! Walking uphill! In the snow! Barefoot!" (Wax n.d.). The image of walking uphill, barefoot, in the snow seems particularly apposite to me as I consider the possibilities—the impossibilities—of knowing *in general* and of knowing the WPS agenda in particular.

I have argued throughout this book that knowing the WPS agenda through a narrative approach enables a productive condition of engagement. It is an ill-disciplined, or perhaps (more generously) a multidisciplinary, approach, attentive to narratology, discourse theory, politics, and policy. It is not an approach that lends itself to certitude, and ultimately mine is an argument about uncertainty and the multiple images and imaginings of WPS that constitute its realities, now and in the future. It might be difficult for those trained in and wedded to the Euro-American model of conventional social science research and method elaborated by Law (2004). But to work within and alongside uncertainty and undecidability, we might embrace the hard work of mess, chaos, and complexity. The argument I present here implies that those seeking to realize the WPS agenda might need instead to live with the irreconcilable, the irresolvable, and the ambiguous. I have shown how the narratives of the WPS agenda are organized according to plural and undecidable logics and have argued that this plurality, the actually existing complexity, of the agenda cannot—should not—be used as an alibi for limited action or strategic inaction. It is complicated, but that cannot—should not—deflect or diminish sustained engagement with the agenda in its infinite complexity, its intrinsic plurality. The plural logics I identify resist efforts to close down or narrow the meaning of WPS as a policy agenda in global politics, and so effective political engagement—the realization of agenda—depends on sitting with, and finding productive potential in, multiplicity, polysemy, and ambivalence: "[T]oday, you have to go beyond the simple definition. But I don't see where is the problem. The women, peace and security agenda for me has room to capture all this" (Interview, 201601).

Key Provisions of the UN Security Council Resolutions Adopted under the Title of "Women and Peace and Security"

RESOLUTION/ YEAR	KEY ISSUES AND CORE PROVISIONS
S/RES/1325 (2000)	Representation and participation of women in peace and security governance; protection of women's rights and bodies in conflict and post-conflict situations.
S/RES/1820 (2008)	Protection of women from sexualized violence in conflict (SViC); zero tolerance of sexualized abuse and exploitation perpetrated by UN DPKO personnel.
S/RES/1888 (2009)	Creation of office of SRSG-SViC; creation of UN Action; identification of "team of experts"; appointment of women's protection advisers (WPAs) to field missions.
S/RES/1889 (2009)	Need to increase participation of women in peace and security governance at all levels; creation of global indicators to map implementation of UNSCR 1325.
S/RES/1960 (2010)	Development of SViC monitoring, analysis, and reporting arrangements; integration of WPAs to field missions alongside gender advisers.
S/RES/2106 (2013)	Challenging impunity and lack of accountability for SViC.
S/RES/2122 (2013)	Identifies UN Women as key UN entity providing information and advice on participation of women in peace and security governance; whole-of-UN accountability; civil society inclusion; 2015 High-level Review of implementation of UNSCR 1325.
S/RES/2242 (2015)	Integrates Women, Peace and Security (WPS) agenda in all UNSC country situations; establishes Informal Experts Group on WPS; adds WPS considerations to sanctions committee deliberations; links WPS to countering terrorism and extremism.
S/RES/2467 (2019)	Strengthens prosecution/punishment for SViC; opens possibility for sanctions against perpetrators; affirms survivor-centered approach; calls for provision of reparations to survivors.
S/RES/2493 (2019)	Calls on member states to promote women's rights; encourages creation of safe operational environment for those working to promote women's rights; calls for full implementation of all previous WPS resolutions.

List of Resolutions, Reports, and Policy Documents

UN Security Council resolutions (n = 10)

United Nations Security Council (2000) Resolution 1325. S/RES/1325 (2000). Online, at https://undocs.org/S/RES/1325(2000).

United Nations Security Council (2008) Resolution 1820. S/RES/1820 (2008). Online, at https://undocs.org/S/RES/1820(2008).

United Nations Security Council (2009) Resolution 1888. S/RES/1888 (2009). Online, at https://undocs.org/S/RES/1888(2009).

United Nations Security Council (2009) Resolution 1889. S/RES/1889 (2009). Online, at https://undocs.org/S/RES/1889(2009).

United Nations Security Council (2010) Resolution 1960. S/RES/1960 (2010). Online, at https://undocs.org/S/RES/1960(2010).

United Nations Security Council (2013) Resolution 2106. S/RES/2016 (2013). Online, at https://undocs.org/S/RES/2106(2013).

United Nations Security Council (2013) Resolution 2122. S/RES/2122 (2013). Online, at https://undocs.org/S/RES/2122(2013).

United Nations Security Council (2015) Resolution 2242. S/RES/2242 (2015). Online, at https://undocs.org/S/RES/2242(2015).

United Nations Security Council (2019) Resolution 2467. S/RES/2467 (2019). Online, at https://undocs.org/S/RES/2467(2019).

United Nations Security Council (2019) Resolution 2493. S/RES/2493 (2019). Online, at https://undocs.org/S/RES/2493(2019).

UN Security Council presidential statements (n = 15)

United Nations Security Council (2001) Statement by the President of the Security Council. S/PRST/2001/31. 31 October 2001. Online, at https://undocs.org/en/S/PRST/2001/31.

United Nations Security Council (2002) Statement by the President of the Security Council. S/PRST/2002/32. 31 October 2002. Online, at https://undocs.org/en/S/PRST/2002/32.

United Nations Security Council (2004) Statement by the President of the Security Council. S/PRST/2004/40. 28 October 2004. Online, at https://undocs.org/en/S/PRST/2004/40.

United Nations Security Council (2005) Statement by the President of the Security Council. S/PRST/2005/52. 27 October 2005. Online, at https://undocs.org/en/S/PRST/2005/52.

United Nations Security Council (2006) Statement by the President of the Security Council. S/PRST/2006/42. 26 October 2006. Online, at https://undocs.org/en/S/PRST/2006/42.

United Nations Security Council (2007) Statement by the President of the Security Council. S/PRST/2007/5. 7 March 2007. Online, at https://undocs.org/en/S/PRST/2007/5.

United Nations Security Council (2007) Statement by the President of the Security Council. S/PRST/2007/40. 24 October 2007. Online, at https://undocs.org/en/S/PRST/2007/40.

United Nations Security Council (2008) Statement by the President of the Security Council. S/PRST/2008/39. 29 October 2008. Online, at https://undocs.org/en/S/PRST/2008/39.

United Nations Security Council (2010) Statement by the President of the Security Council. S/PRST/2010/8. 27 April 2010. Online, at https://undocs.org/en/S/PRST/2010/8.

United Nations Security Council (2010) Statement by the President of the Security Council. S/PRST/2010/22. 26 October 2010. Online, at https://undocs.org/en/S/PRST/2010/22.

United Nations Security Council (2011) Statement by the President of the Security Council. S/PRST/2011/20. 28 October 2011. Online, at https://undocs.org/en/S/PRST/2011/20.

United Nations Security Council (2012) Statement by the President of the Security Council. S/PRST/2012/3. 23 February 2012. Online, at https://undocs.org/en/S/PRST/2012/3.

United Nations Security Council (2012) Statement by the President of the Security Council. S/PRST/2012/23. 31 October 2012. Online, at https://undocs.org/en/S/PRST/2012/23.

United Nations Security Council (2014) Statement by the President of the Security Council. S/PRST/2014/21. 28 October 2014. Online, at https://undocs.org/en/S/PRST/2014/21.

United Nations Security Council (2016) Statement by the President of the Security Council. S/PRST/2016/9. 15 June 2016. Online, at https://undocs.org/en/S/PRST/2016/9.

UN Secretary-General's reports (n = 28)

United Nations Security Council (2002) Report of the Secretary-General on Women and Peace and Security. S/2002/1154. 16 October 2002. Online, at https://undocs.org/S/2002/1154.

United Nations Security Council (2004) Women and Peace and Security: Report of the Secretary-General. S/2004/814. 13 October 2004. Online, at https://undocs.org/S/2004/814.

United Nations Security Council (2005) Report of the Secretary-General on Women and Peace and Security. S/2005/636. 10 October 2005. Online, at https://undocs.org/S/2005/636.

United Nations Security Council (2006) Report of the Secretary-General on Women, Peace and Security. S/2006/770. 27 September 2006. Online, at https://undocs.org/S/2006/770.

United Nations Security Council (2008) Women and Peace and Security: Report of the Secretary-General. S/2008/622. 25 September 2008. Online, at https://undocs.org/S/2008/622.

United Nations Security Council (2009) Report of the Secretary-General Pursuant to Security Council Resolution 1820. S/2009/362. 15 July 2009. Online, at https://undocs.org/S/2009/362.

United Nations Security Council (2009) Women and Peace and Security: Report of the Secretary-General. S/2009/465. 16 September 2009. Online, at https://undocs.org/S/2009/465.

United Nations Security Council (2010) Women and Peace and Security: Report of the Secretary-General. S/2010/173. 6 April 2010. Online, at https://undocs.org/S/2010/173.

United Nations Security Council (2010) Women's Participation in Peacebuilding: Report of the Secretary-General. A/65/354-S/2010/466. 7 September 2010. Online, at https://undocs.org/en/S/2010/466.

United Nations Security Council (2010) Women and Peace and Security: Report of the Secretary-General. S/2010/498. 28 September 2010. Online, at https://undocs.org/en/S/2010/498.

United Nations Security Council (2010) Report of the Secretary-General on the Implementation of Security Council Resolutions 1820 (2008) and 1888 (2009). A/65/592–S/2010/604. 24 November 2010. Online, at https://undocs.org/en/S/2010/604.

United Nations Security Council (2011) Report of the Secretary-General on Women and Peace and Security. S/2011/598. 29 September 2011. Online, at https://undocs.org/en/S/2011/598.

United Nations Security Council (2012) Conflict-Related Sexual Violence: Report of the Secretary-General. A/66/657-S/2012/33. 13 January 2012. Online, at https://undocs.org/en/S/2012/33.

United Nations Security Council (2012) Report of the Secretary-General on Women and Peace and Security. S/2012/732. 2 October 2012. Online, at https://undocs.org/en/S/2012/732.

United Nations Security Council (2013) Sexual Violence in Conflict: Report of the Secretary-General. A/67/792-S/2013/149. 14 March 2013. Online, at https://undocs.org/en/S/2013/149.

United Nations Security Council (2013) Report of the Secretary-General on Women and Peace and Security. S/2013/525. 4 September 2013. Online, at https://undocs.org/en/S/2013/525.

United Nations Security Council (2014) Conflict-Related Sexual Violence: Report of the Secretary-General. S/2014/181. 13 March 2014. Online, at https://undocs.org/en/S/2014/181.

United Nations Security Council (2014) Report of the Secretary-General on Women and Peace and Security. S/2014/693. 23 September 2014. Online, at https://undocs.org/en/S/2014/693.

United Nations Security Council (2015) Conflict-Related Sexual Violence: Report of the Secretary-General. S/2015/203. 23 March 2015. Online, at https://undocs.org/en/S/2015/203.

United Nations Security Council (2015) Report of the Secretary-General on Women and Peace and Security. S/2015/716. 16 September 2015. Online, at https://undocs.org/en/S/2015/716.

United Nations Security Council (2016) Report of the Secretary-General on Conflict-Related Sexual Violence. S/2016/361. 20 April 2016. Online, at https://undocs.org/en/S/2016/361.

United Nations Security Council (2016) Report of the Secretary-General on Women and Peace and Security. S/2016/822. 29 September 2016. Online, at https://undocs.org/en/S/2016/822.

United Nations Security Council (2017) Report of the Secretary-General on Conflict-Related Sexual Violence. S/2017/249. 15 April 2017. Online, at https://undocs.org/en/S/2017/249.

United Nations Security Council (2017) Report of the Secretary-General on Women and Peace and Security. S/2017/861. 16 October 2017. Online, at https://undocs.org/en/S/2017/861.

United Nations Security Council (2018) Report of the Secretary-General on Conflict-Related Sexual Violence. S/2018/250. 23 March 2018. Online, at https://undocs.org/en/S/2018/250.

United Nations Security Council (2018) Report of the Secretary-General on Women and Peace and Security. S/2018/900. 9 October 2018. Online, at https://undocs.org/en/S/2018/900.

United Nations Security Council (2019) Women and Peace and Security: Report of the Secretary-General. S/2019/800. 9 October 2019. Online, at https://undocs.org/en/S/2019/800.

United Nations Security Council (2019) Conflict-Related Sexual Violence: Report of the Secretary-General. S/2019/280. 29 March 2019. Online, at https://undocs.org/en/S/2019/280.

UN Security Council transcripts of Open Debates (n = 41; 59 separate documents due to resumptions)

United Nations Security Council (2001) Fifty-sixth year. 4402nd meeting. Wednesday, 31 October 2001. S/PV.4402. Online, at https://undocs.org/en/S/PV.4402.

United Nations Security Council (2002) Fifty-seventh year. 4589th meeting. Thursday, 25 July 2002. S/PV.4589. Online, at https://undocs.org/en/S/PV.4589.

United Nations Security Council (2002) Fifty-seventh year. 4589th meeting. Thursday, 25 July 2002. S/PV.4589 (Resumption 1). Online, at https://undocs.org/S/PV.4589%20(Resumption%201).

United Nations Security Council (2002) Fifty-seventh year. 4635th meeting. Monday, 28 October 2002. S/PV.4635. Online, at https://undocs.org/en/S/PV.4635.

United Nations Security Council (2002) Fifty-seventh year. 4635th meeting. Tuesday, 29 October 2002. S/PV.4635 (Resumption 1). Online, at https://undocs.org/S/PV.4635%20(Resumption%201).

United Nations Security Council (2002) Fifty-seventh year. 4641st meeting. Thursday, 31 October 2002. S/PV.4641. Online, at https://undocs.org/S/PV.4641.

United Nations Security Council (2003) Fifty-eighth year. 4852nd meeting. Wednesday, 29 October 2003. S/PV.4852. Online, at https://undocs.org/en/S/PV.4852.

United Nations Security Council (2003) Fifty-eighth year. 4852nd meeting. Wednesday, 29 October 2003. S/PV.4852 (Resumption 1). Online, at https://undocs.org/S/PV.4852%20(Resumption%201).

United Nations Security Council (2004) Fifty-ninth year. 5066th meeting. Thursday, 28 October 2004. S/PV.5066. Online, at https://undocs.org/en/S/PV.5066.

United Nations Security Council (2004) Fifty-ninth year. 5066th meeting. Thursday, 28 October 2004. S/PV.5066 (Resumption 1). Online, at https://undocs.org/S/PV.5066%20(Resumption%201).

United Nations Security Council (2005) Sixtieth year. 5294th meeting. Thursday, 27 October 2005. S/PV.5294. Online, at https://undocs.org/en/S/PV.5294.

United Nations Security Council (2005) Sixtieth year. 5294th meeting. Thursday, 27 October 2005. S/PV.5294 (Resumption 1). Online, at https://undocs.org/S/PV.5294%20(Resumption%201).

United Nations Security Council (2006) Sixty-first year. 5556th meeting. Thursday, 26 October 2006. S/PV.5556. Online, at https://undocs.org/en/S/PV.5556.

United Nations Security Council (2006) Sixty-first year. 5556th meeting. Thursday, 26 October 2006. S/PV.5556 (Resumption 1). Online, at https://undocs.org/S/PV.5556%20(Resumption%201).

United Nations Security Council (2007) Sixty-second year. 5636th meeting. Wednesday, 7 March 2007. S/PV.5636. Online, at https://undocs.org/en/S/PV.5636.

United Nations Security Council (2007) Sixty-second year. 5766th meeting. Tuesday, 23 October 2007. S/PV.5766. Online, at https://undocs.org/en/S/PV.5766.

United Nations Security Council (2007) Sixty-second year. 5766th meeting. Tuesday, 23 October 2007. S/PV.5766 (Resumption 1). Online, at https://undocs.org/S/PV.5766%20(Resumption%201).

United Nations Security Council (2008) Sixty-third year. 5916th meeting. Thursday, 19 June 2008. S/PV.5916. Online, at https://undocs.org/en/S/PV.5916.

United Nations Security Council (2008) Sixty-third year. 5916th meeting. Thursday, 19 June 2008. S/PV.5916 (Resumption 1). Online, at https://undocs.org/S/PV.5916%20(Resumption%201).

United Nations Security Council (2008) Sixty-third year. 6005th meeting. Wednesday, 29 October 2008. S/PV.6005. Online, at https://undocs.org/en/S/PV.6005.

United Nations Security Council (2008) Sixty-third year. 6005th meeting. Wednesday, 29 October 2008. S/PV.6005 (Resumption 1). Online, at https://undocs.org/S/PV.6005%20(Resumption%201).

United Nations Security Council (2009) Sixty-fourth year. 6180th meeting. Friday, 7 August 2009. S/PV.6180. Online, at https://undocs.org/en/S/PV.6180.

United Nations Security Council (2009) Sixty-fourth year. 6180th meeting. Friday, 7 August 2009. S/PV.6180 (Resumption 1). Online, at https://undocs.org/S/PV.6180%20(Resumption%201).

United Nations Security Council (2009) Sixty-fourth year. 6195th meeting. Wednesday, 30 September 2009. S/PV.6195. Online, at https://undocs.org/en/S/PV.6195.

United Nations Security Council (2009) Sixty-fourth year. 6196th meeting. Monday, 5 October 2009. S/PV.6196. Online, at https://undocs.org/en/S/PV.6196.

United Nations Security Council (2009) Sixty-fourth year. 6196th meeting. Monday, 5 October 2009. S/PV.6196 (Resumption 1). Online, at https://undocs.org/S/PV.6196%20(Resumption%201).

United Nations Security Council (2010) Sixty-fifth year. 6302nd meeting. Tuesday, 27 April 2010. S/PV.6302. Online, at https://undocs.org/en/S/PV.6302.

United Nations Security Council (2010) Sixty-fifth year. 6411th meeting. Tuesday, 26 October 2010. S/PV.6411. Online, at https://undocs.org/en/S/PV.6411.

United Nations Security Council (2010) Sixty-fifth year. 6411th meeting. Tuesday, 26 October 2010. S/PV.6411 (Resumption 1). Online, at https://undocs.org/S/PV.6411%20(Resumption%201).

United Nations Security Council (2010) Sixty-fifth year. 6453rd meeting. Thursday, 16 December 2010. S/PV.6453. Online, at https://undocs.org/en/S/PV.6453.

United Nations Security Council (2010) Sixty-fifth year. 6453rd meeting. Friday, 17 December 2010. S/PV.6453 (Resumption 1). Online, at https://undocs.org/S/PV.6453%20(Resumption%201).

United Nations Security Council (2011) Sixty-sixth year. 6515th meeting. Thursday, 14 April 2011. S/PV.6515. Online, at https://undocs.org/en/S/PV.6515.

United Nations Security Council (2011) Sixty-sixth year. 6642nd meeting. Friday, 28 October 2011. S/PV.6642. Online, at https://undocs.org/en/S/PV.6642.

United Nations Security Council (2011) Sixty-sixth year. 6642nd meeting. Friday, 28 October 2011. S/PV.6642 (Resumption 1). Online, at https://undocs.org/S/PV.6642%20(Resumption%201).

United Nations Security Council (2012) Sixty-seventh year. 6722nd meeting. Thursday, 23 February 2012. S/PV.6722. Online, at https://undocs.org/en/S/PV.6722.

United Nations Security Council (2012) Sixty-seventh year. 6722nd meeting. Thursday, 23 February 2012. S/PV.6722 (Resumption 1). Online, at https://undocs.org/S/PV.6722%20(Resumption%201).

United Nations Security Council (2012) Sixty-seventh year. 6759th meeting. Tuesday, 24 April 2012. S/PV.6759. Online, at https://undocs.org/en/S/PV.6759.

United Nations Security Council (2012) Sixty-seventh year. 6852nd meeting. Wednesday, 31 October 2012. S/PV.6852. Online, at https://undocs.org/en/S/PV.6852.

United Nations Security Council (2012) Sixty-seventh year. 6877th meeting. Friday, 30 November 2012. S/PV.6877. Online, at https://undocs.org/en/S/PV.6877.

United Nations Security Council (2013) Sixty-eighth year. 6948th meeting. Wednesday, 17 April 2013. S/PV.6948. Online, at https://undocs.org/en/S/PV.6948.

United Nations Security Council (2013) Sixty-eighth year. 6984th meeting. Monday, 24 June 2013. S/PV.6984. Online, at https://undocs.org/en/S/PV.6984.

United Nations Security Council (2013) Sixty-eighth year. 7044th meeting. Friday, 18 October 2013. S/PV.7044. Online, at https://undocs.org/en/S/PV.7044.

United Nations Security Council (2014) Sixty-ninth year. 7160th meeting. Friday, 25 April 2014. S/PV.7160. Online, at https://undocs.org/en/S/PV.7160.

United Nations Security Council (2014) Sixty-ninth year. 7289th meeting. Tuesday, 28 October 2014. S/PV.7289. Online, at https://undocs.org/en/S/PV.7289.

United Nations Security Council (2015) Seventieth year. 7428th meeting. Wednesday, 15 April 2015. S/PV.7428. Online, at https://undocs.org/en/S/PV.7428.

United Nations Security Council (2015) Seventieth year. 7533rd meeting. Tuesday, 13 October 2015. S/PV.7533. Online, at https://undocs.org/en/S/PV.7533.

United Nations Security Council (2015) Seventieth year. 7533rd meeting. Tuesday, 13 October 2015. S/PV.7533 (Resumption 1). Online, at https://undocs.org/S/PV.7533%20(Resumption%201).

United Nations Security Council (2016) Seventy-first year. 7658th meeting. Monday, 28 March 2016. P/SV.7658. Online, at https://undocs.org/en/S/PV.7658.

United Nations Security Council (2016) Seventy-first year. 7704th meeting. Thursday, 2 June 2016. P/SV.7704. Online, at https://undocs.org/en/S/PV.7704.

United Nations Security Council (2016) Seventy-first year. 7717th meeting. Wednesday, 15 June 2016. P/SV.7717. Online, at https://undocs.org/en/S/PV.7717.

United Nations Security Council (2016) Seventy-first year. 7793rd meeting. Tuesday, 25 October 2016. S/PV.7793. Online, at https://undocs.org/en/S/PV.7793.

United Nations Security Council (2017) Seventy-second year. 7938th meeting. Monday, 15 May 2017. S/PV.7938. Online, at https://undocs.org/en/S/PV.7938.

United Nations Security Council (2017) Seventy-second year. 8079th meeting. Friday, 27 October 2017. S/PV.8079. Online, at https://undocs.org/en/S/PV.8079.

United Nations Security Council (2018) Seventy-third year. 8234th meeting. Monday, 16 April 2018. S/PV.8234. Online, at https://undocs.org/en/S/PV.8234.

United Nations Security Council (2018) Seventy-third year. 8382nd meeting. Thursday, 25 October 2018. S/PV.8382. Online, at https://undocs.org/en/S/PV.8382.

United Nations Security Council (2019) Seventy-fourth year. 8514th meeting. Tuesday, 23 April 2019. S/PV.8514. Online, at https://undocs.org/en/S/PV.8514.

United Nations Security Council (2019) Seventy-fourth year. 8649th meeting. Tuesday, 29 October 2019. S/PV.8649. Online, at https://undocs.org/en/S/PV.8649.

United Nations Security Council (2019) Seventy-fourth year. 8649th meeting. Tuesday, 29 October 2019. S/PV.8649 (Resumption 1). Online, at https://undocs.org/S/PV.8649%20(Resumption%201).

United Nations Security Council (2019) Seventy-fourth year. 8649th meeting. Tuesday, 29 October 2019. S/PV.8649 (Resumption 2). Online, at https://undocs.org/S/PV.8649%20(Resumption%202).

Press statements, reports, and other related policy documents

United Nations (2000) Peace Inextricably Linked with Equality Between Women and Men Says Security Council, In International Women's Day Statement. S/6816 (2000). Online, at https://www.un.org/press/en/2000/20000308.sc6816.doc.html.

United Nations (1996) Report of the Fourth World Conference on Women, Beijing 4–15 September 1995. A/CONF.177/20/Rev.1 (1996). Online, at https://www.un.org/womenwatch/daw/beijing/pdf/Beijing%20full%20report%20E.pdf.

United Nations General Assembly/United Nations Security Council (2000) Windhoek Declaration and the Namibia Plan of Action on Mainstreaming a Gender Perspective in Multidimensional Peace Support Operations. A/55/138-S/2000/693 (2000). Online, at https://www.un.org/documents/ga/docs/55/a55138.pdf.

Notes

Chapter 1

1. Correct at the time of writing. These resolutions, with year of adoption, are as follows: UNSCR 1325 (2000); UNSCR 1820 (2008); UNSCR 1888 (2009); UNSCR 1889 (2009); UNSCR 1960 (2010); UNSCR 2106 (2013); UNSCR 2122 (2013); UNSCR 2242 (2015); UNSCR 2467 (2019); and UNSCR 2493 (2019).

2. The coverage of various security challenges in NAPs is documented and visualized at www.wpsnaps.org.

3. The literature on global governance is vast, and I cannot possibly survey it here. A small sample of some excellent works in this field includes Wilkinson and Hughes, eds. 2002; Barnett and Duvall, eds. 2005; Diehl, ed. 2005; Rai and Waylen, eds. 2008; O'Brien, Goetz, Scholte and Williams 2009; Neumann and Sending 2010; Weiss 2011; Weiss and Wilkinson, eds. 2014; Hudson, Rönnblom and Teghtsoonian, eds. 2017; Weiss and Wilkinson 2019.

4. See, for example, and in addition to the literature engaged in the following chapter: Wibben 2011; Miskimmon, O'Laughlin and Roselle 2013; Stanley 2014, 2016; Inayatullah and Dauphinee, eds. 2016; Mac Ginty and Firchow 2016; Stanley and Jackson 2016; Ravecca and Dauphinee 2018; Hagström and Gustafsson 2019; Ling and Nakamura 2019; Mehta and Wibben 2019; Ravecca 2019; Krystalli 2020.

5. I am grateful to Ole Wæver for encouraging me to think more carefully about the work that concepts of narrative, story, and discourse do, and my motivations for using these concepts.

6. This may not be the case more broadly; as Sujatha Fernandes comments, "Scholarly and popular non-fiction works, storytelling manuals, and storytelling strategists often extrapolate from the Western experience to present the idea of storytelling as universal and timeless" (2017a, 5).

7. This is not necessarily to claim that there exist universal story forms or patterns. In fact, "[t]he notion of a prototypical, conflict-driven story is a construct, which serves to impose order on what is an incoherent, widely divergent set of narrative practices" (Fernandes 2017a, 5).

8. Relatedly, there are stories of other complex governance systems that interact and intersect with the WPS agenda, which could be analyzed using the approach I elaborate here. But those are not the stories of this book, either.

9. I discuss the concept of logics further in chapter 2. I first used the concept in earlier work on security (Shepherd 2008b), in which I argued that security discourses are commonly organized around particular logics, which structure the organization of subjects and objects within that discourse, creating associative chains of value and

hierarchy. These different logics inform different discourses of security that have radically different effects; a discourse on national security, for example, underpinned by a logic of state centrism and a logic of anarchy, produces very different political possibilities (and policy prescriptions) than a discourse on human security, underpinned by a logic of equality and a logic of dignity. Since developing this argument, though, I have worked with a brilliant PhD student, Lucy Hall, whose work on the discursive construction of gender and protection in humanitarian normative frameworks pushed me to think further about conceptualizing logics and how they work; I must therefore acknowledge the intellectual debt that this book owes Lucy and her work. If you are looking for a sophisticated and exhaustive analysis of the logics of protection in the governance of humanitarian crisis, Lucy is your woman, and I am grateful to have had the opportunity to work with her and learn from her.

Chapter 2

1. Roland Bleiker, following Franz Kafka, refers to these artifacts and agents as "doorkeepers," which is particularly charming (1997, 63–64).
2. Describing the collections of essays published in *Autobiographical International Relations: I, IR* (Inayatullah, ed. 2011) and *Narrative Global Politics* (Inayatullah and Dauphinee, eds. 2016) as "generative and sometimes difficult" is woefully inadequate. Each of the authors writes their stories with disarming, gentle courage and a sharp critical eye, drawing connections between self and situation in ways that further the reader's understanding of both and of the broader context that is the edifice of knowledge production, which seeks to delegitimize their endeavors as "navel gazing" and "vanity" (Inayatullah 2011, 7–8). Everyone should read these books.
3. As Naeem Inayatullah says: "Academic writing supposes a precarious fiction. It assumes the simultaneous absence and presence of the writer within the writing. The writer presents herself/himself as absent, as distant, and as indifferent to the writing and ideas. . . . The fictive distance, as we all know, dominates academic prose. And yet the reader always uncovers the presence of a particular person in the writing" (2011, 5). Narrative analysis brings to the foreground those communicative modes that center the writer(/speaker) and thus undoes that precarious fiction at which Inayatullah takes aim.
4. I choose not to use Bal's conceptualization of "story," as it sits alongside and resonates powerfully with the way that I understand and deploy the concept of discourse in this investigation.
5. A third element commonly developed in narrative theory is focalization, which is the process through which the focal point(s) of the *fabula* is constructed and how they change over time (Herman and Vervaeck 2007, 223–225). Again, to avoid constructing an overly weighty and cumbersome theoretical framework, I focus on the elements of the *fabula* that are most closely aligned with the storytelling dynamics I identify.
6. In analytical terms, articulation "has a nice double meaning because to 'articulate' means to utter, to speak forth, to be articulate. It carries that sense of language-ing, of

expressing, etc. But we also speak of an 'articulated lorry' (truck): a lorry where the front (cab) and back (trailer) can, but need not be connected to one another" (Stuart Hall, quoted in Weldes 1996a, 285).

7. This should have been obvious to me, but I have always been both ambitious and optimistic in my research practices.

8. The interviews took place over a six-year period between 2013 and 2019; some research participants were interviewed more than once over the life of the project, and some interviews involved pairs or groups of research participants rather than individuals. The interviews lasted anywhere between half an hour and an hour and a half. The audio recordings of the interviews were transcribed, and research participants were offered the chance to review, and if necessary redact elements of, the transcripts before the texts were subjected to analysis.

9. I collected the data and worked on parts of the analysis with a postdoctoral research associate, Caitlin Hamilton, whose contribution to this project was immense and immensely valuable.

10. The analytical and political salience of "common sense" must not be underestimated; Stuart Hall famously called the formation of common sense "a moment of extreme ideological closure," arguing that the "regime of the 'taken for granted'" (1985, 105) should be the target of all critical investigations.

Chapter 3

1. The government of Namibia's discourse about the significance of Windhoek to the WPS agenda is fascinating and provides a sharp counterpoint to the erasure of Windhoek from the agenda over time. In April 2019, as the Namibian government was launching its own NAP to govern the implementation of UNSCR 1325, the ambassador and permanent representative of the Namibian government made the following comments at the Security Council Open Debate on UN Peacekeeping Operations: "In May 2000, the first deliberations of the Women, Peace and Security agenda took place, giving birth to the Windhoek Declaration. At the time, Namibia realized that the international community needed to properly take into account the role of women, as serious stakeholders in peacekeeping, peacebuilding, decision making and mediation. The Windhoek Declaration thus formed the basis for the drafting of resolution 1325. In October 2000, Namibia was President of the Security Council and successfully oversaw the unanimous adoption of the historic 1325 resolution" (Permanent Mission of the Republic of Namibia to the United Nations 2019). Later that same month, the representative of South Africa referred to Namibia as having "pioneered" resolution 1325 (S/PV.8514 2019, p. 28). The claims and counterclaims about origins and influence are intriguing, to say the least, but I am not focused on state discourse in this project. This is a rabbit hole down which I will have to tumble some other time.

2. This dynamic continues in WPS practice today, as I elaborate throughout the book (and for a particularly compelling analysis, see Cook 2016).

3. This formulation does raise the question of what other kinds of change might exist.

4. The centrality of the efforts by the Women's International League for Peace and Freedom and other actors involved in the advocacy for resolution 1325, per the origin story of the resolution, also reproduces this rights dimension of the agenda (see Shepherd 2008, 135–145).
5. "General Recommendations clarify the scope of the Convention and provide detailed guidance to States on how to implement the obligations of the Convention" (UN Women/Swaine and O'Rourke 2015, 9).

Chapter 4

1. My interest in the structure of reporting success grew from an offhand, marginal comment in relation to the 2014 Secretary-General's report, in which I noted: "[R]eports always conclude with some version of 'we have made progress but it's all still a bit rubbish'—what's that about?" I return to the question of rubbish progress in the following chapter.
2. This is an interesting and unusual report in all kinds of ways. It has a very different tempo and tone from the other reports. As noted previously, the report is limited in scope to include only "information on the impact of armed conflict on women and girls in situations of which the Security Council is seized" (S/2009/465, para. 1); this language derives from the Presidential Statement released in October 2008 (S/PRST/2008/39) and is not used in this configuration in any of the other Secretary-General's reports. While the word "seized" is used, and at times mention is made of the Council being "seized of" various related matters, the phrasing "of which the Security Council is seized" does not appear elsewhere across the corpus of reports. I speculate that the formulation of the Presidential Statement in 2008 was heavily influenced by the Chinese government, as China held the presidency of the Security Council in October 2008; the Chinese position vis-à-vis WPS has long been that the agenda should be tightly circumscribed to relate only to situations of armed conflict, which would account for the framing. Having rendered the 2008 Presidential Statement using this language, it makes sense that this phraseology would carry through to the 2009 report. The report also presents a noteworthy perspective on the challenges faced in implementation. As discussed in the following chapter, much evaluation of the challenges in, and shortcomings of, implementation relate to capacity, political will, and resources, but the 2009 report presents a subtle critique of the agenda itself and the implementation plans: "Some emanate from the very nature of armed conflict which creates social, economic and political instability and disrupts existing social networks, infrastructure and economic and social activities. Others relate to the breadth of resolution 1325 (2000), which requires novelty and creativity to address these challenges. Yet others arise from a weak implementation framework and the absence of clear targets and reliable data" (S/2009/465, para. 60). There is also a clear attempt to draw boundaries around the agenda, limiting its applicability to the impact of war on women and the
n of women in peace processes: "The significance of resolution 1325 (2000)
e way it links the impact of war and conflict on women on the one hand, and

promotes their participation in various peace and security processes such as in peace negotiations, constitutional and electoral reforms and reconstruction and reintegration on the other" (S/2009/465, para. 77). This story of what WPS is affixes the agenda carefully to war/postwar and ignores the dimension of conflict prevention that logically precedes either, according to a linear temporality of violence.

3. This work is very demanding for those involved. When I was in New York in 2016, and again (though less surprisingly) in 2019, people were already talking in detail about preparation for the 2020 anniversary, and most of them expressed a real sense of fatigue, even exhaustion, at the ramifications of the anniversary effect: "With the 20th anniversary, I mean I don't actually really know because I haven't been so engaged in the discussions around 2020 but I hope they're not planning for another big review because it does feel like we just finished one" (Interview, 201907). The 2020 anniversary was somewhat subsumed by the Covid-19 pandemic, though an October debate was held virtually by video conference. Russia (who held the presidency) proposed a new resolution, but with 10 abstentions, it did not pass.

4. I should note at this stage that the "October effect" cuts both ways; the specific and exclusive focus on October as the month marker of WPS does not necessarily engender sustained attention to WPS for the other eleven months of the year. As one research participant commented in frustration: "[M]ember states can say a nice, warm, and fluffy statement in October and then 1st November, that's WPS done for another year" (Interview, 201910). I discuss this issue, which I identify as a challenge or shortcoming within the agenda, more fully in the following chapter.

5. My notes on this excerpt include <screaming emoji>.

6. In one noteworthy instance, women's movements are commended for having made "major contributions to building partnerships for peace"; the language is identical in at least two reports (S/2004/814, para. 27; S/2008/622, para. 9). Either this is evidence of discursive convergence, or it's a copy/paste error.

7. There are spaces where these parallel tracks meet, cross, and even become entangled: the briefing of the Security Council by representatives of civil society organizations, for example, each October during the Open Debates, is a moment of collision between these two different worlds. I am grateful to one of the two very generous and engaged reviewers of this manuscript for encouraging me to think about the connections between these communities.

Chapter 5

1. At the time of writing, only eleven member states have invested in the Global Acceleration Instrument (now called the Women's Peace and Humanitarian Fund): Australia, Austria, Canada, Ireland, Japan, Liechtenstein, Lithuania, the Netherlands, Norway, Spain, and the United Kingdom.

2. Academic research on the political economy dimensions of the WPS agenda has not been extensive, but there is an exciting body of literature emerging on this theme. See, for example, True 2012, 2015; Basu 2017; Bergeron, Cohn and Duncanson 2017; Tanyag 2018; Duncanson 2019; Martín De Almagro and Ryan 2019.

3. This means that the individual would wear two or three "hats" while on mission, that is, have two or three different—and demanding and often diverse—roles.

4. This quote has been put to excellent use by Marysia Zalewski in her article " 'I Don't Even Know What Gender Is': A Discussion of the Connections Between Gender, Gender Mainstreaming and Feminist Theory" (2010), which is where I first came across it.

5. Moreover, "there's still a lack of understanding of how gender expertise and being female aren't the same thing" (Interview, 201910), which I unfortunately don't have the space to discuss here.

6. Obviously, while elbows deep in coding for this book, I began to refer to this discursive motif as the "Groundhog Day problem," in reference to the film of the same name in which Bill Murray plays a television personality cursed to relive the same day again and again until he learns the lesson that life is trying to teach him. Or something. It has been a while since I saw it.

Chapter 6

1. The "prevention of sexual violence" or "protection" resolutions are UNSCR 1820 (2008); UNSCR 1888 (2009); UNSCR 1960 (2010); UNSCR 2106 (2013); and UNSCR 2467 (2019). It actually makes more sense to refer to them as prevention (of sexual violence) resolutions because of the institutional bifurcation of the agenda that was structurally embedded with the creation of the Office of the Special Representative of the Secretary-General on Sexual Violence in Conflict (which was established in UNSCR 1888; see S/RES/1888, para. 4). Further, responsibilities for forwarding the agenda were divided at the time of drafting UNSCR 1820, with the representatives of the US government taking the lead on the resolution. The United States continues to act as "pen-holder" on sexual violence issues before the Council, while the UK is formally the pen-holder on women's participation, although any UN Security Council member can act as pen-holder on an issue that concerns them and, as a result of the British government's political interest at the time, the UK took the lead on UNSCR 2016 in 2013, which is indubitably a sexual violence resolution (Crawford 2017, 102).

2. "P3" is shorthand for the three permanent members of the UN Security Council that historically were supporters of the agenda (UK, USA, France).

3. I should say, control, count, and *militarise*. One research participant commented on this directly: "I find it very interesting how there is this continuous perception from women's organizations that the 1325 agenda has been narrowed down by men enactors to be a military project, and to have more women soldiers" (Interview, 201604).

4. It bears noting that this discursive move is resisted in later reports, with, for example, the 2010 report—which was presented also to the General Assembly—noting, "While the scope of the present report is confined to situations on the Council's agenda, it bears noting that sexual violence occurs in other situations of conflict and concern" (SA/65/592-S/2010/406, para. 3).

5. I must reflect also on the fact that I *did not* speak to permanent representatives, mission staff, or government officials in country capitals. Remember that this is a story about how UN staff working on WPS, and those with whom they work closely, tell WPS stories.

6. The subtitle of the heading references Marysia Zalewski's brilliant essay on IR theory, which in turn references a note pinned to the office noticeboard of her then colleague, Nick Wheeler: "All these theories, yet the bodies keep piling up . . ." (Zalewski 1996, 353n5).

7. Cook notes, in a footnote to the quoted passage, "This argument had been successfully used by a small group of NGOs in 2006 to block an earlier attempt to adopt a similar resolution" (Cook 2009, 127n13).

Chapter 7

1. Interestingly, the alienation and disaffection felt by the (exclusively) female representatives from civil society organizations who speak at the Open Debates have become more apparent over time. In 2015 there was evident frustration and irritation in the statement from Julienne Lusenge, director of the Congolese Women's Fund and the president of Solidarité Féminine pour la Paix et le Développement Integral, who also briefed the Council on behalf of the NGO Working Group on Women, Peace and Security: "Seven years ago, in 2008, I came to New York to speak in the Security Council. I described the conflict in my country, the Democratic Republic of the Congo. I set out in detail the sexual violence, murders and massacres. I came to ask for concrete action for the implementation of resolution 1325 (2000) and the integration of the fight against sexual violence in peacekeeping missions. Today, 15 years after the adoption of resolution 1325 (2000) and seven years after my first briefing to the Council, I am once again addressing this body. I thought long and hard before deciding to come back here, and wondered whether or not it was worth the effort" (S/PV.7533 2015, p. 6).

2. The concept of "expert by experience" was developed in social work and mental health care, as part of a broader shift away from a medical model of service delivery—which positioned doctors and allied professionals as experts on service-users—toward a "recovery model," which centers recovery as a process and positions service users as experts in their own lives and needs. See work by Hugh McLaughlin (2009), Tehseen Noorani (2013), and Jijian Voronka (2016).

3. There are glimpses of this multiplicity; when reading and re-reading the Secretary-General's reports, for example, it is possible to identify different writing styles and turns of phrase. My comments on the 2010 report include the marginal annotation *"this concluding paragraph is almost poetic, I don't know who's writing these reports now but it's 100% not the same people/team who were writing in 2009"* next to the text: "Peace, justice and security are interdependent: there can be no peace without the peace of mind that enables women to undertake their daily tasks, no justice without a national capacity to deliver justice, and no security without women's security" (A/65/

592–S/2010/604, para. 47). Perhaps I am wrong about that, of course, and this is just a poetic turn of phrase that had a lucky escape after similar words were excised from earlier reports.

4. This literature is too extensive to do justice to it here, so I have listed just a few examples in each category. For scholarship on the gendered dynamics of claiming and occupying intellectual space, see Hawkesworth 1989; Harding 1991; Rose 1994; Harris 2007; Altamirano-Jiménez and Kermoal 2016; Pereira 2017. For scholarship on the gendered dynamics of navigating physical space, see Gill 1989, 1993; Massey 1994; Domosh and Seager 2001; Mahler and Pessar 2001. For scholarship on the gendered dynamics of the corporeality of occupying space, see Orbach 1978, 2018; Moss and Dyck 2002; Bordo [1993] 2003; Gay 2017.

Chapter 8

1. And here I tip my hat to Louise Allen, former director of the NGO Working Group on Women, Peace and Security and someone whose wisdom, insight, and friendship I have come to value very much over the course of this research.

References

Abbot, H. Porter (2008) *The Cambridge Introduction to Narrative*. 2nd edition. Cambridge, UK: Cambridge University Press.

Abbott, H. Porter (2007) "Story, Plot and Narration," 39–51 in David Herman, ed. *The Cambridge Companion to Narrative*. Cambridge. UK: Cambridge University Press.

Agathangelou, Anna and L.H.M. Ling (2004) "The House of IR: From Family Power Politics to the Poisies of Worldism," *International Studies Review*, 6(1): 21–49.

Åhäll, Linda and Stefan Borg (2012) "Predication, Presupposition and Subject Positioning," 196–207 in Laura J. Shepherd, ed. *Critical Approaches to Security: An Introduction to Theories and Methods*. London: Routledge.

Aharoni, Sarai B. (2014) "Internal Variation in Norm Localization: Implementing Security Council Resolution 1325 in Israel," *Social Politics: International Studies in Gender, State & Society*, 21(1): 1–25.

Altamirano-Jiménez, Isabel and Nathalie Kermoal (2016) "Introduction: Indigenous Women and Knowledge," 3–18 in Nathalie Kermoal and Isabel Altamirano-Jiménez, eds. *Living on the Land: Indigenous Women's Understanding of Place*. Edmonton, AB: AU Press.

Ansell, Christopher and Robert Geyer (2017) "'Pragmatic Complexity' a New Foundation for Moving Beyond 'Evidence-Based Policy Making?,'" *Policy Studies*, 38(2): 149–167.

Ansell, Christopher K., Jarle Trondal, and Morten Øgård, eds. (2017) *Governance in Turbulent Times*. Oxford: Oxford University Press.

Arat, Zehra F. Kabasakal (2015) "Feminisms, Women's Rights, and the UN: Would Achieving Gender Equality Empower Women?," *American Political Science Review*, 109(4): 674–689.

Archer, Colin (2013) "Military Spending and the UN's Development Agenda," *Peace Review*, 25(1): 24–32.

Aroussi, Sahla, ed. (2017) *Rethinking National Action Plans on Women, Peace and Security*. Amsterdam: IOS Press.

Ashley, Richard K. and R.B.J. Walker (1990) "Speaking the Language of Exile: Dissident Thought in International Studies," *International Studies Quarterly*, 34(3): 259–268.

Atef, Ali (2008) "'Women and Security': Interview with Anne Marie Goetz," *United States Institute of Peace*. Online, at: https://www.usip.org/sites/default/files/missing-peace/Goetz%20interview.pdf.

Babík, Milan (2019) *The Poetics of International Politics: Fact and Fiction in Narrative Representations of World Affairs*. London: Routledge.

Baden, Sally and Anne Marie Goetz (1997) "Who Needs [Sex] When You Can Have [Gender]? Conflicting Discourses on Gender at Beijing," *Feminist Review*, 56: 3–25.

Bal, Mieke (2017) *Narratology: Introduction to the Theory of Narrative*. 4th edition. Toronto, ON: University of Toronto Press.

Bang, Henrik Paul, ed. (2003) *Governance as Social and Political Communication*. Manchester: Manchester University Press.

Barnes, Karen (2011) "The Evolution and Implementation of UNSCR 1325: An Overview," 15–34 in 'Funmi Olonisakin, Karen Barnes and Eka Ikpe, eds. *Women, Peace and Security: Translating Policy into Practice*. London: Routledge.

Barnett, Michael and Raymond Duvall, eds. (2005) *Power in Global Governance*. Cambridge, UK: Cambridge University Press.

Barthes, Roland (1974) *S/Z*, trans. Richard Miller. Oxford, Blackwell.

Basini, Helen and Caitlin Ryan (2016) "National Action Plans as an Obstacle to Meaningful Local Ownership of UNSCR 1325 in Liberia and Sierra Leone," *International Political Science Review*, 37(3): 390–403.

Basu, Soumita (2016a) "The Global South Writes 1325 (Too)," *International Political Science Review*, 37(3): 362–374.

Basu, Soumita (2016b) "Gender as National Interest at the UN Security Council," *International Affairs*, 92(2): 255–273.

Basu, Soumita (2017) "The UN Security Council and the Political Economy of the WPS Resolutions," *Politics & Gender*, 13(4): 721–727.

Basu, Soumita and Catia C. Confortini (2017) "Weakest 'P' in the 1325 Pod? Realizing Conflict Prevention through Security Council Resolution 1325," *International Studies Perspectives*, 18(1): 43–63.

Basu, Soumita, Paul Kirby and Laura J. Shepherd (2020) "Women, Peace and Security: A Critical Cartography," 1–28 in Soumita Basu, Paul Kirby, and Laura J. Shepherd, eds. *New Directions in Women, Peace and Security*. Bristol: Bristol University Press.

Bell, Christine and Catherine O'Rourke (2010) "Peace Agreements or Pieces of Paper? The Impact of UNSC Resolution 1325 on Peace Processes and Their Agreements," *International & Comparative Law Quarterly*, 59(4): 941–980.

Bergeron, Suzanne, Carol Cohn and Claire Duncanson (2017) "Rebuilding Bridges: Toward a Feminist Research Agenda for Postwar Reconstruction," *Politics & Gender*, 13(4): 715–721.

Bjarnegård, Elin and Meryl Kenny (2016) "Comparing Candidate Selection: A Feminist Institutionalist Approach," *Government and Opposition*. 51(3): 370–392.

Björkdahl, Annika and Johanna Mannergren Selimovic (2019) "WPS and Civil Society," 428–438 in Sara E. Davies and Jacqui True, eds. *The Oxford Handbook of Women, Peace and Security*. Oxford: Oxford University Press.

Black, Renee (2009) "Mainstreaming Resolution 1325? Evaluating the Impact on Security Council Resolution 1325 on Country-Specific UN Resolutions," *Journal of Military and Strategic Studies*, 11(4). Online, at: https://jmss.org/article/view/57612/43283.

Bleiker, Roland (1997) "Forget IR Theory," *Alternatives: Global, Local, Political*, 22(1): 57–85.

Bleiker, Roland (2001) "The Aesthetic Turn in International Political Theory," *Millennium: Journal of International Studies*, 30(3): 509–533.

Bleiker, Roland (2009) *Aesthetics and World Politics*. Basingstoke: Palgrave Macmillan.

Bode, Ingvild (2020) "Women or Leaders? Practices of Narrating the United Nations as a Gendered Institutions," *International Studies Review*, 22(3): 347–369.

Bordo, Susan ([1993] 2003) *Unbearable Weight: Feminism, Western Culture, and the Body*. Berkeley, CA: University of California Press.

Bousquet Antoine, and Simon Curtis (2011) "Beyond Models and Metaphors: Complexity Theory, Systems Thinking and International Relations," *Cambridge Review of International Affairs*, 24(1): 43–62.

Bridgeman, Teresa (2007) "Time and Space," 52–65 in David Herman, ed. *The Cambridge Companion to Narrative*. Cambridge, UK: Cambridge University Press.

Campbell, David (1998) *Writing Security: United States Foreign Policy and the Politics of Identity*. Revised edition. Minneapolis, MN: University of Minnesota Press.

Chandler, David (2014a) "Beyond Neoliberalism: Resilience, the New Art of Governing Complexity," *Resilience*, 2(1): 47–63.

Chandler, David (2014b) *Resilience: The Governance of Complexity*. London: Routledge.

Charlesworth, Hilary and Christine Chinkin (2013) "The New United Nations 'Gender Architecture': A Room with a View?," 3–60 in Armin von Bogdandy, Anne Peters, Rüdiger Wolfrum and Christiane E. Philipp, eds. *Max Planck Yearbook of United Nations Law*. Leiden: Koninklijke Brill.

Chinkin, Christine (2019) "Adoption of 1325 Resolution," 26–37 in Sara E. Davies and Jacqui True, eds. *The Oxford Handbook of Women, Peace and Security*. Oxford: Oxford University Press.

Cockburn, Cynthia (2013) "War and Security, Women and Gender: An Overview of the Issues," *Gender & Development*, 21(3): 433–452.

Cohn, Carol (1987) "Sex and Death in the Rational World of Defence Intellectuals," *Signs: Journal of Women in Culture and Society*, 12(4): 687–718.

Cohn, Carol (2008) "Mainstreaming Gender in UN Security Policy: A Path to Political Transformation?," 185–206 in Shirin M. Rai and Georgina Waylen, eds. *Global Governance: Feminist Perspectives*, Basingstoke: Palgrave Macmillan.

Cohn, Carol (2017) "Beyond the 'Women, Peace and Security' Agenda: Why We Need a Feminist Roadmap for Sustainable Peace," *Consortium on Gender, Security, and Human Rights*. Online, at http://genderandsecurity.org/sites/default/files/Cohn_-_Beyond_the_Women_Peace_and_Security_Agenda_Why_We_Need_a_Feminist_Roadmap_for_Sustainable_Peace.pdf.

Cohn, Carol, Helen Kinsella and Sheri Gibbings (2004) "Women, Peace and Security: Resolution 1325," *International Feminist Journal of Politics*, 6(1): 130–140.

Cook, Sam (2009) "Security Council Resolution 1820: On Militarism, Flashlights, Raincoats, and Rooms with Doors—A Political Perspective on Where It Came from and What It Adds," *Emory International Law Review*, 23(1): 125–140.

Cook, Sam (2016) "The 'Woman-in-Conflict' at the UN Security Council: A Subject of Practice," *International Affairs*, 92(2): 353–372.

Cook, Sam (2019) "Marking Failure, Making Space: Feminist Intervention in Security Council Policy," *International Affairs*, 95(6): 1289–1306.

Coomaraswamy, Radhika et al. (2015) *Preventing Conflict, Transforming Justice, Securing the Peace: A Global Study on the Implementation of United Nations Security Council Resolution 1325*. New York, NY: UN Women. Online, available at http://wps.unwomen.org/en.

Crawford, Kerry F. (2017) *Wartime Sexual Violence: From Silence to Condemnation of a Weapon of War*. Washington, DC: Georgetown University Press.

Culler, Jonathan (1997) *Literary Theory: A Very Short Introduction*. Oxford: Oxford University Press.

Culler, Jonathan (2002) *The Pursuit of Signs: Semiotics, Literature, Deconstruction*. Ithaca, NY: Cornell University Press.

Dauphinee, Elizabeth (2013) *The Politics of Exile*. London: Routledge.

Davies, Sara E. and Jacqui True (2017) "Norm Entrepreneurship in Foreign Policy: William Hague and the Prevention of Sexual Violence in Conflict," *Foreign Policy Analysis*, 13(3): 701–721.

Davies, Sara E. and Jacqui True (2019a) "WPS: A Transformative Agenda?," 3–14 in Sara E. Davies and Jacqui True, eds. *The Oxford Handbook of Women, Peace and Security*, Oxford: Oxford University Press.

Davies, Sara E. and Jacqui True, eds. (2019b) *The Oxford Handbook of Women, Peace and Security*. Oxford: Oxford University Press.

Davies, Sara E., Kimberly Nackers and Sarah Teitt (2014) "Women, Peace and Security as an ASEAN Priority," *Australian Journal of International Affairs*, 68(3): 333–355.

de Jonge Oudraat, Chantal (2013) "UNSCR 1325—Conundrums and Opportunities," *International Interactions*, 39(4): 612–619.

Der Derian, James (2012) *Project Z*. Film, dir. Phillip Gara. Oley, PA: Bullfrog Films.

Derrida, Jacques (1972) *Positions*. Chicago, IL: University of Chicago Press.

Derrida, Jacques (1974) *Of Grammatology*, trans. Gayatri Chakravorty Spivak. Baltimore, MD: Johns Hopkins University Press.

Diehl, Paul F., ed. (2005) *The Politics of Global Governance: International Organizations in an Interdependent World*. Boulder, CO: Lynne Rienner.

Dillon, Michael (1998) "The Scandal of the Refugee: Some Reflections on the 'Inter' of International Relations and Continental Thought," *Refuge*, 17(6): 30–39.

Diop, Bineta (2011) "The African Union and Implementation of UNSCR 1325," 173–183 in 'Funmi Olonisakin, Karen Barnes and Eka Ikpe, eds. *Women, Peace and Security: Translating Policy into Practice*. London: Routledge.

Domosh, Mona and Joni Seager (2001) *Putting Women in Place: Feminist Geographers Make Sense of the World*. New York, NY: Guilford Press.

Doty, Roxanne Lynn (1993) "Foreign Policy as Social Construction: A Post-Positivist Analysis of US Counterinsurgency Policy in the Philippines," *International Studies Quarterly*, 37(3): 297–320.

Doty, Roxanne Lynn (1996) *Imperial Encounters: The Politics of Representation in North-South Relations*. Minneapolis, MN: University of Minnesota Press.

Douglas, Sarah and Cécile Mazzacurati (2017) "Financing for Gender-Responsive Peacebuilding: Setting Financial Targets as a Tool for Increasing Women's Participation in Post-Conflict Recovery," 227–246 in Zora Khan and Nalini Burn, eds. *Financing for Gender Equality: Realising Women's Rights through Gender Responsive Budgeting*. Basingstoke: Palgrave Macmillan.

Drumond, Paula and Tamya Rebelo (2020) "Global Pathways or Local Spins? National Action Plans in South America," *International Feminist Journal of Politics*, 22(4): 462–484.

Duncanson, Claire (2019) "Beyond Liberal vs Liberating: Women's Economic Empowerment in the United Nations' Women, Peace and Security Agenda," *International Feminist Journal of Politics*, 21(1): 111–130.

Dutt, Mallika (1996) "Some Reflections on U.S. Women of Color and the United Nations Fourth World Conference on Women and NGO Forum in Beijing, China," *Feminist Studies*, 22(3): 519–528.

Edkins, Jenny (2013) "Novel Writing in International Relations: Openings for a Creative Practice," *Security Dialogue*, 44(4): 281–297.

Egnell, Robert (2016) "Gender Perspectives and Military Effectiveness: Implementing UNSCR 1325 and the National Action Plan on Women, Peace, and Security," *Prism*, 6(1): 72–89.

Eisenstein, Hester (1996) *Inside Agitators: Australian Femocrats and the State*. Philadelphia, PA: Temple University Press.

El-Bushra, Judy (2007) "Feminism, Gender, and Women's Peace Activism," *Development and Change*, 38(1): 131–147.

Enloe, Cynthia (1996) "Margins, Silences and Bottom Rungs: How to Overcome the Underestimation of Power in the Study of International Relations," 186–202 in Steve Smith, Ken Booth, and Marysia Zalewski, eds. *International Theory: Positivism and Beyond*. Cambridge, UK: Cambridge University Press.

Esplen, Emily and Patti O'Neill (2017) "From Commitment to Action: Aid in Support of Gender Equality and Women's Rights in the Implementation of the Sustainable Development Goals," 205–225 in Zohra Khan and Nalini Burn, eds. *Financing for Gender Equality: Gender, Development and Social Change*. Basingstoke: Palgrave Macmillan.

Fernandes, Sujatha (2017a) *Curated Stories: The Uses and Misuses of Storytelling*. Oxford: Oxford University Press.

Fernandes, Sujatha (2017b) "Stories and Statecraft: Afghan Women's Narratives and the Construction of Western Freedoms," *Signs: Journal of Women in Culture and Society*, 42(3): 643–667.

Ford, Liz (2019) "UN Waters Down Rape Resolution to Appease US's Hardline Abortion Stance," *The Guardian*, 24 April 2019. Online, at https://www.theguardian.com/global-development/2019/apr/23/un-resolution-passes-trump-us-veto-threat-abortion-language-removed.

Foucault, Michel ([1976] 2000) "Truth and Power," in J.D. Faubion, ed. *Power: Essential Works of Michel Foucault 1954–1984*, Volume 3. London: Penguin.

Franklin, M.I., ed. (2015) *Resounding International Relations: On Music, Culture, and Politics*. Basingstoke: Palgrave Macmillan.

Fritz, Jan Marie, Sharon Doering and F. Belgin Gumru (2011) "Women, Peace, Security and the National Action Plans," *Journal of Applied Social Science*, 5(1): 1–23.

Frost, Robert (1979) *The Poetry of Robert Frost*, ed. Edward Connery Latham. New York, NY: Henry Holt.

Fuijo, Christy (2008) "From Soft to Hard Law: Moving Resolution 1325 on Women, Peace and Security Across the Spectrum," *Georgetown Journal of Gender and the Law*, 9(1): 215–236.

Gay, Roxane (2017) *Hunger*. New York, NY: HarperCollins.

George, Nicole and Laura J. Shepherd (2016) "Women, Peace and Security: Exploring the Implementation and Integration of UNSCR 1325," *International Political Science Review*, 37(3): 297–306.

George, Nicole (2016) "Institutionalising Women, Peace and Security in the Pacific Islands: Gendering the 'Architecture of Entitlements'?," *International Political Science Review*, 37(3): 375–389.

George, Nicole and Pauline Soaki (2020) "'Our Struggle, Our Cry, Our Sweat': Challenging the Gendered Logics of Participation and Conflict Transition in Solomon Islands," *International Feminist Journal of Politics*, 22(4): 572–593.

Gerring, John (2012) *Social Science Methodology: A Unified Framework*. Revised edition. Cambridge, UK: Cambridge University Press.

Gibbings, Sheri Lynn (2011) "No Angry Women at the United Nations: Political Dreams and the Cultural Politics of United Nations Security Council Resolution 1325," *International Feminist Journal of Politics*, 13(4): 522–538.

Gizelis, Theodora-Ismene and Louise Olsson, eds. (2015) *Gender, Peace and Security: Implementing UN Security Council Resolution 1325*. London: Routledge.

Grey, Rosemary (2014) "Conflicting Interpretations of 'Sexual Violence' in the International Criminal Court," *Australian Feminist Studies*, 29(81): 273–288.

Grey, Rosemary (2019) *Prosecuting Sexual and Gender-Based Crimes at the International Criminal Court: Practice, Progress and Potential*. Cambridge, UK: Cambridge University Press.

Guerrina, Roberta and Katharine A.M. Wright (2016) "Gendering Normative Power Europe: Lessons of the Women, Peace and Security Agenda," *International Affairs*, 92(2): 293–312.

Haastrup, Toni (2019) "WPS and the African Union," 375–387 in Sara E. Davies and Jacqui True, eds. *The Oxford Handbook of Women, Peace, and Security*. Oxford: Oxford University Press.

Hagen, Jamie J. and Toni Haastrup (2020) "Global Racial Hierarchies and the Limits of Localisation via National Action Plans," 133–152 in Soumita Basu, Paul Kirby, and Laura J. Shepherd, eds. *New Directions in Women, Peace and Security*. Bristol: Bristol University Press.

Hagström, Linus and Karl Gustafsson (2019) "Narrative Power: How Storytelling Shapes East Asian International Politics," *Cambridge Review of International Affairs*, 32(4): 387–406.

Hall, Nina and Jacqui True (2009) "Gender Mainstreaming in a Post-conflict State," 159–174 in Bina D'Costa and Katrina Lee-Koo, eds. *Gender and Global Politics in the Asia-Pacific*. Basingstoke: Palgrave Macmillan.

Hall, Stuart (1984) "The Narrative Construction of Reality," *Southern Review*, 17: 3–17.

Hall, Stuart (1985) "Signification, Representation, Ideology: Althusser and the Post-Structuralist Debates," *Critical Studies in Mass Communication*, 2(2): 91–114.

Halley, Janet (2006) *Split Decisions: How and Why to Take a Break from Feminism*. USA: Princeton University Press.

Hans, Asha and Swarna Rajagopalan, eds. (2016) *Openings for Peace: UNSCR 1325, Women and Security in India*. New Delhi: SAGE.

Hansen, Lene (1997) "A Case for Seduction? Evaluating the Poststructuralist Conceptualization of Security," *Cooperation and Conflict*, 32(4): 369–397.

Hansen, Lene (2006) *Security as Practice: Discourse Analysis and the Bosnian War*. London: Routledge.

Haraway, Donna J. (1988) "Situated Knowledges: The Science Question in Feminism and the Privilege of Partial Perspective," *Feminist Studies*, 14(3): 575–599.

Harding, Sandra (1986) *The Science Question in Feminism*. Ithaca, NY: Cornell University Press.

Harding, Sandra (1991) *Whose Science? Whose Knowledge? Thinking from Women's Lives*. Ithaca, NY: Cornell University Press.

Harman, Sophie (2019) *Seeing Politics: Film, Visual Method, and International Relations*. Montreal, QC: McGill Queens University Press.

Harman, Sophie and Leanne Welham (2017) *Pili*. Film, dir. Leanne Welham. London: Studio Soho Distribution.

Harrington, Carol (2011) "Resolution 1325 and Post-Cold War Feminist Politics," *International Feminist Journal of Politics*, 13(4): 557–575.

Harris, Tina M. (2007) "Black Feminist Thought and Cultural Contracts: Understanding the Intersection and Negotiation of Racial, Gendered, and Professional Identities in the Academy," *New Directions for Teaching and Learning*, 110: 55–64.

Harrison, Neil, ed. (2006) *Complexity in World Politics: Concepts and Methods of a New Paradigm*. New York, NY: SUNY Press.

Hawkesworth, Mary E. (1989) "Knowers, Knowing, Known: Feminist Theory and Claims of Truth," *Signs: Journal of Women in Culture and Society*, 14(3): 533–557.

Heathcote, Gina (2011) "Feminist Politics and the Use of Force: Theorising Feminist Action and Security Council Resolution 1325," *Socio-Legal Review*, 7: 23–43.

Heathcote, Gina (2012) "Naming and Shaming: Human Rights Accountability in Security Council Resolution 1960 (2010) on Women, Peace and Security," *Journal of Human Rights Practice*, 4(1): 82–105.

Heathcote, Gina (2018) "Security Council Resolution 2242 on Women, Peace and Security: Progressive Gains or Dangerous Development?," *Global Society*, 32(4): 374–394.

Hemmings, Clare (2011) *Why Stories Matter: The Political Grammar of Feminist Theory*. Durham, NC: Duke University Press.

Hendrick, Rebecca M. and David Nachmias (1992) "The Policy Sciences: The Challenge of Complexity," *Policy Studies Review*, 11(3/4): 310–328.

Hendricks, Cheryl and Romi Sigworth, eds. (2016) *Gender, Peace and Security in Africa*. Abingdon: Routledge.

Herblinger, Andreas T. and Claudia Simons (2015) "The Good, the Bad, and the Powerful: Representations of the 'Local' in Peacebuilding," *Security Dialogue*, 46(5): 422–439.

Herman, David (2007) "Introduction," 3–21 in David Herman, ed. *The Cambridge Companion to Narrative*. Cambridge, UK: Cambridge University Press.

Herman, Luc and Bart Vervaeck (2007) "Ideology," 217–230 in David Herman, ed. *The Cambridge Companion to Narrative*. Cambridge, UK: Cambridge University Press.

Hill, Felicity, Mikele Aboitiz, and Sara Poehlman-Doumbouya (2003) "Nongovernmental Organizations' Role in the Build-up and Implementation of Security Council Resolution 1325," *Signs: Journal of Women in Culture and Society*, 28(4): 1255–1269.

Højlund Madsen, Diana (2018) "'Localising the Global'—Resolution 1325 as a Tool for Promoting Women's Rights and Gender Equality in Rwanda," *Women's Studies International Forum*, 66(1): 70–78.

Hudson, Christrtline, Malin Rönnblom, and Katherine Teghtsoonian, eds. (2017) *Gender, Governance and Feminist Analysis: Missing in Action?* London: Routledge.

Hudson, Natalie Florea (2009) "Securitizing Women's Rights and Gender Equality," *Journal of Human Rights*, 8(1): 53–70.

Hudson, Natalie Florea (2010) *Gender, Human Security and the United Nations: Security Language as a Political Framework for Women*. London: Routledge.

Hudson, Natalie Florea (2015) "The Social Practice of Securitizing Women's Rights and Gender Equality: 1325 Fifteen Years On," 167–184 in Joel R. Pruce, ed. *The Social Practice of Human Rights*. Basingstoke: Palgrave Macmillan.

Hudson, Natalie Florea and Anne Marie Goetz (2014) "Too Much That Can't Be Said," *International Feminist Journal of Politics*, 16(2): 336–346.

Hughes, Langston and James Mercer (1994) *The Collected Poems of Langston Hughes*, ed. Arnold Rampersad and David Roessel. New York, NY: Vintage Classics.

Hunt, Swanee and Alice Wairimu Nderitu (2019) "WPS as a Political Movement," 76–87 in Sara E. Davies and Jacqui True, eds. *The Oxford Handbook of Women, Peace and Security*, Oxford: Oxford University Press.

Hutchison, Andrew John, Lynne Halley Johnston, and Jef David Breckon (2010) "Using QSR-NVivo to Facilitate the Development of a Grounded Theory Project: An Account of a Worked Example," *International Journal of Social Research Methodology*, 13(4): 283–302.

Inayatullah, Naeem (2011) "Falling and Flying: An Introduction," 1–12 in Naeem Inayatullah, ed. *Autobiographical International Relations: I, IR*. London, Routledge.

Inayatullah, Naeem (2013) "Pulling Threads: Intimate Systematicity in *The Politics of Exile*," *Security Dialogue*, 44(4): 331–345.

Inayatullah, Naeem and Elizabeth Dauphinee (2016a) "Permitted Urgency: A Prologue," 1–4 in Naeem Inayatullah and Elizabeth Dauphinee, eds. *Narrative Global Politics: Theory, History and the Personal in International Relations*. London: Routledge.

Inayatullah, Naeem and Elizabeth Dauphinee, eds. (2016b) *Narrative Global Politics: Theory, History and the Personal in International Relations*. London: Routledge.

Irvine, Jill A. (2012) "Leveraging Change: Women's Organizations and the Implementation of UNSCR 1325 in the Balkans," *International Feminist Journal of Politics*, 15(1): 20–38.

Jackson, Patrick T. (2010) *The Conduct of Inquiry in International Relations: Philosophy of Science and Its Implications for the Study of World Politics*. London: Routledge.

Jackson, Richard (2014) *Confessions of a Terrorist*. London: Zed.

Jahn, Manfred (2007) "Focalization," 94–108 in David Herman, ed. *The Cambridge Companion to Narrative*. Cambridge, UK: Cambridge University Press.

Jansson, Maria and Maud Eduards (2016) "The Politics of Gender in the UN Security Council Resolutions on Women, Peace and Security," *International Feminist Journal of Politics*, 18(4): 590–604.

Jarvis, Lee (2009) *Times of Terror: Discourse, Temporality and the War on Terror*. Basingstoke: Palgrave Macmillan.

Jauhola, Marjaana (2016) "Decolonizing Branded Peacebuilding: Abjected Women Talk Back to the Finnish Women, Peace and Security Agenda," *International Affairs*, 92(2): 333–351.

Johnson-Freese, Joan (2019) *Women, Peace and Security: An Introduction*. London: Routledge.

Jonjić-Beitter, Andrea, Hanna Stadler, and Flora Tietgen (2020) "Civil Society and Its Role Within UNSCR 1325 National Action Plans," 177–199 in Manuela Scheuermann and Anja Zürn, eds. *Gender Roles in Peace and Security*. Cham: Springer.

Kavalski, Emilian (2007) "The Fifth Debate and the Emergence of Complex International Relations Theory: Notes on the Application of Complexity Theory to the Study of International Life," *Cambridge Review of International Affairs*, 20(3): 435–454.

Kirby, Paul (2015) "Ending Sexual Violence in Conflict: The Preventing Sexual Violence Initiative and Its Critics," *International Affairs*, 91(3): 457–472.

Kirby, Paul and Laura J. Shepherd (2016) "The Futures Past of the Women, Peace and Security Agenda," *International Affairs*, 92(2): 373–392.

Koester, Diana, Emily Esplen, Karen Barnes Robinson, Clare Castillejo, and Tam O'Neil (2016) "How Can Donors Improve Their Support to Gender Equality in Fragile Settings? Findings from OECD Research," *Gender & Development*, 24(3): 353–373.

Koomen, Jonneke (2019) "WPS and the International Criminal Court," 351–363 in Sara E. Davies and Jacqui True, eds. *The Oxford Handbook of Women, Peace and Security*. Oxford: Oxford University Press.

Krystalli, Roxani (2019) "Narrating Violence: Feminist Dilemmas and Approaches," 173–188 in Laura J. Shepherd, ed. *Handbook on Gender & Violence*. Cheltenham: Edward Elgar.

Labonte, Melissa and Gaynel Curry (2016) "Women, Peace, and Security: Are We There Yet?," *Global Governance*, 22(3): 311–320.

Laclau, Ernesto (2006) "Ideology and Post-Marxism," *Journal of Political Ideologies*, 11(2): 103–114.

Laclau, Ernesto and Chantal Mouffe ([1985] 2001) *Hegemony and Socialist Strategy: Towards a Radical Democratic Politics*. Revised edition. London: Verso.

Law, John (2004) *After Method: Mess in Social Science Research*. London: Routledge.

Law, John and John Urry (2004) "Enacting the Social," *Economy and Society*, 33(3): 390–410.

Lee-Koo, Katrina (2014) "Implementing Australia's National Action Plan on United Nations Security Council Resolution 1325," *Australian Journal of International Affairs*, 68(3): 300–313.

Lee-Koo, Katrina (2016) "Engaging UNSCR 1325 Through Australia's National Action Plan," *International Political Science Review*, 37(3): 336–349.

Lee-Koo, Katrina and Barbara K. Trojanowska (2017) "Does the United Nations' Women, Peace and Security Agenda Speak with, for or to Women in the Asia Pacific? The Development of National Action Plans in the Asia Pacific," *Critical Studies on Security*, 5(3): 287–301.

Lewis, Dustin A (2009) "Unrecognized Victims: Sexual Violence Against Men in Conflict Settings under International Law," *Wisconsin International Law Journal*, 27(1): 1–50.

Ling, L.H.M. and Mari Nakamura (2019) "Popular Culture and Politics: Re-narrating the Senkaku/Diaoyu Islands Dispute," *Cambridge Review of International Affairs*, 32(4): 541–558.

Lipton, Briony and Elizabeth Mackinlay (2016) *We Only Talk Feminist Here: Feminist Academics, Voice and Agency in the Neoliberal University*. Cham, Switzerland: Palgrave Macmillan.

Lorde, Audre (1984) *Sister Outsider: Essays and Speeches*. Berkeley, CA: Crossing Press.

Lowndes, Vivien and Mark Roberts (2013) *Why Institutions Matter: The New Institutionalism in Political Science*. Basingstoke: Palgrave Macmillan.

Lubell, Mark (2013) "The Ecology of Games Framework," *Policy Studies Journal*, 41(3): 537–559.

Mac Ginty, Roger (2015) "Where Is the Local? Critical Localism and Peacebuilding," *Third World Quarterly*, 36(5): 840–856.

Mac Ginty, Roger and Pamina Firchow (2016) "Top-down and Bottom-up Narratives of Peace and Conflict," *Politics*, 36(3): 308–323.

Mahler, Sarah J. and Patricia R. Pessar (2001) "Gendered Geographies of Power: Analyzing Gender Across Transnational Spaces," *Identities*, 7(4): 441–459.

Manchanda, Rita (2017) "Introduction," xv–xl in Rita Manchanda, ed. *Women and Politics of Peace: South Asia Narratives on Militarization, Power, and Justice*. New Delhi: SAGE.

Manjoo, Rashida, and Calleigh McRaith (2011) "Gender-Based Violence and Justice in Conflict and Post-Conflict Areas," *Cornell International Law Journal*, 44(1): 11–32.

Margolin, Uri (2007) "Character," 66–79 in David Herman, ed. *The Cambridge Companion to Narrative*. Cambridge, UK: Cambridge University Press.

Martín De Almagro, María (2018a) "Producing Participants: Gender, Race, Class, and Women, Peace and Security," *Global Society*, 32(4): 395–414.

Martín De Almagro, María (2018b) "Lost Boomerangs, the Rebound Effect and Transnational Advocacy Networks: A Discursive Approach to Norm Diffusion," *Review of International Studies*, 44(4): 672–693.

Martín De Almagro, María and Caitlin Ryan (2019) "Subverting Economic Empowerment: Towards a Postcolonial-Feminist Framework on Gender (In)securities in Post-war Settings," *European Journal of International Relations*, 25(4): 1059–1079.

Massey, Doreen (1994) *Space, Place and Gender*. Cambridge, UK: Polity.

McLaughlin, Hugh (2009) "What's in a Name: 'Client', 'Patient', 'Customer', 'Consumer', 'Expert by Experience', 'Service User'—What's Next?," *The British Journal of Social Work*, 39(6): 1101–1117.

McLeod, Laura (2013) "Back to the Future: Temporality and Gender Security Narratives in Serbia," *Security Dialogue*, 44(2): 165–181.

McLeod, Laura (2015) *Gender Politics and Security Discourse: Personal-Political Imaginations and Feminism in "Post-Conflict" Serbia*. Abingdon: Routledge.

Mehta, Akanksha and Annick T.R. Wibben (2019) "Feminist Narrative Approaches to Security," 48–58 in Caron E. Gentry, Laura J. Shepherd, and Laura Sjoberg, eds. *Handbook on Gender & Security*. London: Routledge.

Merry, Sally Engle (2016) *The Seductions of Quantification: Measuring Human Rights, Gender Violence, and Sex Trafficking*. Chicago, IL: University of Chicago Press.

Miller, Barbara, Milad Pournik, and Aisling Swaine (2014) *Women in Peace and Security Through United Nations Security Resolution 1325: Literature Review, Content Analysis of National Action Plans, and Implementation*. Online, at: https://giwps.georgetown.edu/resource/women-in-peace-and-security-through-united-nations-security-resolution-1325-literature-review-content-analysis-of-national-action-plans-and-implementation/.

Milliken, Jennifer (1999) "The Study of Discourse in International Relations," *European Journal of International Relations*, 5(2): 225–254.

Miskimmon, Alister, Ben O'Loughlin, and Laura Roselle (2013) *Strategic Narratives: Communication Power and the New World Order*. London: Routledge.

Moisander, Johanna K., Heidi Hirsto, and Kathryn M. Fahy (2016) "Emotions in Institutional Work: A Discursive Perspective," *Organization Studies*, 37(7): 963–990.

Moss, Pamela and Isabel Dyck (2002) *Women, Body, Illness: Space and Identity in the Everyday Lives of Women with Disabilities*. Lanham, MD: Rowman and Littlefield.

Muehlenhoff, Hanna (2017) "Victims, Soldiers, Peacemakers and Caretakers: The Neoliberal Constitution of Women in the EU's Security Policy," *International Feminist Journal of Politics*, 19(2): 153–167.

Naraghi Anderlini, Sanam (2007) *Women Building Peace: What They Do, Why It Matters*. Boulder, CO: Lynne Rienner.

Naraghi Anderlini, Sanam (2019) "Civil Society's Leadership in Adopting 1325 Resolution," 38–52 in Sara E. Davies and Jacqui True, eds. *The Oxford Handbook of Women, Peace and Security*. Oxford: Oxford University Press.

Naumes, Sarah (2015) 'Is All 'I' IR?,' *Millennium: Journal of International Studies*, 43(3): 820–832.

Neumann, Iver B. and Ole Jacob Sendinng (2010) *Governing the Global Polity: Practice, Mentality, Rationality*. Ann Arbor, MI: University of Michigan Press.

Noorani, Tehseen (2013) "Service User Involvement, Authority and the 'Expert-by-Experience' in Mental Health," *Journal of Political Power*, 6(1): 49–68.

Nwangwu, Chikodiri and Christian Ezeibe (2019) "Femininity Is Not Inferiority: Women-Led Civil Society Organizations and 'Countering Violent Extremism' in Nigeria," *International Feminist Journal of Politics*, 21(2): 168–193.

O'Brien, Robert, Anne Marie Goetz, Jan Aart Scholte, and Marc Williams (2000) *Contesting Global Governance: Multilateral Economic Institutions and Global Social Movements*. Cambridge, UK: Cambridge University Press.

O'Brien, Robert, Anne Marie Goetz, Jan Aart Scholte, and Marc Williams (2009) *Contesting Global Governance: Multilateral Economic Institutions and Global Social Movements*. Revised edition. Cambridge, UK: Cambridge University Press.

Olonisakin, 'Funmi, Karen Barnes, and Eka Ikpe, eds. (2012) *Women, Peace and Security: Translating Policy into Practice*. London: Routledge.

O'Rourke, Catherine (2017) "Feminist Strategy in International Law: Understanding Its Legal, Normative and Political Dimensions," *European Journal of International Law*, 28(4): 1019–1045.

Orbach, Susie (1978) *Fat Is a Feminist Issue*. New York, NY: Paddington.

Orbach, Susie (2018) *Hunger Strike: The Anorectic's Struggle as a Metaphor for Our Age*. London: Routledge.

Otto, Dianne (2010) "Power and Danger: Feminist Engagement with International Law Through the UN Security Council," *Australian Feminist Law Journal*, 32(1): 97–121.

Otto, Dianne (2014) "Beyond Stories of Victory and Danger: Resisting Feminism's Amenability to Serving Security Council Politics," 157–172 in Gina Heathcote and Dianne Otto, eds. *Rethinking Peacekeeping, Gender Equality and Collective Security*. Basingstoke: Palgrave Macmillan.

Otto, Dianne and Gina Heathcote (2014) "Rethinking Peacekeeping, Gender Equality and Collective Security: An Introduction," 1–22 in Gina Heathcote and Dianne Otto, eds. *Rethinking Peacekeeping, Gender Equality and Collective Security*. Basingstoke: Palgrave Macmillan.

Parashar, Swati (2019) "The WPS Agenda: A Postcolonial Critique," in Sara E. Davies and Jacqui True, eds. *The Oxford Handbook of Women, Peace, and Security*. Oxford: Oxford University Press.

Patten, Pramila (2018) "Unlocking the Potential of CEDAW as an Important Accountability Tool for the Women, Peace and Security Agenda," 171–184 in Fionnuala Ní Aoláin, Naomi R. Cahn, Dina Francesca Haynes, and Nahla Valji, eds. *The Oxford Handbook of Gender and Conflict*. Oxford: Oxford University Press.

Pereira, Maria do Mar (2017) *Power, Knowledge and Feminist Scholarship: An Ethnography of Academia*. London: Routledge.

Permanent Mission of the Republic of Namibia to the United Nations (2019) "Statement by M.E. Mr. Neville Gertze, Ambassador and Permanent Representative, 73rd Session of the United Nations General Assembly at the Security Council on the Open Debate in Connection with the Agenda Item 'United Nations Peacekeeping Operations: Women in Peacekeeping.'" Online, at https://www.un.int/namibia/sites/www.un.int/files/Namibia/Statements/SecurityCouncil/unsc_statement_wps_11_april_2019_women_in_peacekeeping.pdf.

Peterson, V. Spike and Anne Sisson Runyan (1999) *Global Gender Issues*. 2nd edition. Boulder, CO: Westview Press.

Porter, Elisabeth (2003) "Women, Political Decision-Making, and Peace-Building," *Global Change, Peace & Security*, 15(3): 245–262.

Porter, Elisabeth (2007) *Peacebuilding: Women in International Perspective*. London: Routledge.

Pratt, Nicola (2013) "Reconceptualizing Gender, Reinscribing Racial–Sexual Boundaries in International Security: The Case of UN Security Council Resolution 1325 on 'Women, Peace and Security,'" *International Studies Quarterly*, 57(4): 772–783.

Puckett, Kent (2016) *Narrative Theory: A Critical Introduction.* Cambridge, UK: Cambridge University Press.

Puechguirbal, Nadine (2004) "Women and Children: Deconstructing a Paradigm," *Seton Hall Journal of Diplomacy and International Relations*, 5(1): 5–16.

Puechguirbal, Nadine (2012) "The Cost of Ignoring Gender in Conflict and Post-Conflict Situations: A Feminist Perspective," *Amsterdam Law Journal*, 4(1): 4–19.

Rai, Shirin M. and Georgina Waylen, eds. (2008) *Global Governance: Feminist Perspectives.* Basingstoke: Palgrave Macmillan.

Rajagopalan, Swarna (2016) "The 1325 Resolutions: From Thought to Action," in Asha Hans and Swarna Rajagopalan, eds. *Openings for Peace: UNSCR 1325, Women and Security in India.* New Delhi: SAGE.

Ravecca, Paulo (2019) *The Politics of Political Sciences: Re-Writing Latin American Experiences.* London: Routledge.

Ravecca, Paulo and Elizabeth Dauphinee (2018) "Narrative and the Possibilities for Scholarship," *International Political Sociology*, 12(1): 125–138.

Reiling, Carrie (2017) "Pragmatic Scepticism in Implementing the Women, Peace and Security Agenda," *Global Affairs*, 3(4–5): 469–481.

Reilly, Niamh (2009) *Women's Human Rights: Seeking Gender Justice in a Globalizing Age.* Cambridge, UK: Polity.

Rose, Hilary (1994) *Love, Power, and Knowledge: Towards a Feminist Transformation of the Sciences.* Cambridge, UK: Polity.

Rosenau, James (1990) *Turbulence in World Politics: A Theory of Change and Continuity.* London: Harvester Wheatsheaf.

Rosenau, James N. (1990) *Turbulence in World Politics: A Theory of Change and Continuity.* Princeton, NJ: Princeton University Press.

Rosenau, James N. and Ernst-Otto Czempiel, eds. (1992) *Governance Without Government: Order and Change in World Politics.* Cambridge, UK: Cambridge University Press.

Ruby, Felicity (2014) "*Security Council Resolution 1325: A Tool for Conflict Prevention?,*" 173–184 in Gina Heathcote and Dianne Otto, eds. *Rethinking Peacekeeping, Gender Equality and Collective Security.* Basingstoke: Palgrave Macmillan.

Ryan, Marie-Laure (2007) "Toward a Definition of Narrative," 22–38 in David Herman, ed. *The Cambridge Companion to Narrative.* Cambridge, UK: Cambridge University Press.

Safi, Mariam (2016) "Afghan Women and Countering Violent Extremism: What are Their Roles Challenges and Opportunities in CVE?," 118–140 in Naureen Chowdhury Fink, Sara Zeiger, and Rafia Bhulai, eds. *In a Man's World? Exploring the Roles of Women in Countering Terrorism and Violent Extremism.* Abu Dhabi: Hedayah and the Global Center on Cooperative Security.

Särmä, Saara (2014) *Junk Feminism and Nuclear Wannabes - Collaging Parodies of Iran and North Korea.* Doctoral dissertation. Online, at http://tampub.uta.fi/bitstream/handle/10024/95961/978-951-44-9535-9.pdf?sequence=1&isAllowed=y.

Sawer, Marian (1998) "Femocrats and Ecorats: Women's Policy Machinery in Australia, Canada and New Zealand," in Carol Miller and Shahra Razavi, eds. *Missionaries and Mandarins: Feminist Engagement with Development Institutions.* London: ITDG Publishing.

Sawer, Marian (2003) "The Life and Times of Women's Policy Machinery in Australia," 243–262 in Shirin Rai, ed. *Mainstreaming Gender, Democratizing the State: Institutional Mechanisms for the Advancement of Women*. London: Routledge.

Shapiro, Michael J. (2009) *Cinematic Geopolitics*. London: Routledge.

Shawki, Noha (2017) "Implementing the Women, Peace and Security Agenda," *Global Affairs*, 3(4–5): 455–467.

Shekhawat, Seema, ed. (2018) *Gender, Conflict, Peace, and UNSC Resolution 1325*. Lanham, MD: Lexington Books.

Shepherd, Laura J. (2008) *Gender, Violence and Security: Discourse as Practice.* London: Zed Books.

Shepherd, Laura J. (2011) "Sex, Security and Superhero(in)es: From 1325 to 1820 and Beyond," *International Feminist Journal of Politics*, 13(4): 504–521.

Shepherd, Laura J. (2013) *Gender, Violence and Popular Culture: Telling Stories*. London: Routledge.

Shepherd, Laura J. (2016a) "Research as Gendered Intervention: Feminist Research Ethics and the Self in the Research Encounter," *Crítica Contemporánea: Revista de Teoría Política*, No. 6: 1–15.

Shepherd, Laura J. (2016b) "Making War Safe for Women? National Action Plans and the Militarisation of the Women, Peace and Security Agenda," *International Political Science Review*, 37(3): 324–335.

Shepherd, Laura J. (2016c) "Victims of Violence or Agents of Change? Representations of Women in UN Peacebuilding Discourse," *Peacebuilding*, 4(2): 121–135.

Shepherd, Laura J. (2017) *Gender, UN Peacebuilding, and the Politics of Space*. Oxford: Oxford University Press.

Shepherd, Laura J. (2018) "Activism in/and the Academy: Reflections on 'Social Engagement,'" *Journal of Narrative Politics*, 5(1).

Shepherd, Laura J. (2019) "WPS and Adopted Security Council Resolutions," 98–109 in Sara E. Davies and Jacqui True, eds. *The Oxford Handbook of Women, Peace and Security*. Oxford: Oxford University Press.

Singh, Shweta (2017) "Re-thinking the 'Normative' in United Nations Security Council Resolution 1325: Perspectives from Sri Lanka," *Journal of Asian Security and International Affairs*, 4(2): 219–238.

Skjelsbæk, Inger and Torunn L. Tryggestad (2019) "Donor States Delivering on WPS: The Case of Norway," 516–527 in Sara E. Davies and Jacqui True, eds. *The Oxford Handbook of Women, Peace and Security*. Oxford: Oxford University Press.

Smith, Steve (2000) "The Discipline of International Relations: Still an American Social Science?," *British Journal of Politics and International Relations*, 2(3): 374–402.

Smith, Steve (2004) "Singing Our World into Existence: International Relations Theory and September 11," *International Studies Quarterly*, 48(3): 499–515.

Snyder, Jack and Robert Jervis, eds. (1993) *Coping with Complexity in the International System*. Boulder, CO: Westview Press.

Solangon, Sarah and Preeti Patel (2012) "Sexual Violence Against Men in Countries Affected by Armed Conflict," *Conflict, Security & Development*, 12(4): 417–442.

Spehar, Andrea (2018) "The Pursuit of Political Will: Decision Makers' Incentives and Gender Policy Implementation in the Western Balkans," *International Feminist Journal of Politics*, 20(2): 236–250.

Spivak, Gayatri Chakravorty (1988) "Can the Subaltern Speak?," 24–28 in Cary Nelson and Lawrence Grossberg, eds. *Marxism and the Interpretation of Culture*. Basingstoke: Macmillan.

Stanley, Liam (2014) " 'We're Reaping What We Sowed': Everyday Crisis Narratives and Acquiescence to the Age of Austerity," *New Political Economy*, 19(6): 895–917.

Stanley, Liam (2016) "Using Focus Groups to Study Everyday Narratives in World Politics," *Politics*, 36(3): 236–249.

Stanley, Liam and Richard Jackson (2016) "Introduction: Everyday Narratives in World Politics," *Politics*, 36(3): 223–235.

Steans, Jill (2003) "Engaging from the Margins: Feminist Encounters with the 'Mainstream' of International Relations," *British Journal of Politics and International Relations*, 5(3): 428–454.

Subrahmanian, Ramya (2007) "Making Sense of Gender in Shifting Institutional Contexts: Some Reflections on Gender Mainstreaming," in Andrea Cornwall, Elizabeth Harrison, and Ann Whitehead, eds. *Feminisms in Development: Contradictions, Contestations and Challenges*. London: Zed.

Suganami, Hidemi (1999) "Agents, Structures, Narratives," *European Journal of International Relations*, 5(3): 365–386.

Suganami, Hidemi (2008) "Narrative Explanation and International Relations: Back to Basics," *Millennium: Journal of International Studies*, 37(2): 327–356.

Swaine, Aisling (2009) "Assessing the Potential of National Action Plans to Advance Implementation of United Nations Security Council Resolution 1325," *Yearbook of International Humanitarian Law*, 12: 403–433.

Swaine, Aisling (2018) *Conflict-Related Violence Against Women: Transforming Transition*. Cambridge, UK: Cambridge University Press.

Sylvester, Christine (2013) *War as Experience: Contributions from International Relations and Feminist Analysis*. London: Routledge.

Sylvester, Christine (2019) *Curating and Re-curating the American Wars in Vietnam and Iraq*. Oxford: Oxford University Press.

Tanyag, Maria (2018) "Depleting Fragile Bodies: The Political Economy of Sexual and Reproductive Health in Crisis Situations," *Review of International Studies*, 44(4): 654–671.

Thomson, Jennifer (2018) "The Women, Peace, and Security Agenda and Feminist Institutionalism: A Research Agenda," *International Studies Review*, 21(4): 598–613.

Tripp, Aili Mari Tripp (2006) "The Evolution of Transnational Feminism: Consensus, Conflict, and New Dynamics," 51–78 in Myra Marx Ferree and Aili Mari Tripp, eds. *Global Feminism: Transnational Women's Activism, Organizing, and Human Rights*. New York, NY: New York University Press.

True, Jacqui (2008) "Gender Specialists and Global Governance: New Forms of Women's Movement Mobilisation?," 91–104 in Sandra Grey and Marian Sawer, eds. *Women's Movements: Flourishing or in Abeyance?* London: Routledge.

True, Jacqui (2012) *The Political Economy of Violence against Women*. Oxford: Oxford University Press.

True, Jacqui (2015) "A Tale of Two Feminisms in International Relations? Feminist Political Economy and the Women, Peace and Security Agenda," *Politics & Gender*, 11(2): 419–424.

True, Jacqui (2016) "Explaining the Global Diffusion of the Women, Peace and Security Agenda," *International Political Science Review*, 37(3): 307–323.

True, Jacqui and Michael Mintrom (2001) "Transnational Networks and Policy Diffusion," *International Studies Quarterly*, 45(1): 27–57.

True, Jacqui and Antje Wiener (2019) "Everyone Wants (a) Peace: The Dynamics of Rhetoric and Practice on 'Women, Peace and Security,'" *International Affairs*, 95(3): 553–574.

Tryggestad, Torunn L. (2009) "Trick or Treat? The UN and Implementation of Security Council Resolution 1325 on Women, Peace, and Security," *Global Governance: A Review of Multilateralism and International Organizations*, 15(4): 539–557.

Tuhiwai Smith, Linda (20120) *Decolonizing Methodologies*. 2nd edition. London: Zed.

UN Women/Swaine, Aisling and Catherine O'Rourke (2015) *Guidebook on CEDAW General Recommendation No. 30 and UN Security Council Resolutions on Women, Peace and Security*. Online, at http://www.unwomen.org/en/digital-library/publications/2015/8/guidebook-cedawgeneralrecommendation30-womenpeacesecurity.

Valentine, Gill (1989) "The Geography of Women's Fear," *Area*, 21(4): 385–390.

Valentine, Gill (1993) "(Hetero)Sexing Space: Lesbian Perceptions and Experiences of Everyday Spaces," *Environment and Planning D: Society and Space*, 11(4): 395–413.

Voronka, Jijian (2016) "The Politics of 'People with Lived Experience': Experiential Authority and the Risks of Strategic Essentialism," *Philosophy, Psychiatry, & Psychology*, 23(3/4): 189–201.

Waldron, Thea and Erin Baines (2019) "Gender and Embodied War Knowledge," *Journal of Human Rights Practice*, 11(2): 393–405.

Wax, Dustin (n.d.) "Advice for Students: 10 Steps Toward Better Research," *Lifehack*. Online, at https://www.lifehack.org/articles/communication/advice-for-students-10-steps-toward-better-research.html.

Weber, Cynthia (2011) *"I Am an American": Filming the Fear of Difference*. London and Chicago, IL: Intellect Books UK and University of Chicago Press.

Weiss, Thomas G. (2011) *Thinking about Global Governance: Why People and Ideas Matter*. London: Routledge.

Weiss, Thomas G. and Rorden Wilkinson (2014) *International Organization and Global Governance*. London: Routledge.

Weiss, Thomas G. and Rorden Wilkinson (2019) *Rethinking Global Governance*. Cambridge, UK: Polity Press.

Weldes, Jutta (1996a) "Constructing National Interests," *European Journal of International Relations*, 2(3): 275–318.

Weldes, Jutta (1996b) *Constructing National Interests: The United States and the Cuban Missile Crisis*. Minnesota, MN: University of Minnesota Press.

What's in Blue (2019) "In Hindsight: Negotiations on Resolution 2467 on Sexual Violence in Conflict," *What's in Blue*, 2 May 2019. Online, at https://www.whatsinblue.org/2019/05/in-hindsight-negotiations-on-resolution-2467-on-sexual-violence-in-conflict.php#.

Wibben, Annick T.R. (2011) *Feminist Security Studies: A Narrative Approach*. London: Routledge.

Wibben, Annick T.R. (2016) "Female Engagement Teams in Afghanistan: Exploring the 'War on Terror' Narrative," 57–75 in Annick T.R. Wibben, ed. *Researching War: Feminist Methods, Ethics, and Politics*. London: Routledge.

Wilkinson, Rorden and Steve Hughes, eds. (2002) *Global Governance: Critical Perspectives*. London: Routledge.

Young, Iris Marion (2003) "The Logic of Masculinist Protection: Reflections on the Current Security State," *Signs: Journal of Women in Culture and Society*, 29(1): 1–25.

Young, Oren (2017) *Governing Complex Systems: Social Capital for the Anthropocene.* Cambridge, MA: MIT Press.

Zalewski, Marysia (1996) "'All These Theories Yet the Bodies Keep Piling Up': Theory, Theorists, Theorising," 340–353 in Steve Smith, Ken Booth, and Marysia Zalewski, eds. *International Theory: Positivism and Beyond.* Cambridge, UK: Cambridge University Press.

Zalewksi, Marysia (2010) "'I Don't Even Know What Gender Is': A Discussion of the Connections Between Gender, Gender Mainstreaming and Feminist Theory," *Review of International Studies*, 36(1): 3–27.

Index